Enjoy the Rea
Best Wishes
Rosemary Brierley

A Bletchley Park Wren Overseas

ROSEMARY BRIERLEY

A Bletchley Park Wren Overseas
by Rosemary Brierley

First published in 2018

A catalogue card for this book is available from the British Library.

Paperback ISBN: 978-1-9996788-9-0

Publication support
TJ INK
tjink.co.uk

Printed and bound in Great Britain by
TJ International, Padstow, Cornwall

Cover by Wileman Design

A Bletchley Park Wren Overseas

The diary and reminiscences of

Flora Crossley
who served at Bletchley Park
and its overseas outstations
in Africa and Ceylon
during World War II

A BLETCHLEY PARK WREN OVERSEAS

CONTENTS

THE DIARY

It is one day in 2004 when we are expecting the gasman that I first hear this story. My aunt, by then in her late 80s, likes me to be with her when people she doesn't know come to call. We have been waiting a couple of hours, when she goes over to the sideboard and takes out a large brown envelope. Inside are two hardbacked exercise books, which she hands to me.

'You might like to read this. But you must remember it is a bit naïve, not too well written, but I was very young at the time.'

She allows me to take it home, saying that it would be better if I read it now, rather than after she's passed away. That way if there is anything that puzzles me, I can ask her about it.

In places the diary is a bit hard to follow, because there is a lot I don't know about the Second World War and there are terms I don't understand, but the story itself is fascinating. I don't go to bed until I come to the end.

Shortly afterwards, my aunt has a mild stroke; she is less steady on her feet after that, but the main effect is on her speech. She can remember everything quite clearly in her head, knows exactly what she wants to say, but can't always find the word she's looking for. The speech therapist says she should practise at home and talk to the flowers. My aunt has no intention of talking to flowers, so instead she talks to me. This serves two purposes: Aunt Flora finds the words she had lost, and I have the beginnings of a book.

The diary begins when she boards a troopship bound for Mombasa in February 1943, but the story begins long before that. Aunt Flora shares her memories with me in the living room of her one-bedroomed flat. When I arrive, the tray, covered with a hand-embroidered tray cloth and laid with china teacups and saucers, is ready on the low table in front of the settee. In the kitchen, the kettle has boiled and the teapot is warming, lid open waiting for a spoon of Orange Pekoe from the caddy beside it. Since the stroke I carry the gleaming silver-plated tea service and set it down beside the cups. As always, she says, 'Shall I be mother?'

Milk first, of course, then she places the tea strainer over the cups, pours the tea, then returns the strainer with the unwanted tea leaves to its metal holder. She always offers me sugar from the oval bowl with swan-neck handles, even though she knows I don't take it. With silver sugar tongs, she helps herself to two cubes and uses the spoon waiting in the saucer to stir. As I balance my teacup in one hand, she offers me a ginger biscuit or a garibaldi from a plate with a paper doily.

Aunt Flora tells her story in short scenes, digressing forwards and backwards in time as a suddenly-remembered incident springs to mind. It wouldn't be right to use a recorder or write anything down, so I store everything she says in my head, then pour it all out onto paper when I get home. Later, I rearrange it into chronological order and transfer it to the computer.

PROLOGUE

May 1945

Under cover of darkness, the heavy cruiser *Haguro* and the destroyer *Kamikaze* sneaked through the Straits of Malacca. Only white water feathering out as the bows sliced through the grey sea and a trail of foam from the stern marked their position. The throb of their engines evaporated into the dark tropical night, unheard on the far-distant shores of Malaya and the island of Sumatra. Below deck on the *Haguro*, a wireless operator flipped the pages of the current code book, noting the five-digit numbers representing the Japanese symbols that made up the message. Then he selected a starting point, anywhere in a book of 100,000 random numbers, and added these to the code numbers. With his index finger he began to transmit the dots and dashes that represented these totals.

A wireless operator, more than 1,000 nautical miles away on the island of Ceylon, rotated the dial. The Morse signal became clearer – this was the one they'd been waiting for. She recognised his fist, his rhythm in tapping out Morse – each operator had their own distinctive touch. The pencil in her right hand flew across the paper as she wrote the groups of five numbers in the columns on the intercept form. When the message ended, she waved the form in the air.

A WRNS petty officer collected the intercept form and took it over to the cryptanalysts in the adjacent single-storey, wooden building. A man in civvies looked up as she entered and nodded. They had probably already managed to replicate sufficient of the current Japanese code book to crack this one… all thanks to the Hollerith.

Meanwhile, housed in another hut close by, where every inch of wall space was lined with shelves piled high with boxes of the punch-cards that recorded every intercepted signal, the Holleriths kept on clattering. Wrens worked in silence, intent on their task of satisfying these electro-mechanical tabulating machines' insatiable appetite for these seven-by-three-inch cards. They collected and refiled the ones it spewed out, then checked the printer. A printout of several messages that included the same sequence would eventually reveal the Japanese symbols encrypted in these five-digit numbers.

On 15 May 1945, the 26th Destroyer Flotilla was dispatched to the Straits of Malacca. At 2 a.m. on the 16th, 50 miles south-west of Penang, the *Haguro* was hit by several torpedoes and sank within minutes.

One of the Wrens who minded the Hollerith machine was my Aunt Flora.

PART 1: BRITAIN
CHAPTER 1
Halifax

When Flora – my grandmother's third surviving child, another daughter – was born, the First World War still had another two and a half years to run before the Armistice was signed on 11 November 1918. Although Flora was too young to recall what actually happened, she grew up amidst talk of the war. Her father had magazines describing the Somme, Ypres and Passchendaele, bound in leather and once – once only – the girls had peeked at the grim pictures. Halifax, where the family lived, was a garrison town and troops from the Duke of Wellington's regiment would regularly march from the barracks down Gibbet Street and into the town. When Flora heard the rhythmic beat of their boots on the cobbles she'd avert her eyes from the khaki uniforms and puttees.

Despite her mother's reassurance that The Great War was the war to end wars, as a child Flora decided what to do if it ever happened again. The family had a fairly comfortable lifestyle: her father, a wholesale fruit and vegetable merchant, sold bananas from the Canaries, strawberries from Wisbech, and oranges from Spain in the Piece Hall. They owned an end-terraced house in a tree-lined avenue, one end of which was closed off with tall iron gates, only ever opened for weddings and funerals. And they had a car: an open-topped Buick.

On bank holidays the family piled in: Father, David and Mother, Esther, with baby Jessie on her knee in the front, and the three girls Vera, Louie and Flora in the back. Sometimes they drove across the moors to Skipton. As she gazed across the rugged landscape at Flappit, Flora's eyes rested on boulders, large enough to hide behind, and made up her mind: when the sirens sounded, this was where she would come.

***

At 2.30 a.m. on 4 September 1939, the stuttering wail of the sirens resonated through Halifax. Flora was 23 and had a full-time job, so fleeing to Flappit was not an option. At 11.15 a.m. the previous day, a Sunday, Esther and her daughters – her husband had passed away four years earlier – had gathered round the radio. The prime minister announced that, as the ultimatum to withdraw troops from Poland had been ignored, a state of war now existed between Britain and Germany.

Esther led the way down the stone steps to the cellar, and muttered that she never did trust that man Chamberlain with his false promise of peace in our time. She was followed by just two of her daughters: the eldest, Vera, was still in her bedroom, refusing to venture down to the cold, claustrophobic cavern. Louie, my mother, was now married and living in Cornwall. So just Flora and her younger sister, Jessie, waited and listened with their mother. Even their golden Labrador, Rajah, wouldn't join them; he lay across the doorway at the top of the stone steps. It was almost two hours before the continuous wail of the siren announced the all clear. The following day, word spread that it had been a false alarm, but Esther said it was as well to be prepared.

In fact, Britain had been preparing itself for war since the beginning of the year. The family's cellar had been inspected by the local air-raid warden and pronounced suitable to withstand bomb damage. Esther had set the maid to work scrubbing and laying a rug over the flagstone floor. She'd furnished it with discarded armchairs, collected a Primus stove, cups, candles, hot water bottles and blankets. However, these small comforts were never sufficient to persuade Vera to heed the sirens and leave the warmth of her bed to spend a cold and damp night in the cellar.

When she read in the *Halifax Courier* of the need for volunteers, Flora applied to assist with air raid precautions: after work, she could be found knocking on doors, issuing gas masks and filling in record cards. During the day, she was employed in the office at the Paton & Baldwin's woollen mill. From the age of 11 she'd been a day-girl at Crossley & Porter fee-paying school, a large ornate sandstone building surrounded by trees in the corner of Saville Park. She'd excelled at algebra and geometry, the subjects that challenged her powers of reasoning and deduction; she'd enjoyed geography, which instilled in her the desire to travel the world. If it hadn't been for the epidemic of diphtheria which closed the school in the winter of 1931/2, she would have stayed on to take her leaving certificate. However, when the school reopened shortly before her 16th birthday, her parents decided not to send her back for the last two terms, but arranged instead for her to receive private tuition in shorthand and typing. This led to her job at Paton & Baldwin.

In 1939, Flora was working in the Home Trade department. Her role was to arrange appointments and accommodation for the firm's reps, who travelled the country demonstrating knitting yarns and patterns at Women's Institutes. However, with the outbreak of war, petrol was rationed, the salesmen signed up and most of the wool the factory now produced was khaki, navy or air-force blue, so Flora was transferred to stock control.

In the evening, when she arrived home from work, her mother and two sisters would be sitting around the table or in armchairs beside the range in the living-kitchen at the back of the house. Often a man would be with them. No. 32 Milton Place, a four-bedroom house occupied only by a widow and her three grown-up children, was considered a suitable billet for officers from the local barracks. As well as a bedroom, Esther offered her house guests meals on their own in the dining room and the sole use of the drawing room, but most of them preferred the warmth and companionship of the kitchen. Flora remembers three guests in particular. One was the son of a hotelier in Scarborough. Another, a minister's son, was with them for only three weeks before he was posted overseas. After he was reported killed in action, his parents made a special trip to thank Esther; his letters home said how well she had looked after him. Both these men were conscripts in their late teens. The third house guest was an older man, a captain in the regular army. He used to sigh and say that these conscripts had no idea what they were going out to, but he knew…

***

Although the main headline on page 6 of the *Halifax Courier* on 31 May 1940 announced ALLIES HOLD SOLIDLY TO DUNKIRK AREA, a smaller heading further down conceded: *Evacuation Under Blizzard of Bombs*. Two days later, troop trains began to arrive at Halifax station. The remnants of the British Expeditionary Force, their uniforms torn and frayed, sea-water dried into salt ripples on the khaki, cluttered the town. They sat on the pavements, their damp, rotting boots stretched out into the road, their unshaven faces etched with fear, defeat and confusion. People said the troops were arriving back on the south coast faster than the authorities could deal with them. The regiments were all mixed up, so, to keep the ports clear, batches of men were put on trains going anywhere.

Halifax was an obvious destination, but there was no room in the barracks. A schoolroom on Hopwood Lane was cleared to accommodate them. Esther went along with flasks of tea and the best cups and saucers. Later, two of the enlisted men collected up the china and came across to return it. The next day, they were back to borrow a broom. These soldiers became regular visitors to the house, and there's a photograph of them crouched down either side of Rajah, in front of a tub of geraniums in the back yard.

Esther would shake her head and complain about rationing. How could you entertain these military visitors on rations of two ounces of tea for each household member per week? How were you supposed to make cakes with only four ounces of butter and eight ounces of sugar per person? It didn't matter that they now said there'd be no candied peel, crystalized cherries or icing sugar. She would stand in the pantry and count the Kilner jars: now, only half of them contained bottled fruit. On the radio it had said that no more fresh or tinned fruit would be imported. All because of those U-boats prowling beneath the waves, sending precious cargos to the bottom of the ocean.

As dusk turned to darkness in the Atlantic, lookouts would scour the dark waters for telltale signs of impending destruction, while at home the country lived in fear of the Luftwaffe. It was the summer of 1940, and the Battle of Britain had begun.

***

After work, Flora walked down Crossley Street to the town hall, where she descended the steps to the basement. Here, civilian volunteers manned the telephones and stuck pins in a map of the Yorkshire Dales. On nights when the skies overhead were clear of enemy aircraft, they'd compete at the dartboard, knit socks and balaclavas, and drink weak tea.

Flora took her turn answering the phones. When reports came in of planes crossing the coast, she'd ring round the air-raid wardens and first aid posts to inform them of a yellow alert. It was always yellow, never red in all the time she was there. Intent on their targets in Manchester and Liverpool, enemy planes flew straight past the mill chimneys nestled in the Calder Valley beneath a blanket of soot, smoke and smog. There were thirteen bomb incidents in Halifax throughout the whole of the war. However, most of the explosions occurred on sparsely-populated moorland, and censorship restrictions meant that the incidents could only be reported as occurring in a 'northern town'. Therefore, Flora remembers only two.

On the evening of 24 August 1940, the family spent an evening with neighbours, singing along as the tunes encoded in raised dots on the rolls of stiff paper wound their way through the Pianola. Next morning, when Esther opened the front door, a passer-by enquired if she'd seen it. He pointed in the direction of the moors and explained that incendiaries had landed on Southowram; probably just jettisoned by the Germans on their way home. They struck an overhead cable and lit the place up like Blackpool illuminations.

The second was on 22 November in the same year, and this time they couldn't miss the screech of the approaching bomb, the thunderous crack as it detonated. They felt the ground shudder, heard the splintering of glass, the crash of falling masonry. A cloud of smoke billowed from the drawing room fireplace as the blast forced its way down the chimney. A 220-pounder had landed only a few streets away, in Hanson Lane. A memorial and a plaque recording the names of the eleven who died remains to this day. It was the only bomb to cause civilian casualties in Halifax in the whole of the war – in fact, more casualties occurred on the roads during the blackout.

When her shift ended at 10 p.m., Flora emerged from the town hall to total darkness. At the bus stop she listened for the sound of the approaching bus, and peered into the night for the thin crosses of light which peeped through the layers of newspaper covering the headlights. Once aboard, it was even more difficult to judge when she'd reached her stop. She lost count of the number of times she missed it and had to walk back along Hopwood Lane. Not a chink of light was visible from the houses on both sides of their street. The shutters on the ground floors were closed, black paper fastened down the centre to prevent light seeping out where they didn't quite meet; upstairs, the blackout curtains were tightly drawn. Flora counted the gateways until she reached No. 32. She could no longer run her fingers along the railings the way she had as a child. They were gone, sawn off and taken away to be melted down to make guns, fighter aircraft and battleships; only stumps of metal remained in the low wall to indicate where they'd once been.

Flora let herself in and closed the front door before switching on the light, careful to avoid stubbing her toe on the stirrup pumps and buckets of sand, which stood in a row against the wall. Knowing that the lady at No. 32 was always up as soon as the sirens sounded, the local vicar and part-time air-raid warden had asked if he could leave his equipment in her hallway, where it was kept till the end of the war.

The war dragged on into 1941. As well as working in the basement of the town hall in the evening, Flora did her stint in the services canteen on a Sunday morning, selling baked beans on toast for threepence. But she began to wonder whether she should be contributing more to the war effort. Then the decision was taken out of her hands. On 18 December 1941, the National Service Act was passed: all single women between the ages of 20 and 30 would be called up.

Esther was relieved that three of her daughters were exempt: Vera on the grounds of ill health, Louie was married with a young baby, and Jessie was employed as a bookkeeper in an engineering firm, a reserved occupation. She looked at her one remaining daughter and hoped that by the time Flora's name came up, the war would be over.

But Flora didn't wait for the call-up letter. The following Monday, she joined a queue of young women at Wards End. As they inched forward, the sickly smell of fermenting hops from Ramsdens Brewery hung in the frosty air. Once inside the labour exchange she stamped her numb feet, cupped her hands round her mouth and exhaled on her blue fingers. At last it was her turn.

When Flora said she'd like to volunteer for the Women's Royal Navy, the counter clerk shook her head and replied that they were no longer recruiting. She suggested the Auxiliary Territorial Service instead.

Flora had already decided she didn't want to join the ATS and wear that coarse khaki uniform. She didn't want to sign up for the Women's Auxiliary Air Force either, not after hearing from a friend in the WAAF that it was awful living in those huts on the airbase.

The counter clerk said the only other option was munitions.

Flora was certainly not going to work in a factory. She turned and walked out of the labour exchange.

CHAPTER 2

Bletchley Park

Extract from a letter to 10 Downing Street:

Secret and Confidential
Prime Minister only

Hut 6 and Hut 8
(Bletchley Park)

21st October 1941

Dear Prime Minister,

Some weeks ago you paid us the honour of a visit and we believe that you regard our work as important... We think, however, that you ought to know that this work is being held up, and in some cases not done at all, principally because we cannot get sufficient staff to deal with it...

We cannot help feeling that with a Service matter of this kind it should have been possible to detail a body of WRNS for this purpose, if sufficiently urgent instructions had been sent to the right quarters...

Churchill's response: a memo to his chief military assistant:

ACTION THIS DAY

Make sure they have all they want on extreme priority and report to me that this has been done.

When Flora returned from the labour exchange, she went to her bedroom to write a letter to the Women's Royal Naval Service (WRNS) head office in London. When a reply in an OHMS envelope arrived, it caused quite a stir in the household. Until then, her mother and sisters had no idea that Flora had already tried to enlist. When they saw that the letter was about joining the Wrens, Esther gasped and asked her daughter if she would have to go to sea. Her sisters did their best to dissuade her, Vera citing the HMS *Hood*, which had been sunk the previous May, and Jessie the *Ark Royal*, which went down before Christmas.

The interview was in Leeds a few weeks later. Flora wore her best outfit, a light grey dress and bolero jacket in a fine wool material, the neckline and front edges appliqued with red ivy leaves. Vera accompanied her on the train journey. When they left, her mother said that if it had anything to do with guns, Flora must tell the interview panel that she no longer wished to join up.

The recruiting officer assured Flora that the work had nothing at all to do with guns, and added that for the whole of the time she was in the navy she would never see the sea – more than that, the officer couldn't say. Flora would undergo two weeks' basic training, at the end of which, if suitable, she could decide if she wanted to stay on.

***

It was August 1942 when Flora, wearing the same grey outfit and matching hat, arrived at New College, 527 Finchley Road, Hampstead, North West London. Altogether there were fourteen probationary Wrens attending the two-week induction into the navy. Their billet was a former theological college surrounded by streets, houses and shops – miles from the sea. Nevertheless, the rooms where they slept were called cabins, the floors referred to as decks, the common room was the foc'sle, officers spent their off duty in the ward room, and they all ate in the mess.

'Wakey-wakey' was at half past six every morning, except Sunday, when it was an hour later. The would-be recruits had to tidy their cabins and make up their berths with precision before covering them with a blue-and-white striped bedspread, the naval crest centred and the right way up. Later, they would be inspected by the petty officer and if she wasn't satisfied, she'd rip off the covers. Only once did Flora return to find this had happened to her – she never did understand why.

Then they donned blue and white overalls to peel potatoes in the galley or get down on their knees to scrub the decks. Again, the petty officer hovered and if a stone step wasn't scoured to her liking, she made the culprit do it again.

Domestic tasks completed, the girls changed back to civvies for squad drill – no uniforms were to be issued until the successful completion of training. Most of the girls wore their best clothes, including a hat. As they marched up and down Finchley Road they attracted puzzled stares; the only thing to explain what they were doing was a navy-blue armband with WRNS in large letters.

The category designated to six of the recruits, including Flora, was Special Duty X, but during the whole two weeks they never found out what that meant. Other probationers who hoped to become writers practised their typing or bookkeeping; those bound for the supply branch had lectures on the checking of invoices and issuing of stores; but all the SDX recruits learnt was naval etiquette. Flora memorised the different ranks in the navy as well as the army and air force, so she'd know who to salute, a practice compulsory even off duty. In the few hours they were allowed out, Flora and a friend took routes through the back streets of Hampstead, hoping to avoid the 'gold braid' so they wouldn't have to decide whether they required a salute. Only once did the situation arise, and the young officer looked rather startled when they raised their hands to their civilian hats!

The lecture on discipline and procedure which came towards the end of the fortnight's training was no doubt taken from *BR 1077: Regulations and Instructions for the Women's Royal Naval Service*, and was based on the following paragraphs:

15. Conduct to be Observed *– Every person in the Women's Royal Naval Service is to conduct herself with the utmost respect to her superior officer and with strict obedience to his or her orders. She is at all times to discharge every part of her duty with zeal and alacrity and to strive to promote the interests of the Naval Service.*

2. Every member will on all occasions endeavour to uphold the honour of the W.R.N.S. and, by the good order and regularity of her conduct, prove herself to be worthy of the Service to which she belongs. She will remember that persons in uniform are always conspicuous and that members of the W.R.N.S. must avoid any behaviour which, even if not undesirable in itself, may cause adverse criticism of the Service.

3. Members of the W.R.N.S. in uniform are not to indulge in rowdy or noisy behaviour in public. They must in every way consider the comfort and convenience of the public and help the local authorities in maintaining good order.

4. W.R.N.S. ratings must not loiter about the men's quarters, workshops, parade grounds or dockyard gates. Ratings moving from one part of a Naval Establishment to another should do so in a smart and dignified manner.

5. No member of the W.R.N.S. may engage in any money-lending or betting business, nor shall they act as agents in a Naval Establishment for any commercial undertaking.

6. It is the duty of all members of the W.R.N.S. to return punctually from their leave, and offenses of absence without leave are punishable by deductions from pay in addition to other punishments.

At the end of the training only one of the group, a delicate girl with blond hair, decided that the hard work and strict discipline of the navy weren't for her. The rest pledged their allegiance to king and country, were enrolled into the WRNS, allocated a service number and issued with a pay book. Those Wrens in supply and writer categories were given a badge embroidered in light blue with an S or a W surrounded by a star, to sew on the right sleeve of their uniform. Requests by SDX Wrens for their badge were just met with shrugs, blank stares and the words: 'I don't think there is one', or 'What do you do anyway?' – a question they weren't able to answer.

From then on, they wore naval uniform. The hat was a flat-topped cap, very similar to that worn by sailors, with HMS in gold letters at the front. The double-breasted navy-blue serge jacket had six black horn buttons down the front – not until they became petty officers could they exchange these for brass ones. There was a matching straight skirt, also sailor's bell-bottoms that fastened at the front with a square flap that came up from the crotch and buttoned onto the waistband. The four white shirts were issued with nine detachable collars. These were held in place by studs that were difficult to do up and dug in at the neck. There were also the navy drill dresses, so unflattering they soon became known as 'glamour gowns'. The long-legged, navy-blue knickers, nicknamed 'blackouts', weren't compulsory. Unlike other servicewomen, the Wrens were issued with coupons to buy their own underwear and black lisle stockings.

Great excitement accompanied the trying on of their new outfits. Only later did they realise that all civilian clothing had to be packed in their suitcases and sent back home. Never again while they served with the navy in Britain would they be able to wear their own clothes. Not only that, but *Regulations and Instructions for the Women's Royal Naval Service* stated:

> ***16. Uniform***
>
> *3. Jewellery (with the exception of wedding, engagement and signet rings), furs, handbags, umbrellas, scent and coloured fingernails are forbidden when uniform is worn. Stockings are not to be transparent. Make-up, if used, is to be discreet. Hair must be neat and must not fall over the collar.*

One day it was the passing-out parade, the next the six recruits for Special Duty X packed their bags, grabbed their gas masks and climbed aboard naval transport. No one told them their destination, but when the army driver dropped them off at Euston station, they agreed it couldn't be Portsmouth. Each time the train stopped they would crowd round the window and peer out for a clue as to where they were going. The previous year, however, when the country lived in fear of invasion, all station signs had been removed so that, if they did come, the Germans wouldn't know where they were. At an unnamed destination the petty officer gave the order to disembark, and the Wrens were marched to the transport for the journey through country lanes to their billet.

Crawley Grange was an ivy-covered Elizabethan mansion with Tudor chimney stacks and stone-mullioned windows. On the ground floor was a ballroom, the high ceiling edged with a decorative cornice, the walls oak-panelled; the tall windows reached down to the parquet floor. For the duration of the war this magnificent room was used as a dormitory, except for one night, when the Wrens removed the rows of bunks, restored it to its former glory, and invited GIs stationed nearby to a ball.

Crawley Grange

Henceforth, Crawley Grange would be known as the Wrennery. The elegant dining room where waiters once hovered became the mess, where everyone queued up with their plates. Each girl's two-ounce weekly ration of butter, carefully weighed out onto a saucer labelled with their name, was returned to the sideboard after each meal. Flora's berth was in a cabin – a large bedroom on the first floor, that she shared with twenty-five other Wrens. Even here in the heart of the Buckinghamshire countryside, the illusion that they were at sea was maintained – they were now aboard HMS *Pembroke V*.

The 'liberty boat' – the naval term for the requisitioned bus that ferried them back and forth – arrived next morning. The new recruits still weren't told where they were going. After an hour bouncing on slatted wooden seats, as they wound their way through the Buckinghamshire lanes, they reached their destination. On that hot August day, Flora shivered: the gates were guarded by armed soldiers; the perimeter fence was well above head-height; the concrete posts were even higher and angled outward with three rows of barbed wire stretched between them.

They waited while their passes were checked, then the soldiers waved the bus through. They drove up a short driveway bordered by elm and lime trees, then veered left partway around a small circular lawn and drew to a halt. As they waited for orders, Flora surveyed the grand mansion.

***

More than sixty years later, I stand in the circular drive where the Wrens of '42 disembarked the 'liberty boat', and study the architecture. The front façade, the product of money rather than taste, has an air of pretentious indecision. In the centre the style is mock Tudor with timbered gables. To one side it becomes medieval, with battlements above the stone-mullioned bay windows that surround the right-hand corner of the house. Similar ramparts are supported by pillars either side of a front door. On the other side, the design is neo-Gothic, the left-hand gable wrapped round with a two-storey hexagonal tower topped by a verdigris-encrusted copper dome. Stone griffins stand guard on either side of the stone archway, leading to a second front entrance.

Bletchley Park Mansion

The house is exactly the same as a photograph taken when the codebreakers arrived in 1939. During the war years, wooden huts sprung up next to the stables; concrete office blocks rose alongside the lake. Then when the war was over, Churchill ordered all evidence of what went on here to be destroyed. When the Bletchley Park Trust was formed in 1991, only skeletons remained of the original wooden huts and the bomb-proof concrete walls of the new blocks, where more than 9,000 people had once worked.

***

A petty officer led the newly arrived Wrens away from the house, across a patch of bare earth with a few tufts of grass and well-trodden pine cones. The officer told them that here work continued around the clock; they'd be expected to do shift work, including nights. It was monotonous and they'd be on their feet most of the time. She paused to allow her words to sink in.

When one of the stragglers muttered that they might as well have gone into munitions, the officer stopped and turned around. She glared at the girl before walking on in silence.

Flora glanced to her right at the fading pre-war splendour of the estate. Stone steps led down from the circular drive to an overgrowth of what must once have been a well-tended lawn and precisely clipped yew hedges. Beyond it, ducks and geese swam on a lake; neglected shrubs spread out to overhang yellow irises at the water's edge. In the distance, tall poplars and pine trees stretched up into a clear blue sky.

They arrived at a cluster of huts, the walls constructed of horizontal wooden slats, the pitched roofs blackened with tar; thick electrical cables hung between them. The petty officer opened a door into one of these drab, makeshift buildings and led the way down a central corridor into one of several rooms which led off it. Once inside, she pointed to a stack of folding wooden chairs, telling them to take one and sit down. Someone would be along to talk to them shortly.

For a while, all the girls sat in silence. Then one of them asked what they thought was going on, why was it so secret, and pointed to the poster:

You
know more
than other people.
You are in a position of trust
so don't let the forces down.
A few careless words
may give something away
that will help the enemy
and cost us lives
Above all be careful
what you say to strangers and in public.

But they didn't know anything, and if they'd asked they wouldn't have been given any answers.

***

'So, when did you find out what was going on?' I ask.

We are sitting on the settee drinking tea, having just returned from a shopping trip. Aunt Flora runs her hand over her neatly trimmed, silver-grey hair. She is wearing a tailored navy jacket and a pleated plaid skirt.

'We didn't know, not really,' she says.

'But you must have guessed it was something to do with intercepting German messages.'

'But not the details. What the messages were about.'

'But you found out later?'

'After the war I never spoke about it, and neither did anyone else. Then in the early '70s there was this book by Group Captain Winterbotham. I couldn't believe it. It was all about what went on at Bletchley.'

'You read it?'

'I bought it.' Aunt Flora gets up and goes over to the bookshelves, and runs her finger along the spines. 'Here it is... and there was another one, but that didn't come out until the late '90s.' She adjusts her glasses. 'Yes, *Station X* by Michael Smith.'

'Can I borrow them?'

'Yes of course, but I must have them back.'

***

Since the beginning of the war, German messages, enciphered then transmitted in Morse, were intercepted at Y stations dotted all over Britain – from huts battered by North Sea winds on cliffs near Scarborough to another stone frigate, HMS *Flowerdown*, in the heart of the English countryside near Winchester. Wireless operators at these secret listening posts would transcribe the dots and dashes and pass them on to the Government Code and Cypher School (GC&CS) at this estate in Buckinghamshire. Here in the huts, these strings of nonsensical five-letter groups were scrutinised by the most brilliant minds in Britain until the original message emerged. In September 1941, Churchill himself had made his first official visit to Bletchley Park, and by the time Flora arrived he was already referring to what went on in the huts as his 'most secret source'.

In the summer of 1940, Hut 6 had deciphered and read the signals from Goering to the Luftwaffe, alerting Dowding of Germany's plans to 'wipe the British Air Force out of the sky' in the Battle of Britain. A year later, they were deciphering the signals sent by Donitz to his fleet, below the waves, in time for the Admiralty to divert Atlantic convoys away from the U-boats.

In July 1942, when Flora and the other Wrens arrived at Bletchley, Hut 6 had turned their attention towards North Africa and were reading signals from Kesselring to Rommel, giving precise details of Mediterranean convoys. Ultra top secret signals intelligence were able to alert the British Navy and Air Force, thus depriving the Africa Korps of spare parts for their tanks, fuel and food. This, together with information about strength and positions in signals between Rommel and his Panzer divisions, would contribute to Montgomery's victory at El Alamein later in the year.

But the Wrens of '42 knew nothing of this – just that it was hush-hush. And so it had to be. Britain couldn't risk the chance of the Germans finding out that their secret code wasn't secure. Even when the German messages had been deciphered and left Bletchley Park, elaborate plans were in place to disguise the source: fictitious agents were thanked in sham radio messages which the British knew the Germans would be able to decode. Reconnaissance planes flew over convoys whose positions had already been pinpointed.

***

'Sugar?' Aunt Flora holds out the silver bowl with the swan-neck handles.

She's not forgetful, just polite, brought up always to offer to guests before helping herself.

I wait until she has caught two sugar cubes with the sugar tongs, stirred her tea and replaced the teaspoon in her saucer.

'The books you lent me are fascinating. The German Enigma machine. When you were at Bletchley did you known about that?'

'Not really.' Aunt Flora shakes her head. 'Until I read the books I never knew it was called Enigma. A good name, though: the ancient Greek word for a puzzle.' She picks up the plate with the doily. 'Garibaldi?'

'Thank you.' I take a biscuit.

Aunt Flora helps herself. 'I believe it was something like a typewriter with rotors and wires which changed the letter they typed in to another one, so the jumble of letters they ended up with made no sense at all.'

'That's right,' I nod. 'And I'd like to find out more. Can I keep the books a bit longer?'

'Of course.'

***

The German Army, Navy and Air Force all had these portable, battery-operated Enigma machines – about 50,000 in all. What these cipher machines were designed to do was substitute one letter for another: the operator pressed a key and another letter – never the same one – lit up on the lampboard behind the keyboard. Which letter depended on the route an electrical current had taken through a scrambler and a plugboard the Germans called a Stecker – and there were 158 million, million, million possibilities.

The German Enigma Machine

This was achieved because of the order in which three out of five possible rotors were slotted onto a spindle of the scrambler (sixty possible combinations). Each rotor could be adjusted by means of the Ringstellung to any one of twenty-six starting positions, thus raising the number of possibilities to 1,054,560. To compound this even further, opening a flap beneath the keyboard revealed the Steckerboard, where twenty-six sockets labelled with letters could be coupled by ten leads with a jack plug at each end in 150,738,274,937,250 different ways.

158 million, million, million different settings, and once the machine was set up, the routes the current took kept changing; each time a key was pressed, the rotors moved on a notch, which meant that a different letter would light up the next time the same key was used.

To decipher the message, the machine had to be set up in exactly the same way: the scrambler with the same rotors in the same order, each adjusted to the same setting, and the same sockets connected on the Steckerboard. If this was done correctly, then pressing the first letter of an enciphered message on the keyboard would light up the first letter of the original plaintext message on the lampboard. So, deciphering an Enigma signal was simple – provided you knew the settings. However, these changed every twenty-four hours at midnight, according to a list issued at the beginning of each month to all German senders and recipients of Enigma messages, with strict orders to destroy the list in the event of capture. The Germans knew that to work out these settings, before the messages hidden behind them were yesterday's news, was an impossible task, even for the most brilliant of minds. Therefore, they believed Enigma to be impregnable. However, they hadn't reckoned with Bletchley Park and the Bombes.

CHAPTER 3

The Bombe

I place the receipts on the kitchen table and count out the change. Aunt Flora checks it. Then I put the potatoes and carrots in the vegetable rack, the bread in the terracotta crockpot, the bananas and Granny Smiths in the cut-glass fruit bowl. She unwraps the quarter of potted beef and the two slices of cooked ham and inspects them as she transfers them onto saucers. Then she covers them with more odd saucers and puts them in the fridge. Today, I have been shopping on my own. The biting wind is too much for Aunt Flora's angina.

I pour boiling water onto the tea leaves then carry the ready-prepared silver tea tray into the sitting room. Aunt Flora follows with the cream cakes – today I chose chocolate eclairs – on china plates. She lays them on the coffee table and goes over to the sideboard for cake forks, and lines them up alongside our plates as she sits down next to me on the settee.

We chat about the dreadful weather. She tells me that she beat her friends at Scrabble again. When there's a lull, I steer the conversation around to her time in the Wrens.

'You had to sign the Official Secrets Act.'

Aunt Flora stares across the room, trying to remember. 'I don't think we did at Bletchley. That was later, before we went overseas.'

'But you were told the work you were doing was secret.'

'Yes, that first day a naval officer gave us this lecture. Said we'd never be able to tell anyone what we were doing. Not friends. Not family. Not even other people who also worked in the park. Nor could we ask anyone else what they did. Once outside the door of the hut, we kept our mouths shut.'

'And what did he say would happen if you didn't?'

'We would be guilty of high treason. Could be sent to prison.'

'How did you all feel about that?'

'Frightened. Wondered what we had let ourselves in for. Especially when he said we'd be there for the rest of the war. There'd be no transfers and little chance of promotion.'

***

When the briefing was over, the petty officer came to fetch them and led the way along a gravel path beside the tennis courts. On the right was a hut similar to the one they'd just left, but apart from a small gap for the door it was protected by a brick blast-wall which reached up to the eaves, completely obscuring the windows. As they passed, a man in khaki came out; he had three pips on his epaulette, which signified a captain. Flora began to raise her right arm, but her hand hesitated at waist level. The man didn't look up, before he disappeared into a hut directly in front of them. There was no reprimand – later, she found out that no one saluted at Bletchley. A man in air-force blue walked past and also ignored them. Other people were hurrying around the Park but only these two were in uniform, and they weren't navy.

They followed the path round to the left, then the petty officer brought the group to a halt in front of a brick and cement building labelled Hut 11. Before they went inside, the Wrens were warned once again never to mention to anyone anything they saw or heard behind these doors.

From her time at Paton & Baldwin, Flora was familiar with industrial odours and noises – the sickly smell of warm oil, the continuous whirr of spinning machines on the shop floor – but the racket that hit them when they entered this confined space, which they would soon be referring to as the 'hell hole', was altogether different. The machines not only whirred continuously, they also clicked, not in unison, but out of time, like an orchestra in need of a conductor.

The only light came from fluorescent tubes hung from the very low ceiling. The four windows, each one no more than eighteen inches square, down two sides of the room, were too high for the inquisitive to look in – or for the workers to see out. Nevertheless, they were still covered by thick black-out blinds.

In the gloom, Flora could make out six machines. Each one, the size of a very wide wardrobe, was minded by two Wrens. Beads of perspiration collected on the girls' foreheads, damp hair clung to the backs of their necks. They didn't look up but remained engrossed in their task, which involved row upon row of saucer-sized rotors whirring round on the front of the machine and a tangle of wires at the back.

Flora began her training on the machines. From the racks that lined the walls, she learnt to select the correct rotors: red, maroon, green, yellow or brown. These heavy metal disks, a good two inches in depth and almost a hand span in diameter, each with all twenty-six letters of the alphabet around the circumference, had to be pushed onto spindles at the front of the machine in a specified order.

At the top of the machine was a bank of thirty-six rotors arranged in three rows of twelve. Flora now knew why they'd asked her height at the interview: at 5ft 7ins, she had to stretch up to reach the top row. There was a similar bank of thirty-six at waist level, and another below it; to

Wrens operating the Bombe
Reproduced by courtesy of the Bletchley Park Trust

load this, it was necessary to crouch down. In all, 108 rotors, and each one had to be turned around so that the correct letter was at the starting position, then clipped in place. If not properly secured, when the machine was switched on they'd rotate out of control. All this clipping on and off resulted in bruised and sore fingers, which Flora and the other Wrens suffered in silence.

Then they went around to the back of the machine.

***

Sixty years later, as we walk to the shops, Aunt Flora says, 'It was just like that.' In front of us, the door of one of those green boxes you see in the middle of the pavement is open, a British Telecom engineer peering inside, tweaking the wires. 'Only much bigger – much, much bigger – and a lot more wires.'

'How did you know where they all went?' I ask.

Aunt Flora shakes her head. 'It's a long time ago. You forget.'

'It must have been very complicated.'

'We had "menus". Don't know why they called them that. Looked more like a map of the underground, but with letters instead of stations. The things we plugged in were like combs, attached to lots of wires plaited like hair – twenty-six wires, I think, like the letters of the alphabet, though I never counted them.'

Over a cup of tea, I ask Aunt Flora to tell me more about the Bombes.

'To us they were just machines. We never called them Bombes – a good name, though, as they were always ticking.'

'What did you do after you'd put the rotors on the front and wired up the back?'

'At one end of the machine there was an input register, four vertical columns of twenty-six switches, one for each of the letters of the alphabet. The "menu" would tell us which ones to turn on.'

'And then?'

'When we'd finished, the whole setup had to be checked. One Wren called out Apple or Banana, Charlie, Dan, Edward, Freddie or George.' Aunt Flora smiles. 'Mostly boys' names!'

'All this must have taken ages.'

She nods. 'Then, when we were sure we'd got it right, we'd go round the side and switch on the power and the motor, then back to the front to press the ON button. Then the rotors would start to spin: the top row very fast, the middle row clicked round a bit slower, the bottom one slower still.'

'How long did that go on for?'

'A run was about half an hour.'

'So you had time for a break?'

She shakes her head. 'No time for chatting. Anyway, with all that racket going on, it was impossible to hear what anyone said… and then there were the "stops".'

'You mean the machine stopped? So what did you do then?'

'There were three extra rotors, gold ones, permanently fixed alongside the middle bank. We had to write down the three letters where they had stopped. Then we went round the side of the machine and looked at the indicator unit and wrote down the letter which was underneath the metal pointer. The petty officer in charge would then pass the piece of paper with these four letters on through the hatch to the checking room.'

'Then what?'

'We'd start the machine whirring again and wait for the verdict.'

'The verdict?'

'Well, what we hoped for was "Strip down. Job's up." That meant we'd cracked it, but more often than not it was "Continue with the same setup." And we'd just carry on passing on more "stops" for checking.' Aunt Flora pauses, her eyes staring out of the window, her mind back in the 1940s, remembering. 'Sometimes it would be "corrupt" and the order would be given to change the setup. Most annoying of all was when the "stops" kept coming every few minutes because we hadn't put a rotor on properly. Or when it was a short circuit and we'd have to wait for an RAF engineer to come and fix it, and the run would have to be started all over again from the beginning.'

'So how many runs did you do in a shift?'

She shrugs. 'When one run finished, a row of twelve rotors had to be taken off and another set put on, and the whole cycle repeated. And so it went on, sometimes for days.'

***

At the end of her training, Flora had to take an exam. By nature a meticulous and methodical person, she always followed the 'menus' to the letter. Thoroughly familiar with this whirring machine, she was aware of its idiosyncrasies. She knew that the rotors should always be turned forwards, not backwards, so the twenty-six piano-wire brush connections didn't get bent out of line. Even then, it was prudent to check each rotor before it was replaced on the rack. If a wire was at slightly the wrong angle, it had to be stroked back into place with eyebrow tweezers to avoid a short circuit and a false 'stop' the next time it was used.

Although she passed the exam and was an expert in operating the machine, Flora didn't understand how it worked. She wondered who drew up these strange 'menus'. Was it the eccentric intellectuals she'd seen with heads down, deep in thought wandering the park, or eating in silence in the canteen? Most of them were older than she was, but others looked not long out of school. What did they do before the war?

Bletchley was chosen as the Government Code and Cypher School (GC&CS) because it was midway between Oxford and Cambridge, a convenient location for academics. There were mathematicians and musicians; some had a degree in classics or were chosen for their aptitude for crosswords or chess. These were the men – and a few women – who wrote the 'menus' for the army and air force ciphers in Hut 6 and naval ciphers in Hut 8. But how did they do it?

The one flaw in Enigma was that no letter could be enciphered as itself – if the operator pressed A on the keyboard, A would never light up on the lampboard, and the same applied for every other letter of the alphabet. This on its own, however, wasn't sufficient to provide a clue to the settings. What was needed was a 'crib', a section of ciphered text for which the original plaintext was known or could be worked out. It could be a weather report, which often included the heading *Wettervorhersage*, or routine reports like *Keine besondere Ereignisse*, which told the recipient that nothing was happening. It could be a 'kiss', a message enciphered twice, once in Enigma and again in another cipher that was easy to read. Knowing that it was impossible to have the same letter in the same position in the original message and the enciphered message, then by comparing the two, it was possible to make assumptions, thus reducing the number of possibilities from millions of millions to the tens of thousands the machines could test.

It would have taken human brains weeks, months even, to plough their way through all these possible settings, but the Bombes could do it in a fraction of that time. Each bank of the Bombe had thirty-six rotors, which simulated the action of twelve Enigma machines and could cycle through 17,576 possible settings in half an hour. The only problem was that each day several thousand signals were coming into Bletchley by dispatch-rider and teleprinter. Even though these were sorted so that only those likely to yield useful information were tested, there still weren't enough Bombes. At the end of August 1942 there were thirty, and each one was being operated round the clock.

About 200 Wrens manned them in watches. The first week was the day watch: eight o'clock until four o' clock, not that much different from the hours Flora had worked at Paton & Baldwin, and at least it was daylight for the hour's journey back and forth between their billet at Crawley Grange and Bletchley Park.

The second week was the afternoon watch: four o'clock until 12 o'clock, with its midnight dash for the 'liberty boat' to get a seat at the front, be first off when they arrived back at the Wrennery, and beat the others to claim the scraps from supper left out on the scrubbed stone slabs in the kitchen. Many a time Flora grabbed a wedge of pale, stodgy sponge pudding and took it into a corner to share with her friends.

The third week was the night watch: midnight until eight o'clock in the morning. It wasn't easy to sleep in the day, when others in the cabin kept coming and going. The last three days of the rota were the worst: eight hours on, eight hours off, and it took all of the following four days' leave to get their sleep pattern back to normal.

A cabin shared with Wrens all on different watches was no place for resting, so most of them went ashore. London was favourite. They'd come straight off watch, run down the path to Bletchley station, and call in at the buffet to buy the bar of chocolate, wrapped in greaseproof paper – red for plain, blue for milk – available off ration to those going on leave. In the train toilet they'd change from the thick lisle to silk stockings, which some obliging Bletchley shopkeepers would sell in exchange for the navy-issue coupons.

The return train fare, however, cost ten shillings, almost all of a Wren's weekly wage, and the journey was never easy: no announcements where trains were going, timetables didn't exist and cancellations were frequent. There was a much quicker way.

Bletchley was on the Great North Road, the A5, and it was easy to get a lift, or so the other Wrens had said. Flora stood at the kerbside wearing her uniform with her gas mask case over her shoulder, her overnight clothes inside. She'd ignored the posters which warned: *Hitler will send no warning. Always carry your gas mask*, and had left it back at the Wrennery. This hitchhiking wasn't as easy as she'd been led to believe. Then an airman, hoping for a lift going in the opposite direction, came across the road and showed her how to wave a thumb in the direction she wanted to go.

This was the first of many hitchhiking trips to London. Once, Flora travelled on the back of a motorbike; another time, she was offered a lift in a lorry, provided she would take the box lying on the passenger seat on her knee – it was a present for the driver's small children. They were well on the way before he mentioned it contained two white mice. Flora, who had a lifelong fear of rodents, asked him to drop her at Edgware and took the Tube.

Sometimes they hitched in groups. Once, a party of six got a ride on the back of a truck. One of the girls had an accordion and they all sang along for the whole of the 50-mile journey. When they stopped at traffic lights, war-weary Londoners smiled and joined in with 'It's a Long Way to Tipperary' and 'Lily of Laguna'.

It was easy to find somewhere to stay: service clubs or the YWCA charged about two shillings a night. Free theatre tickets were available for service personnel; you just asked at reception. On one occasion, the receptionist told Flora about a French-Canadian army officer staying at the hotel who was looking for someone to show him around London.

As they walked through Hyde Park, he suggested taking a boat out on the Serpentine; fortunately, he was a good rower, because Flora wasn't. He'd always wanted to see Madame Tussaud's, particularly the Chamber of Horrors. She went with him, but soon left him to it and went upstairs to visit the royal family instead. In the evening he invited her to a musical recital, held at the Canadian Embassy. He took her arm and led her up the wide, curved staircase across thick carpets into an anteroom, the walls lined with gilt mirrors. A crowd of people he seemed to know were already there; Flora stood close by his side and forced a smile. To her relief, it wasn't long before the doors opened and they were led into another room with chairs in rows and a quartet in the corner.

The following morning, Flora took the Tube to High Barnet, walked to the by-pass and stuck out her thumb.

And so back aboard: another month with only one day off a week.

CHAPTER 4

Wavendon

When I return Aunt Flora's copy of *Station X* by Michael Smith, I open it at page 180 and ask, 'Why have you underlined *Eric Jones, the head of Hut 3*?'

'Because I remember him.' She takes the book from me with one hand and with the other raises her spectacles to look through the lower half of her bifocal lenses, then looks up and says, 'A squadron leader in the air force. Wore uniform all the time, not like a lot of the others who were quite scruffy. Such a nice person. He used to come into Hut 11 and always had a word for us girls. Had a Lancashire accent.'

'Yes,' I say. 'It says he came from Macclesfield.'

'Did well for himself.' Aunt Flora nods. 'He left school at 14, worked in the cotton industry before the war. Then afterwards, when it was all over, he became director of the Government Cypher Headquarters in Cheltenham.'

'So, what did he do at Bletchley Park?'

'All I knew at the time was that he was in charge of Hut 3, but I didn't know what they did in there, of course. But it says in that book they translated the deciphered army and air force messages from German into English, then passed any important information on to those who needed to know.'

When I ask about the other characters, Aunt Flora racks her brains trying to remember, but without success. Hardly surprising, as apart from the other Wrens on B watch, she never got chance to talk to anyone else.

***

The Wrens got off the 'liberty boat' and walked straight to Hut 11. The machines could never be left idle, so the half an hour mid-watch breaks were taken in rotation. For some unknown reason, the new canteen had been built outside the gates of the Park, so precious minutes were lost as the guards checked their passes. Once outside, there was a choice: they could either make a mad dash down the path to Bletchley station, where WVS ladies in the buffet sold beans on toast for fourpence; or risk what was on offer in the canteen. Woolton pie – an amalgam of pastry, cheese and onion – and salads with an excess of grated carrot made regular appearances at lunchtime, Welsh Rarebit or kidneys on toast at four in the morning. Flora would consider the poster: *Better pot luck with Churchill today than humble pie under Hitler tomorrow. Don't waste food*, and do her best.

When the petty officer in charge asked if anyone on B watch could type, Flora was the only one to raise her hand. From then on there was an occasional welcome respite, when another Wren took over the clipping and plugging so she could type memos and notices. She was also the first one to be considered when there were requests from other huts for someone to help out.

On one occasion, she was taken to a room in Hut 6 where she sat on a folding wooden chair, a strange machine on a trestle table in front of her. It resembled a typewriter, but with drums, the size of a large tin of peaches, on either side of the keyboard. One of the men standing behind her asked if she'd used a Type-X cipher machine before and, when Flora shook her head, reassured her all she needed to do was type. He clipped a sheet of foolscap paper, divided into columns by four red lines, onto the machine. Pencilled into the columns were meaningless groups of five letters. All Flora had to do was work her way across the columns, typing in these letters, and then move down to the next row and continue. The men peered over her shoulder as her fingers moved over the keys, much slower than usual as she wasn't used to typing nonsense.

The men examined the tickertape that snaked out from the 'tin of peaches' and one of them asked Flora if she could read German. When she replied that she couldn't, he held the tickertape up so she could see the letters and said, 'Well, this is German.'

Type-X cipher machine

Her next assignment had nothing to do with typing. She had to complete a crossword puzzle, but there were no clues – just a long string of letters. These had to be copied out into the blank squares of the grid, working from the top to the bottom of the first column then moving on to the second. Flora always enjoyed puzzles, but became rather worried when no words, not even any which looked remotely German, emerged. When she'd finished, an officer inspected her work, then pointed to four letters running horizontally and said, 'MARU. That's Japanese for ship.'

If this extracurricular work was to continue, Flora would have liked to stay on at the Park, but that wasn't to be. In the autumn of 1942, another consignment of Bombes arrived. It was considered foolhardy to keep all their eggs in one basket, a sitting target for the Luftwaffe, so they were installed at outstations. Flora was posted to Wavendon.

Wavendon estate was about five miles to the north-east of Bletchley. As the property had only recently been requisitioned, it was totally unspoiled. In the grounds were mature trees, the leaves turning from green to gold and falling to be scattered by autumn winds, which blew ripples across the lake: a vast lake, where swans emerged from the bulrushes to glide over the water.

Wavendon House

The two-storey mansion which became the Wrennery was set back from the road at the end of a long drive. Above the entrance was a stone parapet, supported on either side by two stone pillars. Inside, a magnificent staircase with a wrought-iron balustrade led up to a minstrel's gallery, but the Wrens never set foot on it – they had to use the back stairs. Flora was delighted, however, to find she was sharing a cabin with only one other Wren. They had proper beds and a bedroom suite, the wardrobe more than adequate to hang all their uniform.

Behind the house was a stable block, empty at that time, but when more girls were drafted later in the war it was converted into cabins, two, sometimes four Wrens occupying the space of one horse. But in Flora's time at Wavendon the stables were only ever used as kennels, by a girl who brought her golden retrievers with her from Scotland.

The only building work that had been carried out at Wavendon prior to the first Wrens' arrival in autumn 1942 was a concreted brick and steel bunker with high windows, to house the Bombes. The work was the same as at Bletchley Park, but seemed easier as there was no travelling to and from watches.

At Bletchley, the Bombes had been christened with names like Agnes, Victory, Havoc, Panic and Chaos. At Wavendon, they were signs of the zodiac. One day, as Flora stood behind Leo fitting plugs into the correct sockets, an electrical current shot up her arm and down her legs, leaving her shocked and shaking. The RAF technician called in to investigate said it was because they'd just washed the concrete floor.

While at Wavendon, Flora was trained to provide cover for the girls on the checking machine, and so she discovered what happened to the 'stops', the four letters they wrote down when the Bombe came to a halt. It was a relief not to have to stand throughout the watch: she was able to sit down, as this machine was small enough to fit easily on a trestle table.

The Checking Machine

The checking machine used only four rotors, not the 108 she was used to. The work involved selecting the appropriate rotors, putting them on the machine in the right order and adjusting them according to the letters of the 'stop'. A row of twenty-six typewriter keys labelled A to Z ran along the bottom of the machine, with a similar alphabet of bulbs above. If when a letter which appeared on the 'menu' was pressed, the next one on the 'menu' lit up, then pressing this letter lit up the next one and so on, right around the loop, until pressing the last letter lit up the first one, then this indicated a possible setting for the Enigma machine. This was a good 'stop' and was passed on to Hut 6 or Hut 8 at Bletchley Park.

For years, Aunt Flora could only guess at what happened after that. I turn to the books and the Internet to find out if her suppositions are correct. In fact, from a number of good 'stops' the logical minds in these huts at the Park could deduce probable Stecker pairs and rotor settings on Enigma. The next step was to try them out on the Type-X, a British cipher machine adapted to mimic the Enigma. If typing in an enciphered message resulted in German words on the tickertape which snaked out of the machine, then they'd got it right. All the German signals sent on the same day with the same settings could then be read, and the order 'Job's up. Strip down' was relayed back to the Bombe operators.

In the autumn of '42, the rotors they loaded onto the Bombes weren't just chosen from the usual five – red, maroon, green, yellow and brown – there were also blue, black and silver. They were working on Shark. At Bletchley they'd worked on this setting, but not always. There'd been Chaffinch II, for signals from Kesselring to inform Rommel about his supply convoys in the Mediterranean; and Phoenix, to direct the operations of his Panzer divisions in North Africa. They'd regularly discovered these army settings but not the naval ones used by the U-boats to report their positions and by their commander, Karl Donitz, to order them into wolf packs around Allied convoys, way out in the Atlantic.

The number of U-boats had more than doubled since the beginning of the year, to more than 200. One in three convoys was now stalked by these torpedo-laden piranhas, and their 'kills' had quadrupled: nearly 500 ships were sunk between July and December 1942. B-Dientz, the German deciphering service, had begun to read British naval signals, but Bletchley Park was still struggling to crack Shark.

Not only were there eight rather than five rotors to choose from, the German Navy had introduced a modified Enigma machine which used four rather than the usual three rotors, thus making the chances of finding Shark settings even slimmer. Since then, the Bombes had provided the answer on only three occasions, the last being way back in March when the 'kiss' came directly from Donitz, who boasted his promotion to admiral in signals encrypted not only in Shark, but also in Dolphin: the Home Waters setting which the Bombes were regularly revealing.

October dragged into November, and the first words uttered by the relief watch would be, 'Still Shark?' The Wrens due to stand off would simply nod.

Flora's four days' leave were coming up – time to make the journey home to Halifax. She collected her travel warrant the day before, packed her kitbag and took it with her on watch. The Wren due to relieve her agreed to come in early, so Flora could make it to Woburn Sands station in time to catch the train supposed to leave Bletchley at four o'clock. So far, so good; she sat in a compartment of a no-corridor carriage, impatient as the train stopped at every station on the branch line to Bedford. The service from St Pancras was late, so she made the connection and they arrived at Leeds, with time for a cup of tea in the buffet, before boarding the train for Halifax. It never came. She shivered on the platform for over an hour, before giving up and settling down on a wooden bench in the Ladies waiting room, then caught the first train next morning.

There was no way to let the family know she'd been delayed, so when her mother answered her knock on the door at 32 Milton Place, a smile of relief banished the worried frown and lit up her eyes, darkened from a long, sleepless night. She hustled her daughter into the kitchen and put on the kettle.

While she made the tea, Flora reached for her kitbag and took out a parcel. Her mother was delighted with the four small tablets of soap. It was more than a month's ration for all three of them, that's if the shops had any. Her sister, Vera, wanted to know how she'd got hold of it, and Flora replied there was plenty where she worked.

And where was that? Vera wanted to know. Flora was torn between wanting to tell the family about the strange mansion and the huts in the Park where she worked, and the importance of keeping the secret and what might happen if she spoke out of turn. She just said they already knew that she was stationed at Bletchley because that's where they sent the food parcels, to PO Box 111, and thanked her mother for sending the Yorkshire parkin: her cabinmate said it was spiffing.

The questions, however, continued that evening, when Jessie arrived home from her shift at the Red Cross. She also wanted to know what her sister did at this place called Bletchley. How was it contributing to the war effort? Flora longed to explain, to prove that she was also playing her part – but even if she could tell her family, what could she say? She spent eight hours a day minding a machine, clipping on rotors, putting plugs into sockets. And what for? She still wasn't sure.

Her mother wanted to know if it was dangerous, were there any bombs.

Flora shook her head. In fact, while she was at Bletchley Park she'd never heard a siren. There was no air raid shelter to go to. Hut 11 and the thick walls surrounding some of the wooden shacks were supposed to be blast-proof; in the other, unprotected huts, workers were told in the event of a raid to don their tin hats and hide under the trestle tables.

Only one stick of six bombs ever fell anywhere near Bletchley Park, and that was in November 1940, eighteen months before Flora arrived. The target was thought to be the marshalling yards at the station, but one just missed the house and lifted Hut 4 clean off its foundations. The next day, workmen hitched it back into place and repaired the shattered windows, while inside naval intelligence continued to translate the deciphered signals and extract the vital information to keep the Admiralty up to date.

As Flora listened to her mother and younger sister's tales of their nights in the cellar, she thought of Wavendon and the secret machines it was hiding, and assured them that there were no bombs where she worked.

Although there was no saluting inside Bletchley Park, it was still compulsory outside, even on leave. Flora remembered just in time as she came out of Lloyds Bank onto Commercial Street and saw a naval lieutenant walking towards her. A girl walked beside him, her arm linked through his. She was a friend who Flora had known since childhood; they had started school on the same day, sat together in class. The girl stopped and introduced her husband. The officer smiled and, noting that she was in the Wrens, asked what category.

Flora turned so her right arm was facing away, hoping he wouldn't notice there was no badge on her sleeve, and said she did clerical work. The officer was serving on a destroyer escorting convoys in the Atlantic; his leave ended the following day. Flora's friend placed a hand on her stomach and said they were both hoping he'd be back when their baby was born.

This was the only one of her contemporaries that Flora met on her two and a half days in Halifax. Most of them had signed up. On the third day, she caught the early train – she couldn't risk getting back late, a charge of being adrift and confinement to barracks. Esther waved her daughter off at the station, consoling herself with the knowledge that, during these dark days, there were secret establishments all over the country.

***

On the afternoon of Sunday, 15 November, Esther and her two daughters stood just inside the open front door. All their neighbours at Milton Place did the same. Just after three o'clock, the tenor in the belfry at St John's began to toll, then one by one the other bells joined in the rejoicing. No one spoke. They just savoured the sound that hadn't been heard since 1939. Church bells had remained silent since the beginning of the war, their peals reserved as the harbinger of a German invasion… or to celebrate a victory.

Churchill had decreed El Alamein to be such a victory: that Desert Fox (Rommel) had been forced back, tail between his legs, into his lair, by Montgomery's Desert Rats. But that wasn't the whole story. Other creatures were involved: the Chaffinch that cheeped, the Phoenix that winged its way across the desert, and even the daily toil of the humble Wren had contributed to Britain's first victory of the war.

The trees in the grounds at Wavendon were completely bare. The swans could be seen wading through shards of ice at the edge of the lake. Flora's cabinmate increased the number of jumpers she wore over her pyjamas from three to four. Wrens on the night shift wore the navy-issue knickers they called 'black-outs' under their bell-bottoms, and watched the hands on the clock creep up to midnight, anxious to be the first back to the Wrennery and into the kitchen to bag a kettle to fill their hot water bottle. Even the ship's cocoa, left bubbling on the range until it turned thick and gluey, became popular.

Then, on 13 December, came the phone order: 'Strip down. Job's up.' Later, word filtered through that Bletchley Park had cracked Shark.

There was no chance of going home for Christmas; the machines couldn't be left idle over the festive season. But there were compensations. Invitations arrived to a dance at the American airbase at Thurleigh. Flora added her name to the list.

The transport, an old charabanc, hijacked from the seaside, deposited the party outside an aircraft hangar. The girls exchanged glances, then the bravest nudged open the door. Inside, smoke swirled in the roving beams of coloured spotlights, a Christmas tree glittered, its upper branches almost touching the ceiling. As soon as they crossed the threshold, each girl was whisked away by a Yank to dance to the sounds of Glenn Miller. When the music changed tempo, Flora declined an invitation to jitterbug and allowed herself to be escorted to the buffet. There was food the Wrens hadn't seen for years: ham, beef and turkey in quantities only available on the black market, the fruit salad was made from fresh fruit. As they left, each Wren was handed two presents. One was a tin of salted peanuts; the other, a sewing kit containing safety pins, needles and thread in the three US uniform colours of black, white and buff. On the front was an eagle, the American Air Force emblem.

The message 'Job's up. Strip down' was frequently relayed to the Wrens on watch in the Bombe block at Wavendon during Christmas 1942. In the huts over at Bletchley Park, they were able to read most of the naval signals enciphered in Shark, before the settings changed at midnight. And the signals were prolific. U-boats reported their positions, Admiral Donitz issued orders. U-boat command became known as 'the most gabby military organisation in all the history of the war'. And so it continued until early March 1943. But by then, Flora – the Wren who was told she would never see the sea – was on a troopship in a convoy on the Atlantic.

CHAPTER 5

Overseas Posting

'So, you were posted abroad,' I say. 'How did that happen?'

We are sitting in deckchairs in the garden behind the sheltered housing complex where Aunt Flora now lives. She is wearing a seersucker dress: navy-blue patterned with wild flowers. Her white, wavy hair is cut short and neat.

'There was a notice up in the foc'sle... I mean the common room... asking for volunteers for an overseas posting. As soon as I saw it I went to Regulating and put my name down.'

'What about the other Wrens. Didn't they want to go too?'

'Yes, several hundred applied, but they only wanted sixteen.' A smile lights up Aunt Flora's face. 'And I was one they chose.'

'How did they choose?'

'They said they were looking for girls with some knowledge of engineering, or mechanical ability.'

Aunt Flora often tackles minor jobs around the house, changing a fuse or rewiring a plug, but as for anything more complicated...

'But when I went before the selection board, there weren't any technical questions.' She gazes around at the mass of orange blooms in the rose bed, the trailing branches of the weeping willow swaying in the gentle breeze. 'I only remember a naval officer looking down at my file, noticing I came from Yorkshire, and saying it was very bleak up there and did I think I could cope with a tropical climate.'

***

The selection board must have decided that Flora wouldn't wilt in the tropics, because not long after, she was ordered to report to Regulating where she was told her request for an overseas posting had been granted. When she asked where she was going, the unit officer shrugged and said that even she didn't know. Flora would do four weeks' training then, after a short embarkation leave, she'd report to an overseas drafting depot in London.

At the beginning of January, the other fifteen successful applicants moved into Wavendon House and the training began. Each morning after breakfast they were driven to Bletchley Park, returning in time for supper: a welcome change from the watches.

The equipment they were taught to operate bore no resemblance at all to the machine they were used to. It was called Hollerith, and included a punch-card machine, a tabulator and a printer. The girls soon realised that from now on they wouldn't be working on alphabetical ciphers, but numerical codes – Japanese codes.

Their instructor was a woman, a civilian, who hovered over them as they struggled to master the punch-card machine. Typewriting skills were no help at all. The keys were numbered one to ten and all were operated by the right hand. The aim was to punch holes in a card seven inches wide and four inches high in the correct row, from zero at the top to nine at the bottom. To practise, each girl was given a string of eighty numbers and each one had to be in the right row in the eighty columns across the width of the card. It was immediately obvious if a card had been punched correctly, because then the holes in these practice cards formed a symmetrical pattern. The attempts by Flora and fourteen of the other Wrens often did not, and then they had to repeat the same exercise all over again.

Not only accuracy but also speed was required; the tap of the keys should be rhythmic and fast. For the beginners, it was erratic and slow. All except one Wren, whose job before the war had been punching these same cards. None of the others would sit next to her to have their laboured efforts compared with her competent clicking.

The punch-card machine

The instructor threatened them with the ruling that at the end of their month's training each girl's performance would be assessed, and they'd be told if they were suitable. If not, it would be back to minding their noisy, clicking machines. At the end of four weeks, Flora still hadn't completed the final practice punch-card correctly, and, like the other fourteen, she feared she'd be left behind when their ship sailed.

Maybe the powers that be decided there was no time to train anyone else: all sixteen were told to report to the overseas drafting depot. In the meantime, they were granted a week's embarkation leave.

As soon as she arrived home, Esther demanded to know where her daughter was going – a question that Flora was unable to answer. She tried to placate her mother by saying she would write as soon as she got there, and she could reply to HMS *Tana*. This didn't help, as her mother was now convinced Flora would be serving aboard a ship, and recounted all the disasters that could happen at sea.

On Monday, there was some respite from the questions. Jessie was at work; her elder sister, Vera, was out shopping; and her mother was in the scullery, supervising the elderly maid with the washing. Flora went up to the bedroom she shared with Jessie and took *Professor Meiklejohn's Comparative Atlas* down from the shelf.

Although they hadn't been told where they were going, she knew the climate was tropical and they'd been trained in the Japanese section. She sat on the bed and opened the atlas at pages 38 and 39: South East Asia. Japan snaked its way down the coast of Manchuria – Manchuko, as the Imperial Emperor had rechristened his conquest. To the east was the Pacific, and off the edge of the page were the islands of Hawaii. Pearl Harbour.

Pearl Harbour: that Sunday, the December before last. The family had been in the living-kitchen when the announcement had come on the nine o'clock news – eighteen warships sunk or crippled, more than 150 aircraft up in flames, almost 2,500 US servicemen dead. Overnight, Japanese carriers and destroyers had crept up on the sleeping islands. At dawn they'd released swarms of aircraft, shoals of torpedoes to devastate the US fleet on Battleship Row. It was Jessie who'd broken the silence by pointing out that at least now the Yanks would have to join the war.

For the next few days, talk at Paton & Baldwin had been of Emperor Hirohito rather than Hitler. Flora had thought the Japanese were too far away to cause the British any harm. She'd been wrong. The following week, as she ate her lunch, one of the typists burst into the canteen with news that the Japs had sunk *The Prince of Wales* and the *Repulse*. Britain's brand-new battleship and a cruiser were at the bottom of the South China Sea.

There'd been no stopping the Japanese. They pushed the British and Indian armies south down the Malay peninsula – Singapore fell on 15 February – north through Burma – Rangoon surrendered on 8 March. By early summer, the Japanese had invaded all the islands south of their homeland down to the north-west coast of Australia, but even that wasn't enough.

She searched the index for the island of Midway and eventually found it on page 51, right in the middle of the Pacific – strategic to the Japanese as a base from which to mount their attack on the west coast of North America. But this time the US forces had been waiting, and the Japs suffered their first defeat. In the eight months since then, the Battle of the Pacific had raged. The Emperor's rampage had been halted by US forces in the south of New Guinea and the Solomon Isles, but as far as she knew Burma, Malaya, the Philippines, French Indo-China and Sumatra, Java, Borneo and other islands of the Dutch East Indies were all in Japanese hands. Flora closed the book.

Flora was still in the bedroom, standing in front of the open wardrobe, when Jessie returned from her shift at the hospital. Her sister pointed to the afternoon dresses, one cotton, one linen, laid out on the bed and asked what they were for. When Flora replied that she was taking them with her as they'd been told there was a social life overseas, Jessie scoffed. Her gaze fell on the long silk dress over her sister's arm, and said she hardly thought Flora would need eveningwear where she was going… who did she think she was: Mata Hari?

Flora pulled a face as the door slammed shut. In the *Instruction for W.R.N.S. Ratings Proceeding Overseas* the list of things to take included two cotton frocks and a civilian suit, as well a bathing suit and cap and dressing gown and slippers. They could each take two suitcases weighing in total up to a hundredweight, so there'd be plenty of room for everything she needed. Petty officers were allocated twice that amount, chief Wrens even more, so goodness knows what they took with them – perhaps the tennis racquet or golf clubs which also appeared on the list!

On the last day of her leave, Flora took a walk alone through the streets of her childhood, past the familiar rows of terraced houses, sooty deposits forming a patchwork of grey on their sandstone-block walls. She crossed Hopwood Lane to People's Park. The railings around it were already gone, and so were the two cannons captured and brought back to Britain when Sebastopol fell almost a century before: all dismantled for the war effort. She sat on a bench on the terrace with its grimy statues of Diana, Apollo and Hercules.

When would she see Yorkshire again? Overseas postings normally lasted two years – maybe, if the war ended, it wouldn't be that long. But the war showed no signs of ending. Even though Montgomery's victory at El Alamein meant that Rommel's retreat from North Africa was on the cards, Germany still occupied France and the Low Countries, and in the east his troops were advancing on Russia. But even if the war in Europe came to an end, what difference would it make? Would she be allowed home? Although US marines had landed at Guadalcanal in the Solomon Islands at the beginning of August last year, the land, air and sea battle had lasted months; only in the last weeks had the Japanese finally relinquished the minutest portion of their ill-gotten gains.

A voice called her name. Flora looked up as the school friend she'd seen on her last leave bent to pull up the brake lever on the pram, then sat down beside her. Flora leant over and cooed at the tiny face peeping out from the blue bonnet, and asked if his dad had managed to get home when he was born.

The new mother shook her head and said that his leave had been cancelled. In the silence that followed, Flora thought of the U-boats in the Atlantic. When she finally replied, to say that he must be delighted to have a son, her friend turned away to hide the tears in her eyes and said she wasn't sure if he knew, she wrote but hadn't heard back. It had now been over three weeks.

Flora gazed across the grass to the bandstand, to the fountain in the middle of the pool where they'd paddled together as children. Beyond it was the lake where they'd fed the swans, the bridge over the stream where they'd played hide and seek. Way back then, in peacetime, there'd been no silences between them. Now, she could think of no words to say.

***

The overseas drafting depot was just off Piccadilly at 32 Golden Square, premises which before the war had been an ear, nose and throat hospital, and still bore the scars: deep scratches on the double doors and chips out of the plaster marked out trolley routes along the corridors. Their cabin was an old Nightingale-style ward with the bedsteads replaced by metal bunks. The sixteen Bletchley Wrens weren't the only ones awaiting shipment abroad. Other Wrens were bound for naval bases where they would take up clerical or administrative duties, or remote Y-stations to become wireless operators. But none of them knew where they were going.

Shortly after they arrived, Flora and the other fifteen from Bletchley were taken by naval transport into central London. Inside a building with high ceilings and wide staircases, the Wrens were read the Official Secrets Act and each given a copy to sign.

They waited.

The days stretched into a week. No squad drill, no cleaning – in fact, no duties at all. The girls were allowed shore leave for short periods, but had to report back by a certain time in case news came in of their posting. Being in London, there was plenty to see, even though many of the attractions were closed during wartime.

Then the group of sixteen was ordered to report to Regulating, and told they would be leaving sometime within the next few days and their destination would be Mombasa. None of the girls had a clue where that was, so Flora told them she thought it was somewhere on the east coast of Africa. They were to tell no one where they were going and, from then on, all shore leave was cancelled.

The next couple of days were hectic: medical examinations and inoculations for typhoid, typhus, tetanus, cholera and smallpox. There were lectures on healthcare in hot countries, how to behave towards the locals, and oblique references to relationships with the opposite sex.

Then they were taken to the clothing depot at Mill Hill, to be kitted-out for the tropics. Much to the girls' disgust, their jaunty sailor caps were replaced by wide-brimmed hats with a 'tidley bow' at the back. Navy was too dark and unsuited to the hot climate, so each girl was given three circular pieces of white material and instructed to use them to cover the crown and to take them off regularly to wash them, then sew them back in place. For the rest of their uniform, white replaced navy-blue: six skirts, six short-sleeved blouses and three cotton dresses. Down the front reveres were a series of holes, for inserting detachable buttons held in place with split rings. The skirts allowed for easier movement than the navy version as they were made up of panels of white drill material, with a slight flare at the hem. There was a white belt, two pairs of white canvas shoes, two pairs of white lisle stockings and four pairs of white ankle socks; most of the girls took up the option of exchanging the socks for stockings, a decision they would later regret.

Each girl received a grant of a guinea to buy extra underwear: one brassiere, four pairs of white rayon knickers and two cellular vests. They were also issued with ten coupons to buy soap, as this had been found to be expensive to purchase abroad. The other essential that it was difficult to buy overseas was sanitary towels, so they were provided with a free three-month supply.

While they were packing their two service-issue suitcases back at the depot in Golden Square, a petty officer came into the cabin carrying sixteen small circles of navy serge embroidered in light blue with a star, a W in the centre. She instructed the girls to sew them on their right sleeve, midway between shoulder and elbow. The Wrens protested that they weren't writers. The officer told them that there would be other troops aboard who'd want to know their category. Officially it was Special Duty X – SDX for short – but they couldn't tell anyone that, and it would be easier to let everyone think they were just typists.

Then, she asked if anyone had a camera, and ordered the Wrens that owned one to hand them over. The girls groaned and unfastened their suitcases once more. Flora located her precious Kodak, which opened out into bellows at the front, a present from her father. She parted with it most reluctantly, hoping that it wouldn't get lost on the journey, and the officer would be able to keep her promise and return it when they arrived in Mombasa.

PART 2: THE VOYAGE

Aunt Flora passes away in 2008, at the age of 92. In a drawer in her bedroom, I find the two volumes of her diary, together with a photograph album. They are wrapped up in a clear plastic bag and tied with ribbon. Attached is a luggage label; neatly printed on it in proud, bold capitals is the following:

WRNS EX BLETCHLEY PARK
AUG 1942–45
BOMBE OPERATOR UNTIL FEB 43
THEN OVERSEAS TO
MOMBASA (ALIDINA) HOLLERITH) JAPANESE
CEYLON, COLOMBO ") INTELLIGENCE

As an afterthought, she has squeezed in the words:

FIRST 16 WRENS TO GO OVERSEAS FROM BP

I take out the two notebooks, one quarto-size, the other foolscap. The corners are battered and reveal thin layers of buff card beneath the scuffed, maroon paper veneer of the hardback covers.

Listed on the inside of the first one, the smaller of the two, are the names of the other Special Duty X Wrens to be sent overseas. Glued beneath it is Aunt Flora's second-class berthing card, completed in blue pencil with D for Deck,

29 for Cabin, 13 for Berth. Next to it is a passport-sized photograph of her in a hat with a wide navy brim, the letters HMS on the navy ribbon above it, and the crown neatly covered with a circular piece of white material. She has a shy smile on her youthful face.

The pages have become yellow over time, their edges beginning to curl. The diary begins when she leaves London to travel to Scotland, to board a troopship at Greenock.

She uses a fountain pen, which makes me wonder where she managed to find a quiet corner to write on a ship overcrowded with troops. Was it in a sheltered spot on deck? But it was February, and she would have had to wrap up in her serge jacket and bell-bottoms if she was to survive the Atlantic winds as the ship rounded the western coast of Ireland. Was it lying on her top bunk? But the writing seems far too neat – no smudges or blots – for such cramped conditions. Perhaps she was lucky and managed to find a table somewhere in the communal rooms on the upper decks, or cleared a space on the dressing table down in the cabin, where she could rest her book and lay out her ink bottle and blotting paper.

This time, I read the diaries with the insight gained from our long chats over tea and biscuits. They tell her story, in parts in great detail, followed by lapses in time. During the last years of Aunt Flora's life, she answered my questions, filled in some of the gaps, retold some of the stories. Sometimes, to jog my memory I have to look back over the notes I made at the time.

Not everything, however, is explained. The places where she was billeted, where she worked, are never named; there is no mention of the work she did. Then, there are the questions I never asked, a couple because I thought they were too personal – that she may find them upsetting and they may lead us in a direction she didn't want to go. And there were those that I never thought about back then. To answer these, I visit the library and surf the net.

CHAPTER 6

Leaving

We left the drafting depot, Golden Square, London in the evening and were taken in lorries to St Pancras station where we were told we would have a long journey up to Greenock. We were all feeling terribly excited on the first stage of our journey, at last we felt we were actually on the way. When the time came for the train to pull out of the station we all crowded into the corridors to watch the last glimpse of London disappear into the night and I think the majority were wondering when they would once more see that city.

– Diary entry, 21 February 1943

Back in the blacked-out, third-class compartment, nobody spoke. The dimmed, blue light bulb concealed a few tears as the excitement of their long-awaited departure gave way to apprehension, not knowing how long it would be before they returned. Flora unwrapped her greaseproof paper parcel of sandwiches. Other Wrens couldn't face the usual coarse brown bread, a scraping of butter and Spam, and devoured their ration of chocolate instead.

One by one, the Wrens fell asleep.

When she woke, Flora's neck was stiff where her head had lolled to one side. She longed to reach down to massage her frozen feet, but didn't, for fear of waking the others. Outside the window, early morning mist swirled over the countryside. The train chugged on through sleepy village stations in the Yorkshire Dales.

In Carlisle, the troops were allowed off the train, where they were given more sandwiches and mugs of tea. Back aboard, rumour circulated that their destination in Greenock was another drafting depot. To the Wrens' delight, however, the transport that picked them up from the station dropped them off within sight of ships' funnels and tall cranes dangling nets of crates and baggage.

They assembled on the dock for roll call, alongside a ship topped with three enormous funnels. Rows of portholes marked out the accommodation decks beneath the two open decks with lifeboats dangling from davits above them. Men from all three services lined the ship's rails. A platoon of Tommys whistled as they embarked through an opening low down in the ship's side. The Wrens were marched up a steep gangway straight onto the open deck. They were now aboard RMS *Strathaird*, a 22,000-ton P&O passenger liner.

RMS Strathaird

Flora wrote in her diary:

What a thrill it was when, after the usual roll calls, at last we embarked and, on arriving on the ship, we were given our cabin and berth numbers. Our cabin was very large, 16 bunks and four mattresses on the floor, there was also plenty of hanging space for clothes and dressing tables in between the bunks. We also had four wash basins with hot and cold water so it seemed luxury to what we had expected. I had visions of being absolutely crowded together with very little room to move about, this seemed a very good beginning. By now it was 4 p.m. and nothing had been mentioned of a meal, except for a cup of tea we had had nothing since breakfast of sandwiches in Carlisle about 8 a.m. so we were all feeling hungry.

The next step was to collect our luggage which the sailors were bringing on board. We went along to the orderly room and what a sight and noise met our eyes and ears. From the stairs sailors were passing down the luggage calling out various names, but as there were approx. 300 Wrens crowded into a few square yards, all trying to retrieve their cases at the same time, once you were in the crowd it was absolutely hopeless trying to move in any direction and impossible to reach one's case. This hubbub went on for quite a while and in the end we were all sent back to our cabins and told the cases would be distributed round the alleyways and could then be collected with ease. What a relief, this was certainly more sensible and eventually our cases were found and safely deposited in our cabins…

At last there was the very welcome sound of the dinner gong and did we make a quick exit and so to the mess which was on "B" deck and was also used by the W.O.'s [warrant officers]. *It was a huge room with tables for 10 and a few for eight and we really did have a marvellous meal and were ready for it!!! It seemed such a change to go into a mess and find the tables all laid with glasses and clean cutlery. Also there were stewards to wait on you, quite unheard of in service life, and to have your meal brought to you instead of continual queues seemed too good to be true. We also had white bread, another war-time luxury and we certainly did justice to that meal and wondered if this service would continue for the whole voyage!!! There were a number of Lascars* [East Indian seamen] *on the ship as stewards and helping with the ship in general, some of them wearing most becoming tunics, vividly embroidered, and small hats…*

Afterwards we went up on deck for a little fresh air, it was bitterly cold so after a short while we returned to the cabin and so to bed. One had almost to be a trapeze artist to climb into the upper bunks, they were exceptionally high and made of iron with rails at the side which one could let down, but mine was so stiff and difficult to move I climbed over the top, trying my best to avoid banging my head on the various pipes running across the roof. In spite of the bed being rather hard and the pillow made of straw with a hard ridge in the middle, I slept very heavily and had a good night's sleep which I definitely felt to need after all the excitement.

The following day, all service personnel were issued with life jackets and ordered to report to emergency stations. As they donned their Mae Wests, the Wrens joked about vital statistics. Then the procedure for abandoning ship, should the vessel be on fire or in danger of sinking, was explained. On dismissal, they couldn't return to their cabins until ship's inspection was complete; Flora and her companions stood by the rail, clutching their life preservers and looked down at the cold, grey sea a long way below.

The Wrens were surprised to find a good canteen aboard where they could buy almost anything, including tins of plums and Carnation cream, which later in the voyage they would purchase to celebrate special occasions. It might be a birthday of someone aboard or back home, and many a time they would eat plums and cream out of mugs in the cabin by torchlight. The canteen also sold chocolate, and they returned regularly after lunch to buy their ration of one bar a day – the meal wasn't complete without it. The barber's shop sold a limited range of cosmetics, and items of clothing like shorts and pumps, but at exorbitant prices; the Wrens came away without making a purchase. Nor would they be back for a shampoo and set: at between eight and nine shillings, it was a sizable chunk out of a week's pay.

In the early hours of Wednesday, 24 February 1943, RMS *Strathaird* weighed anchor and slipped out of the Clyde, past the darkened Isle of Arran and through the North Channel. Out in open sea, she was joined by other vessels, their merchant markings all blotted out with the same grey paint. They lined up: 200 yards of sea separating the stern of one from the bow of the next; nine columns, 500 yards apart. Destroyers, minesweepers and corvettes circled around the perimeter. By daylight, they were on course for the first phase of their voyage round the north-west coast of Ireland.

CHAPTER 7

Aboard a Troopship

During the night we left the shores of Scotland and when we woke up in the morning we found ourselves really at sea and a very choppy sea at that. It was a most peculiar sensation when you got out of bed you more or less rolled across the floor. I imagine it was similar to being drunk as you could not walk straight.

– Diary entry, 24 February 1943

Flora gripped the metal bars and slid down from the bunk. As her feet touched the deck, the ship listed to starboard and she careered across the cabin, narrowly missing other Wrens asleep on mattresses on the floor. With one hand on the bulkhead, she reached the washbasin and, still swaying, managed a quick strip wash.

Breakfast was at eight. With only four basins in the cabin, there were cries of 'Hurry up it's my turn', but late risers didn't even manage to splash their face with cold water before the gong sounded. A few didn't manage to get up at all, just lay in their berths groaning, their faces pale, tinged with green.

After breakfast, the brave but unwashed returned to the cabin and turned on the taps. Nothing came out. Someone complained to the cabin steward, an elderly British merchant seaman. He just shrugged and informed them that while at sea, water for washing was turned off at eight-thirty. Flora resolved from then on to fill her hot water bottle first thing every morning; at least then there'd be a chance of a wash before dinner.

The sea continued to be very choppy. More Wrens took to their beds, leaving more vacant seats in the mess, where the roll of the ship seemed worse and the smell of food didn't help. Flora, however, managed all her meals, but as soon as she rose from the table she always headed straight for the fresh air of the deck. She was immensely relieved that she never succumbed to seasickness, but so sorry for those that did. They looked so terribly ill.

One of their sixteen never emerged from the cabin at all for the first four days. She couldn't eat anything, but the cabin steward kept her supplied with a morning cup of tea and jugs of iced water. He was less sympathetic as he watched the other Wrens ricochet from bulkhead to bulkhead in the gangways on their way back to the cabin. When they asked him how long this dreadful weather was likely to last, he told them that there was much worse to come. And that wasn't all: out there to port, in their pens at Brest, the German U-boats were waiting.

But the Wrens felt too sick to care.

Perhaps the seas became calmer, or maybe the landlubbers gained their sea legs, because within a week the chairs in the mess were occupied again. One place at each table, however, was vacant for most of the meal: it had been decreed that there would no longer be table service. The diners had to take it in turns to collect meals for their companions.

Flora hated all this queuing. Not only did they have to queue up on deck for the tea boat, but now for the meals as well. She never enjoyed a meal by the time she had queued for ten soups, ten main courses and ten sweets, usually having to wait for ages by the hot plates when the food had run out and more had to be fetched up from E deck. After she'd cleared the table she felt quite exhausted. The food itself, though, was an improvement on naval rations, as Flora records in her diary:

> *As far as meals were concerned, they were, on the whole, good, but very little variety, the sweet for lunch was always sago, tapioca or rice (very hard and uncooked) and it was a standing joke that for dinner the menu gave various names for the pudding such as Cumberland, Mansfield,*

Vicarage and several more but the pudding itself was always the same, sponge with fruit and by the time we had had 5 weeks of this we were rather tired of it.

After the daily ten o'clock boat drill, the SDX Wrens' only duty was to practise their punching. They had brought a punch-card machine aboard, with strict instructions to keep it hidden. Each Wren took her turn pressing the keys to produce the elusive patterns on punch-cards. But during the whole of the voyage their skill improved very little: they couldn't concentrate. Could their clicking be heard on the other side of the cabin's thin bulkhead? Would someone demand to know what they were doing? And anyway, there were other ways of passing the time, as Flora describes in her diary:

PT classes were arranged each day and at first were very well attended but, as the climate became more tropical these numbers decreased very rapidly. For myself I had not the energy to rush about in very hot weather… Tombola was also very popular being held several times a week, but it always seemed to be so crowded, I much preferred to be in a cool spot on A deck if possible. After the first few days when the weather began to be warmer most of our time was spent lazing on deck, reading, writing or trying to improve my chess…

We also had several lectures which were very good, "The collapse of France" by a French journalist – he really did his best to stick up for France and explained the position of the country at the outbreak of war – he seemed so pathetic somehow you could not help but feel sorry for him and try to understand his point of view. Another was on "Bomber Command", "Destroyers", "West Africa", "Durban", "The Theatre", all of them very interesting and made a break in the days.

On St David's Day they held an "Eisteddford" in the First Class Mess and it was fine. Various competitions were held and prizes given for the best funny stories, song (male & female), piano solo, choir, poem, limerick and all together we had a first rate concert, there was certainly some talent among both ratings and officers, the room was absolutely crowded and the heat terrific, we were lucky to have seats as quite a number were standing.

A ship's concert party was also formed, at first this consisted of Navy & Airforce and was therefore called "The Blues" but later in the voyage some army personnel also helped. The chorus was entirely Wrens and to say they had very few practices they kept together pretty well and were always welcomed with a cheer from the troops. This concert was given several times on deck for troops in various parts of the ship and they all deserved a pat on the back for all the work and time they put into the show making it a real success.

The audience had to bring their lifebelts along to sit on while they watched the twenty-five turns. The programme of 'The Blues' Concert Party, typed on a sheet of lined foolscap paper, is pasted in Flora's diary. It included a number of singers and stand-up comedians. There was a piano solo, a drummer, a tap dancer and an able seaman who played the spoons, as well as comedy sketches and impressions of Flanagan & Allen, Popeye and Donald Duck. The final item was entitled 'A-Deck Annie'. All the men in the audience roared with laughter as a naval lieutenant recited this poem which involved goings-on inside one of the ship's three funnels. This made no sense at all to the Wrens, but years later Flora discovered that the ship's third funnel was just a dummy, an empty shell, added because three funnels were more impressive than two.

Dances held almost every afternoon on B deck were very popular. Admission was by ticket issued to the various services in turn. The SDX Wrens were among the first to be invited. They discussed what they would wear. Not much choice, really. Some of the girls wore their 'glamour gowns', but even with a white belt they never looked smart. Most opted for the white skirts and blouses, silk stockings if they had them, otherwise they asked one of their friends to draw a straight line in black eyebrow pencil down the centre of each leg.

When they arrived, the troops were already there, Royal Engineers and Royal Army Signals Corps. Flora was asked for the pleasure of the first waltz by a handsome, yet crumpled, lance corporal. As they circled the floor, she learnt of the conditions the troops endured down in the bowels of the ship. Later, she wrote in her diary:

> *Although we had very comfortable quarters and good food I am afraid the same could not be said of the men, they were simply crowded together on the lower decks, sleeping in hammocks, slung almost touching one another with others on the floor underneath them and the first few days when so many were ill with seasickness it really must have been terrible, they did not get much pleasure out of the trip, such conditions should not be allowed even for transporting troops and there should definitely be enough good food for them during the whole voyage. Both officers and Wrens had a hot lunch and also dinner at night whilst the men often only had one (sometimes two) slices of bread and jam or ship's biscuits for supper, it did not seem right somehow when everyone is fighting for the same "Freedom". I wonder when such things will alter. I am sure it is not necessary to have such extremes and it caused much resentment on the ship.*

As he escorted Flora off the floor, her dancing partner asked a favour. Sewing an extra stripe onto his sleeve seemed the least she could do to make the newly-promoted lance corporal's life easier. From then on, the Wrens were kept busy with needle and thread, not only applying insignia, but also replacing buttons, shortening shorts and altering jackets.

With only 300 Wrens and a small contingent of nurses aboard, servicemen outnumbered women by at least four to one. The women were, therefore, in great demand, and tickets for the next dance arrived a few days later. This time it was the turn of the Scottish Horse Guards; a number of the men wore kilts and looked very dashing. Their regiment provided the pipe band and the highland reels were enjoyed by spectators and dancers alike.

On their sixth day at sea, Flora made the mistake of asking the cabin steward where they were. He sucked in his lips and told her they were due east of the Azores… where just last month seven tankers out of a convoy of nine were lost to the U-boats. From then on, their cabin steward became known as Job's Comforter.

Later, as the sun sank lower in the sky, every shadow on the sea was a periscope, every patch of white water a conning tower rising up from beneath the waves. Flora left the other Wrens and went astern to watch the foaming trail, marking out the miles they'd already covered. She took comfort from the other ships: one on each side, one following close behind. She looked into the distance, trying to identify the outlines of gun turrets and radio antennae. Out there circling the convoy, listening, watching and waiting was their protector, the battleship HMS *Malaya*.

The Wrens were only allowed on the starboard deck of the ship – the port side being reserved for the men – and could only be accompanied on the outside decks by officers, not ratings, a rule hard to enforce in total blackout. After the sun set at seven, the troops were allowed to leave their cramped quarters in the bowels of the ship for the fresh air and space on the deck. Although Flora never took advantage of this, some of her friends did, but these secret assignations couldn't last long as the Wrens had to go below at eight. After much protest, this was extended to eight-thirty, but no later as a petty officer was waiting to make sure everyone was present and correct. For the men, however, there was no curfew; some of them stayed and slept beneath the stars until daybreak, when the crew swabbed down the decks.

Down in the cabins, the Wrens lay on their bunks in the sticky evening heat, longing for sleep. The ventilators didn't really help, even when they rigged towels above them, hoping to direct a breeze their way. Flora asked the guard posted outside their door to open the porthole. He looked at the water lapping over the lower rim, smiled, and said if he did they would get very wet.

***

Flora and Pat, one of the other SDX Wrens, stood at the bow and, with one hand shading the sun from their eyes, scanned the horizon. They could just make out the dim outline of mountains. This was their first glimpse of the west coast of Africa, their first sighting of land since they'd left the cold shores of Britain twelve days before. As they sailed closer they could see huts on the beach, palm trees in the background.

Down in the cabin, Job's Comforter explained they would be dropping anchor off Freetown in Sierra Leone. Only very small ships could dock there, so there was no chance of going ashore… and they wouldn't want to. It was a terrible place.

But the locals came to them, as Flora describes in her diary:

No sooner had we dropped anchor than the natives came alongside in tiny canoes, very frail crafts which were continually filling with water and making it necessary for them to bale frantically from time to time with some old tins apparently kept specially for that purpose. They sang, or rather tried to sing "Bless 'em All" and "I've got Sixpence", but one could hardly recognise the tune as they have most unusual voices.

I had always heard of natives diving for money and it really was remarkable the way they dived from their canoes, returning very quickly usually with a coin in their mouths and the way they once more scrambled into their canoes without capsizing them was really a wonder. The water was exceptionally silted so how they found the coins I do not know. They are certainly very cute and would only dive for silver and when someone wrapped a copper in silver paper they knew the difference and the language they used was not very complementary [sic].

A larger boat was heading towards them. It lay low in the water, weighed down by its cargo of bananas. Before the war, bunches had hung in her father's ripening store and had been freely available at home – never absent from the fruit bowl on the dresser. Flora remembered their soft, comforting texture, but what did they taste like? It had been almost two years since they'd been imported into Britain. She had the money to buy them, but no means of hauling them up from the sea so far below. Then, a hatch in the ship's side opened and the cargo was hoisted aboard. Rumour spread that bananas would be on sale in the canteen.

That evening, as they watched a party of lucky Wrens board lifeboats, those left behind muttered that it wasn't fair. Ratings were rowing a girls-only group across to the HMS *Malaya* for a party. A farewell party – for this was where the battleship was to leave them.

As night fell, lights from the shore and the vessels anchored around them twinkled across the water and reminded Flora of peacetime. She thought of everyone back home, and wondered how much longer the blackout would continue.

The night-time curfew was extended to nine o'clock. A small concession, but at least the portholes could be left open to let a little more air into the cabins. They heard the partygoers scramble back aboard. Next morning, there was talk of little else but the food, the dancing and the sailors aboard the Malaya.

***

Three days out of Freetown, two incidents occurred. One morning, they sailed past a shoal of flying fish. Flora had seen pictures of these aquatic aviators in a children's encyclopedia, but they were much smaller than she'd imagined: the size of a small herring. They rose from the water at terrific speed, fanning out their pectoral fins into wings of various shades from deep turquoise to translucent purple. Their silver scales sparkled in the sunlight as they zigzagged over the waves for vast distances, before gliding back into the sea. Sometimes a whole shoal would emerge at the same time and skim the surface, producing a cascade of glittering stars as they re-entered the water.

The second event occurred when the Wrens made their regular visit to the canteen after lunch. The bananas were still green and inedible, but worse than that: the chocolate ration had run out.

As they sailed further south, the Wrens were relieved to be allowed to wear white or navy sports shirts instead of uniform blouses, and short socks instead of lisle stockings. With temperatures in the eighties and nineties, only soldiers under orders and the very keen reported for PE; only those convinced that eventually their numbers would be drawn out of the bag and it would be their turn to call 'House!', could endure the daily games of tombola. If they wanted to buy an iced drink, they had to queue for half an hour in the relentless heat.

The ship's position was never divulged, but it was clear they were now very close to the equator. Rumour had it they would cross the line around midday on 15 March. Tradition dictated that ceremonies should take place, based on ancient maritime rituals: involving sailors painting their faces, dressing up in grass skirts, and much fooling around and immersion in water. Everyone waited for the announcement.

It was after four and still nothing, so one of the Wrens consulted Job's Comforter. He said that most likely there'd be no celebrations – hadn't they noticed the ship zigzagging? There were U-boats about.

But even their pessimistic steward didn't know the whole truth. Not far away, survivors from another troopship were adrift in lifeboats, on Carley floats and rafts, hundreds of miles off the Ivory Coast. Their ship, *Empress of Canada*, had been torpedoed by an Italian submarine, *Leonardo Da Vinci*, just after 11 p.m. on 13 March. Aboard the former luxury liner were Italian prisoners of war, French, Greek and Polish refugees, as well as members of the British Navy and Air Force. Sixteen passengers were women: six of them chief Wrens, who had been among the first party of twenty wireless operators to be sent overseas at the beginning of 1941. Having completed two years' duty in Singapore, Ceylon and Mombasa, they were returning home to Britain. After the first hit, the submarine commander had allowed time for passengers and crew to abandon ship, before firing his second torpedo and sending the 20,000-ton ship to the bottom of the ocean.

As the *Strathaird* approached the equator two days later on 15 March, the survivors were still awaiting rescue, prey to the sharks and barracudas of the South Atlantic waters. They had been spotted by a Sutherland flying boat but were not picked up by HMS *Boreas* until the following day. When they disembarked at Freetown, with sun-scorched skin and parched lips, they would learn that almost 400 passengers and crew had perished.

The *Strathaird* crossed the equator just after 22.00 hours. No celebration. No lights. Even the glow of a cigarette smoked by one of the men sleeping on deck could have given away their position.

The following day, crossing-the-line certificates, rubber-stamped with the commander's signature, were piled up in the canteen. They granted the Freedom of the Seas to all servicemen and women who wished to buy them. The Wrens queued up for their copy and in their neatest handwriting filled in their own name and the date.

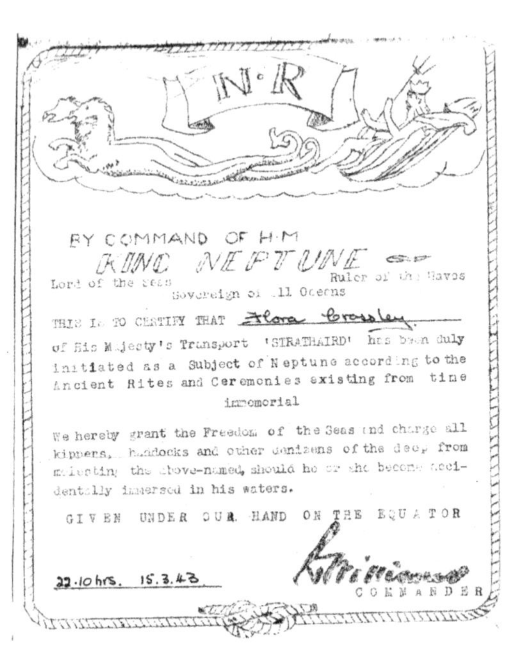

N·R

BY COMMAND OF H·M
KING NEPTUNE
Lord of the Seas   Ruler of the Waves
Sovereign of all Oceans

THIS IS TO CERTIFY THAT Flora Crossley
of His Majesty's Transport 'STRATHAIRD' has been duly initiated as a Subject of Neptune according to the Ancient Rites and Ceremonies existing from time immemorial

We hereby grant the Freedom of the Seas and charge all kippers, haddocks and other denizens of the deep from molesting the above-named, should he or she become accidentally immersed in his waters.

GIVEN UNDER OUR HAND ON THE EQUATOR

22.10 hrs. 15.3.43

COMMANDER

Crossing the Equator Certificate

The Wrens peered across the sea for their first glimpse of Table Mountain. Flora had seen photographs in a children's encyclopedia and knew that the flat top had given the mountain its name. Mist drifted along the vast, horizontal plateau and billowed like smoke down the mountain's steep sides towards Cape Town, the city nestled beneath it, in a semicircle around Table Bay. Both crew and troops had expected the convoy to join the other ships in the harbour, but, to their dismay, they just sailed on past.

***

14 April 2008

I stand at the top of Table Mountain and wonder why the *Strathaird* never docked here sixty-five years ago. It is one of the questions to which I may never find an answer.

I have a picture in my mind of the places Aunt Flora visited, but these are just visions conjured up by words. I need to visit these places and see for myself. Terry, my husband, books us a passage on a ship sailing round the coast of Africa. Our voyage begins in Cape Town.

The cableway we came up on was built in 1929, so it must have been here when my aunt passed by, all those years ago, as must the rugged granite that time has eroded into Lion's Head to our left and Devil's Peak to our right. In the valley between them, however, the city of Cape Town would not have been the high-rise, sprawling city it is today. A mass of dull grey naval vessels and troopships would have been anchored in Table Bay, not the pristine, white passenger liner we board tomorrow.

As we sail out of Table Bay the following day, the tabletop is covered with a cloth of mist, which often happens when the cold air from the sea meets the warm air from the land. We round the headland south-west of the city and the mist begins to lift, just as it did when my aunt sailed by, more than six decades ago. The ship hugs the coast and we gaze upward to the peaks of the twelve apostles, the rocky buttresses extending along the peninsula to the south of Table Mountain. The sun comes out to highlight the steep sides in shades of grey, brown and purple. These craggy slopes descend right to the water's edge, forming the rugged coastline where the cobalt-blue sea bursts into white breakers as it crashes against huge boulders. At intervals, the rough granite gives way to small coves, where gentler waves roll in over yellow, sandy beaches. I can understand what my aunt meant when she wrote in her diary: *it was a sight you could never forget.*

After that, there are no entries in her diary for three days. I suspect I know why. We are sailing round the Cape of Good Hope, where the Atlantic meets the Indian Ocean. Our ship's gross tonnage is 38,000, and there are less than 700 passengers aboard. There's nothing to be done about the pitching – cresting the wave then descending into the depression behind it. However, the stabilisers are out to reduce the side-to-side rolling of the ship. The *Strathaird* was only 22,500 tons, and had about 3,000 troops aboard. Stabilisers weren't fitted on merchant ships until the 1950s.

CHAPTER 8

Durban

What a trade Durban must have done that weekend when the convoy was in, the shops, especially sweet and fruit were besieged, it was such a change to see food so plentiful. [We] *walked along the main road and had not gone far when we were given grapes and bananas by some R.A.F. everyone seemed to be handing things round regardless of whether you knew one another or not, there was definitely a holiday spirit, a feeling of freedom.*

– *Diary entry, 26 March 1943*

After twenty-eight days at sea, the convoy put in to Durban to 'coal ship'. As the *Strathaird* lay in the outer anchorage, waiting her turn to enter the harbour, the Wrens hung over the starboard rail and stared at the sandy beach bordered by a row of brightly-painted buildings. It reminded Flora of Blackpool. Later, she discovered that many of the British settlers in Durban thought the same and, in fact, had nicknamed their seafront the Golden Mile.

Chains rattled and grated as the crew weighed anchor. The ship steered a course past the promenade and the pleasure beach, through the narrow channel into the Bay of Nepal. Battleships, cruisers and destroyers were berthed beside the quays or lay at anchor in this vast, natural harbour. Once inside, *Strathaird* swung hard to starboard and came alongside at Point Docks, on a spit of land that runs from the beach to the harbour entrance and separates the bay from the Indian Ocean.

Only the crew were allowed ashore in the morning; Job's Comforter returned at noon with a box and a large brown-paper parcel – a present for his flock of Wrens. The girls shrieked with delight: inside the box were ten pounds of green grapes, and the parcel contained a dozen lemons.

At last, leave was granted. The road from Point Docks was a moving mass of khaki, air-force blue and navy – everyone heading for the shops. The Wrens were carried along by the crowd. After almost a month crammed together on the ship, where minor irritations festered and arguments mushroomed, at last they were free, all gripes forgotten, all disputes put on hold.

At the top of Point Road, they turned left into West Street, a wide thoroughfare with trolley buses running up the centre and shops under shady awnings lining the pavements. Flora describes their shopping experience in her diary:

> *The most amusing thing was to see the rickshaws and the natives waiting by the road side – the soldiers, sailors and airmen seemed to thoroughly enjoy them. It is surprising the speed the natives can travel, they run along with a most peculiar spring keeping quite a rhythm. Some of them wore fascinating head–dresses of feathers and rows and rows of beads and bracelets, many of them being made of shells. Others had painted their arms and legs with paint, not actually making patterns but just a maze of colours…*
>
> *We went into one large store and the selection of sweets was really astounding, chocolate, Turkish delight, everything you could think of, we finally decided on assorted fudge… it seemed so unfair to have all these luxuries when you cannot get them at all in England. Clothes are fairly expensive and only one article at a time allowed to be purchased but there were plenty of watches china etc.*
>
> *After looking round the shops for a while we went along to the Navy League Canteen for some tea. After ascending about three flights of stone steps we saw a notice pointing the way to the canteen but after one look we turned away hurriedly to find somewhere else as the place seemed to be simply crowded with men and no girls appeared to be in sight. We then heard someone call out that it was quite alright for us to*

go in and upon looking round it was a corporal from our ship whom I had stitched some stripes on for at the beginning of the voyage... He said we must go back as you could have a wonderful meal very reasonable. They had just had what was on the menu as Full House... We finally decided on scrambled egg on toast, fruit salad, ice cream and cream, bread and butter and tea all for 1/-d. It really was good and thoroughly enjoyed, the eggs being fresh and not powdered was such a change and they certainly know how to make ice cream...

While in the canteen several soldiers were asking for the latest news of England they were all so anxious to know if there were any changes, how the food situation was etc. and all tried to talk at once, keeping us quite busy answering all their questions...

The Wrens had been granted shore leave until eight o' clock. Flora and Pat walked along the rutted road, flanked by rusty barbed wire and dirty concrete, back down to Point Docks. On the way up, they had been part of a jubilant throng and hadn't dwelt on the bleak warehouses, the looming cranes. Now, there were few people about, scary shadows. They were glad of the company of two British sailors. Having been at sea aboard a destroyer, HMS *Foxhound*, for eighteen months, they too were anxious for first-hand news about the state of things back in Britain; one of them came from Cleckheaton. They stopped on the way to buy fish and chips, then said goodnight alongside the *Strathaird* just before eight, having arranged a time and place to meet again on Sunday.

The following day, Flora wrote in her diary:

Saturday morning we were divided into three sections, those staying in Durban, others carrying on the Strathaird and approx.100 who were being trans-shipped including our 16. We were then mustered on the dock in exceptional heat and marched along Point Road & the Marine Parade to a Military Depot where we were inoculated. On the way there was one outstanding incident, an elderly lady with pure white hair was leaning from the balcony of one of the hotels waving a Union Jack which somehow made one feel like weeping it was very touching. By the time we arrived at the camp we were feeling absolutely exhausted, dressed in full blues with the heat and not having had any real exercise for a month there was little wonder. However we were feeling slightly refreshed when along came a "Stop me & buy one" Ices and very soon everyone was eating these despite warnings of "----- tummy".

They ate their ices and stared out over the Indian Ocean. Flat-bottomed clouds drifted across the horizon, below a clear azure sky. The sea was a deeper shade of blue, the surface broken by 'white horses', their manes glinting in the sunshine. Waves rolled onto the shore, where rusty, barbed-wire entanglements stretched over the sand. Machine guns, installed in great holes behind the benches on the promenade, pointed out to sea.

As the Wrens licked the last of the ice cream off their fingers, the officer ordered them inside, and made it quite clear that she had warned them and there'd be no reporting in sick tomorrow.

It was just as hot inside the depot, but as they stood in line they were kept supplied with cups of water. Behind the closed door at the head of the queue a medical officer was waiting, hypodermic in hand. The Wrens were here for yellow fever inoculations.

Much to everyone's relief, they weren't expected to march back to the ship after the injections – transport was laid on. Just as well, because Flora needed to be in the centre of Durban by two-thirty for a special service at St Paul's Church. The congregation that afternoon was swelled by large swathes of khaki, patches of navy and a scattering of air-force blue. During their four weeks afloat on the Atlantic, many of the servicemen and women had turned to God for salvation and regularly attended Sunday worship. They were now to be confirmed. Flora watched as several of her fellow Wrens, including her friend Pat, knelt before the altar.

The following day, Flora wrote in her diary:

Sunday morning those who were being trans-shipped were mustered on the docks with gas masks, tin hats and blue uniform. After waiting about 3/4hr with the sun just pouring down we were told to once more go aboard the "Strathaird" as the other ship was not ready for us so once more we returned, to the amusement of all the troops who had been watching with interest. At 11.30am once more we disembarked and marched along the docks and on board a Dutch ship, The Christiaan Huygens.

When the Germans invaded the Low Countries in May 1940, a call had gone out to all Dutch vessels at sea to sail straight to Britain or other Allied countries, rather than return to their home ports and into the hands of the enemy. The *Christiaan Huygens* had responded, and ever since had ferried troops back and forth across the high seas. The servicemen and women aboard this small ship were luckier than most. Flora describes their first impressions in her diary:

We were given cabin numbers as we went on board and when we saw the one we were to have we were thrilled. It was a first class cabin, originally intended for two, but double tier bunks had been put in making accommodation for four. There were two ports, but owing to one of the bunks, only one would open. There was a dressing table/ writing table, fitted wardrobes, shelves and two electric fans which were exceptionally welcome on the journey. We also had a hand basin and good mirrors, a bathroom was attached so was this luxury – it certainly appeared to be a good beginning.

The majority were feeling rather depressed to leave the "Strathaird", but so far as I was concerned although I had enjoyed the trip up to the present I was rather looking forward to another experience and change of ships, and accommodation certainly appeared better. By now it was time for us to go to lunch, what a lovely dining room, the tables were round and held approx. eight but to see them all laid with clean white cloths, clean polished cutlery and glasses was simply overwhelming and we just wondered whether this was to make a good impression and it would soon change and instead of stewards should we once more be serving ourselves?

By the time they had collected their luggage and leave was granted, Flora and Pat were already late. When they arrived at the meeting place there was no sign of the two sailors from HMS *Foxhound* who had escorted them back to the ship on Friday night. This was their last night ashore, with leave extended till 11 p.m., and now, it seemed, they had nowhere to go.

They had heard that it was worth visiting the botanic gardens for a panoramic view down over the city. By the time they found the bus station, it was getting rather late. They sat down on the hard, wooden seats near the back of the bus but the conductor pointed to a sign, saying *Blacks Only,* and sent them to the more comfortable seats at the front. There was just time to admire the view before darkness descended, so they caught the bus back into town. They had dinner at Toc H, an organisation founded by an army chaplain in the First World War to provide soldiers with a touch of home, a haven from war. On the wall outside was a plaque: oval in shape, one half depicted an Aladdin's lamp, the other half the world. Above the door were the words: *All rank abandon, ye who enter here.*

Flora and Pat felt very conspicuous at a table for two, envious of all the other women sharing tables with soldiers or sailors and who, from the noise and laughter, appeared to be having a spiffing time. However, the evening did take a turn for the better, as Flora records in her diary:

> *Whilst we were having dinner a sailor came in and after asking us if we would deliver a message to one of the Wrens on our draft asked if we would go to a concert with them (by this time two of his friends had appeared) at the Jewish Club on the Marine Parade. They were from the* Foxhound & Warspite... *They were exceptionally good company and were telling of all their various experiences. When we arrived at the club the concert room was absolutely packed you could not have put a chair anywhere so we all stood on chairs just between the lounge and the concert hall where we were just able to see. The whole night they kept appearing with ices and fruit drinks for us which were certainly welcome as the heat in that room was terrific.*

The following morning the convoy sailed out of Durban, and Flora wrote in her diary:

> *On the Monday morning 29.3.43 we left Durban and I must say I was extremely sorry to go, it had been such a short stay and I should very much have liked to see some of the beauty spots just outside town. As we left the docks it was a very impressive sight to see the tugs come along and one by one the ships of the convoy move away. A very moving incident was when one of the sopranos of the town (she had been singing in the concert at the Jewish Club) came along to the end of the jetty and as we passed sang "There will always be an England" & "Land of Hope and Glory" and, as she had a megaphone it was marvellous the way her voice carried until we were quite a way out. Everyone seemed very touched by this action and you felt such an impressive atmosphere on the ship as Durban slowly disappeared from view.*

Durban's Lady in White.
Source: the autobiography of Perla Siedle Gibson

***

16 April 2008

A crane is dropping rubble into the sea to reinforce the jetty at the entrance to Durban Harbour – a task no doubt necessary many times since Aunt Flora passed this way more than sixty-five years ago. We sail past into the Bay of Nepal, and dock in Durban Harbour near a bronze statue of Perla Siedle Gibson. Although Aunt Flora doesn't mention her name, a newspaper cutting about this wealthy South African socialite is pasted in her diary. Called the 'Lady in White', she sang to troopships as they sailed in and out of Durban Harbour. We have just a day to find out more.

In the morning, we take a tour of the city. St Paul's Church is marked on the tourist map, but on Field Street modern offices and shops make it hard to pinpoint where No. 25, The Navy League Club used to be.

As the coach travels along Marine Parade, we pass only two rickshaws. The feathers, beads and shells adorning the men who pull them seem less elaborate, the colours decorating their bodies much less vibrant than my aunt described in her diary. Between the high-rise hotels, one single-storey brick building remains. Could it be the military depot the Wrens stood outside, licking ice creams as they waited for their yellow fever injections?

In the afternoon, we hire a taxi to take us to the Memorable Order of Tin Hats museum, because we have heard that the MOTH museum, as it is usually known, is where we might find out more about the Lady in White. It is not as simple as we expect. When we ask at the first two museums the driver takes us to, we are greeted with confused stares and shaken heads. Fortunately, he escorted us to the door and the taxi is still around to take us on to the next one.

When we arrive at Warrior's Gate, the driver pays youths hanging about the street to look after his cab for a third time, then he takes us to a narrow gate set in an arch in a high wall. We peer through the wrought iron to where five people are sitting at a trestle table: two men in coarse khaki uniforms, and behind them two women and a tall man wearing glasses and a baseball hat. The soldiers remain perfectly still but the tall man gets up, comes over to the gate and says in a strong South African accent, 'We're about to close.'

I look at my watch. 'We were told you were open until three.'

He lets us in, warning us not to touch the electric fence which runs along the wall.

As we pass the tin-hatted soldiers they still don't move, and it's only then that I realise they aren't real, and will sit there forever.

The man points to the two small rooms which make up the museum, and I ask about the Lady in White and if they have any information about her.

'Only what you see in there in the glass cases.'

Casually draped white silk provides the backdrop to the display. On a gilt head-and-shoulders hat-stand is a wide-brimmed red hat. A neatly hand-printed card propped against it explains that it is not the original, just a copy of the one worn by Perla Siedle Gibson. Next to it is a hardback book, her autobiography, and beside it a few pages of the original manuscript. In another glass case, alongside a photograph of Perla, her chest covered in medals, is a megaphone – not the one she used to sing to the troops, but the brass one presented to her in the 1950s.

The tall man is anxious to close for the day. As we walk to the gate, I admire the delicate mauve flowers on the creeper which thrives on the electrified wall.

He reaches up and picks a seed pod and hands it to me. 'Amethyst. Wait until the seeds are dry before you plant them.'

When I get home, I do as he says, but the seeds don't germinate. However, on the Internet I do find a copy of the book I saw in the glass case: *Durban's Lady in White*. On reading it, I discover that Perla Siedle Gibson sang for well over 1,000 troopships and 350 hospital ships. She began singing 'It's a long way to Tipperary' and 'Home Sweet Home' in West Street Canteen to the troops stopping over in Durban during the First World War. Then more than twenty years later, when she worked as a volunteer at a dockside canteen, soldiers lining the decks of a departing troopship yelled out, 'Hey Ma! What about a song, Ma,' and her wartime career began. From her villa in the Berea Hills she would watch for arriving and departing convoys, then put on her white volunteers' dress, pick up her unique Durban dockside entertainment pass and drive down to the dock in her black sedan. Perla Siedle Gibson had performed on stage in London, New York and Paris, but her audience of a quarter of a million servicemen and women will never forget her songs on the quayside and at the end of the jetty in Durban.

***

Although the *Christiaan Huygens* was the only vessel bound for Mombasa, for the six-day voyage up the east coast of Africa she remained within the cloak of the convoy, within sight of the three-funnelled liner they had left at Durban. The friends the Wrens had made on board the *Strathaird* were only across the water, but they were now way out of reach. As far as Flora was concerned, she welcomed a change to a smaller ship: the accommodation was certainly much better. Every morning at 10 a.m. they had the usual boat drill while their cabins were inspected, but after that they were free for the rest of the day. Although there were no dances, the Wrens were now allowed in the bathing pool, so Flora went for a swim every day then lay on the deck to soak up the sun. She could quite easily have managed a few more weeks here in the lap of luxury.

However, not everyone agreed, and in Flora's words this: *led to rather a number of arguments and as time went on was rather apt to get on my nerves. We were probably all getting a little touchy with being at close quarters in confined space for several weeks.*

Being so far away from home, when they met someone new the first question everyone asked was where they came from. When Flora said Halifax, John told her he had once been stationed there. It felt good to meet someone who knew her home town, even if not very well, and they became friends straight away. As the convoy made its way at eight knots – the speed of the slowest – through the Mozambique Channel to the west of Madagascar, they met again several times and were joined by two of his friends, also second lieutenants in the Royal Army Service Corps on their way to Abyssinia. When one of them saw Flora and Pat sewing, he asked if they could do anything about his tropical uniform. Flora had to admit that the fit was almost as bad as the outfits the Wrens were expected to wear, and agreed to try. He was very grateful for the small alterations she made. The other lieutenant had them in fits of laughter as he related his experiences with various Wrens on the ship. He asked Flora's advice about the best way of approaching women, and from then on seemed to have more success with the opposite sex.

On the last night, dinner was five courses: St Germain Soup, Braised beef, Coup WRNS (a subtle blend of pineapple, paw-paw and passionfruit), Welsh Rarebit – the not-so-well-connected were assured that a savoury dish at this stage of the meal was the norm in high-class establishments – then fruit to finish. The following morning at breakfast, the cook's hat was passed round to be autographed by all, before being handed back to him by the chief Wren amidst rounds of applause.

The *Christiaan Huygens* altered course away from the convoy. Many of the Wrens stood on the starboard deck and wept as the *Strathaird* became small, then tiny, then the ships of the convoy were just specks on the horizon. They had no idea where the friends they had got to know so well during the first five weeks of the voyage were going, or if they would ever see them again. Flora and Pat stood at the bow of the ship, on lookout for a sign of their final destination. They'd not heard a good word about Mombasa. From all accounts, it was the last place in the world anyone would wish to be stationed.

PART 3: KENYA

At the beginning of 1943, Japan controlled half of the Pacific: from the Aleutian Islands in the north down to the Solomon Islands in the south, across the chain of islands above Australia, through Malaya to Burma, then up along the coast of China – vast expanses of ocean, islands of dense jungle. The only way for Tokyo to communicate with its forces – for admirals to give orders to their fleets, for generals to command their troops – was by radio signals. But others were listening. They had been listening for years.

Since March 1935, at Y-stations in Delhi, Bombay and on Stonecutter's Island in Hong Kong Harbour, Britain's antennae had been tuned in to the bleeps. Wireless operators, deep in concentration, strained to hear, to get it all down. These incomprehensible messages were passed on to the Far East Combined Bureau (FECB) – a vague title to disguise Bletchley Park's overseas outstations.

With the outbreak of war, there was concern that the Japanese might attack Hong Kong. FECB was vulnerable: the personnel knew too much to risk capture. If decrypts fell into Japanese hands, the enemy would know their codes weren't secure. So, both people and papers were shipped back to Singapore. But it wasn't until Christmas Day 1941 that Hong Kong surrendered, and by then Singapore was also under threat. Early in the New Year, FECB sailed west across the Bay of Bengal to Ceylon. Singapore fell six weeks later.

In Ceylon, the antennae were erected at Pembroke College, a requisitioned Indian boys' school, two miles inland from Colombo. The wireless operators were just getting their bearings, becoming more adept at picking up the signals – now much weaker because they were further away – when a message came through loud and clear. The cryptanalysts, still struggling to overcome the setbacks of relocation, managed a partial decode – then froze. A Japanese carrier force was in the Straits of Malacca, its target: Ceylon.

Their advance warning gave Admiral Sir James Somerville, Commander in Chief Eastern Fleet, the chance to put his ships to sea, so that when dive bombers arrived over the port of Colombo on Easter Sunday, and four days later over the harbour at Trincomalee, British naval shipping losses were minimal. Out at sea, however, the cruisers *Dorsetshire* and *Cornwall*, the aircraft carrier Hermes and the destroyer *Vampire* were sunk.

The Eastern Fleet now consisted of only two aircraft carriers, five battleships, five cruisers, fifteen destroyers and seven submarines. No match for the Japanese, so on 25 April 1942 the fleet sailed west again, this time across the Indian Ocean. Once more, FECB packed up its paperwork and went with them, their destination Mombasa, an island on the coast of Kenya.

CHAPTER 9

Mombasa

We were taken in buses from the docks along a very uninteresting road to the W.R.N.S. Quarters and I must say my first impressions were not good, it looked such a desolate place with all the bandas [accommodation] *scattered about and very rough paths, nothing pretty about at all. We were taken along to the recreation room where our luggage was also stacked and we had to wait in long queues and go through the usual procedure of filling in forms, family history etc. One felt to be at a W.R.N.S. Depot on the very first day. After this we collected our bed linen and were directed to our various bandas.*

– Diary entry, 5 April 1943, Mombasa

29 April 2008

Mombasa, a place I never thought I would visit, and indeed I never would have if it hadn't been for Aunt Flora. We are off the coast of Kenya heading for this island, an area less than five square miles. Back home I had stared many times at the map, wondering what it was like. Would the places she had told me about – the requisitioned school where she'd worked, or the *bandas* that she described in the diary – still be there sixty-five years later? I am about to find out.

Our ship sets a course through a gap in the ridge of white water which marks the coral reef that protects the east coast of Kenya, then sails on, between buoys, towards Mombasa. This island, cupped within the coastline, has Tudor Creek, a shallow estuary and the old dhow harbour to the north, and to the south the docks at Kilindini – in Swahili, this means 'very deep water'.

The low cliffs and the lighthouse loom closer, and at the last moment the ship swings hard to port and hugs the island so close that we can see people playing golf and walking along a cliff-top road. Then we are in the narrow approach to Kilindini docks.

The contour on the mainland side is natural and undulating, with palm trees growing down to the water's edge and waves lapping onto sandy beaches; on the island side, it is man-made with straight-sided quays and rusty warehouses. The blue waters of Port Reitz stretch out before us. I try to imagine what it would have been like when the Wrens arrived on 5 April 1943: rows of dismal grey hulls, a forest of funnels, gun turrets and radio masts reaching up above the palm trees to the azure sky.

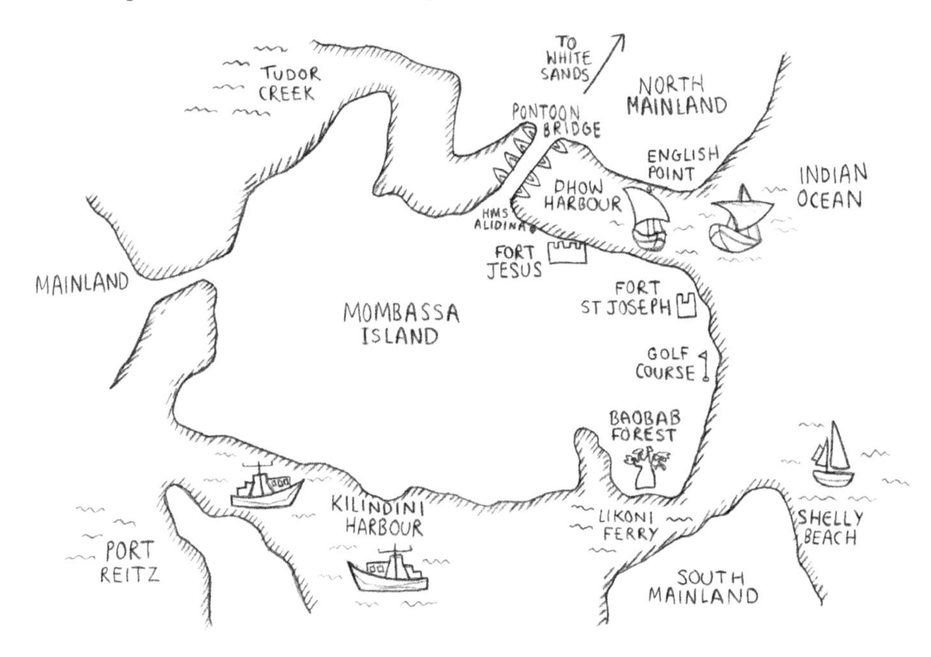

Map of Mombasa 1943 (not to scale). Sketched by Katrina Merkelt

Although Aunt Flora's diary describes where she was billeted, it is never named, but she once let slip that it was called Fort St Joseph.

Before we left home, I borrowed a Kenyan guidebook from the library, but there was no Fort St Joseph marked on the map of Mombasa. There was, however, a 400-year-old Portuguese fortress called Fort Jesus guarding the old harbour.

Aunt Flora rarely got her facts wrong, but the next time I visited her I had to show her the map, point to Fort Jesus and ask, 'Is that where you lived?'

She looked away and adjusted her glasses. 'No,' she said, and bit on her lip.

I waited for her to say more, but she didn't, so I said, 'So it was Fort St Joseph.'

Eventually she whispered, 'We were told never to mention where we were billeted, not to name it in our letters home.'

We begin our search by asking the way to the tourist centre. 'It is on Moi Avenue near the Tuskas,' says a local man. The Tuskas turn out to be two pairs of huge elephant tusks made from sheet-metal welded together, spanning each lane of the dual carriageway to form a large letter M, which is why, when he gave us directions, the man smiled and said, 'Like McDonald's'.

At the tourist office they say they know nothing about British troops billeted here during the war, can't tell us about Fort St Joseph, and suggest we visit Fort Jesus instead: there's a museum, a café and a sound and light show in the evening. When we arrive at Fort Jesus, a young man in an official tour guide T-shirt offers us his services. Omar's English is very good, so I explain that I want to find out more about Fort St Joseph. He shakes his head and says that no one goes there any more – it is in a restricted area. When I ask if there's anywhere I might buy a book about the history of Mombasa, he has an idea and leads us to a two-storey building, its wooden walls worn and bleached with age. Omar tells us that there are many old books here, because during British rule it was the law courts. It appears to have changed little since then, despite the modern sign outside which reads The Centre for Heritage Development in Africa. He speaks to the guard on the door then beckons us to follow him.

Inside it is dark, and a fusty smell hangs in the air. There is no one around, so Omar leads the way up the stairs, turning to us to point out the loose treads.

At the end of the landing is a room where cobwebs hang from the ceiling and rows and rows of hardback books line the walls. He explains what we are looking for to a woman in a sari, and together they begin searching the shelves. I try to help but cannot, as the gilt lettering on the spines of the books is not in English. I feel like an awkward supermarket customer demanding an out of stock item. They produce one English book about the Second World War in Kenya, but there is no reference to FECB or Fort St Joseph. Omar then speaks to a man wearing a long, white *kanzu*. He obviously has a suggestion, because Omar ushers us back along the dusty landing to a small room at the top of the stairs. Inside, a white man sits at an antique desk with a laptop computer open in front of him.

When Omar speaks to him in Swahili, the man's face glows with excitement, he gets up from behind the desk, his arms wide, steps forward to greet us, and to our surprise says, 'God has brought you to me,' in a German accent.

Hans-Martin Sommer is a marine archaeologist working for the National Museums of Kenya, Department of Coastal Archaeology. He is studying the area around Fort St Joseph and has discovered that during WWII navy personnel were billeted there. I can hardly believe it: we have met someone who can confirm where the Wrens were billeted, and now he says he has a permit to enter this restricted area and is offering to take us there.

The taxi takes us along Mama Ngina Drive, past the president's palace and then alongside the restricted area – the police headquarters. Where this secure compound ends and the golf course begins we stop and get out, Hans-Martin shows his pass and a guard unlocks a rusty gate. A path of bare earth winds through coarse grass and low bushes, on a strip of land between the walled police compound and the sea. A cool breeze against my skin is a welcome relief from the scorching sun. All that's left of Fort St Joseph are crumbling stone ramparts and an octagonal lookout post half buried in the cliff, just two sides exposed. Gun-slits frame a view over the old harbour on one side, and on the other, rugged cliffs and the Indian Ocean.

Hans-Martin explains that the naval billet was inside what is now the police compound and, although his permit allows him to enter, he cannot take anyone with him. This is as near as we can get, and we have to make do with peeping through gaps between the lattice of bricks that form the boundary wall. What we see is a dilapidated hut very similar to the one in a photograph in Aunt Flora's album. Could this be one of the *bandas* where the SDX Wrens lived over sixty-five years ago?

***

Bandas – long huts with the walls made out of hessian stiffened with cement, the roof woven from coconut fronds – were scattered about within the compound. Flora found it hard to believe that this was where they would be living for the foreseeable future.

A banda at Fort St Joseph

It took a few moments for their eyes to adjust from bright sunshine to the dim interior – there were windows, just two rows of square holes cut in the walls, but shutters propped open with batons obscured most of the light. At first, they didn't see who was inside, only heard the swish of a broom on the concrete floor. Several of the girls took a step back when the apparition – completely in white, from the small cap on his head to the hem of his ankle-length, flowing robe – emerged from the shadows. He grinned then, with his forearms held one above the other across his chest, he took up his position just inside the door.

There were fifteen beds, with just a chair between them. Flora chose one at the far end and flopped down – too heavily, for the wooden slats beneath the straw-filled mattress creaked in protest. Above each bed was a narrow shelf

– no drawers to be seen. One of the girls pulled back a curtain suspended with string along the far wall: behind it were a couple of partitions, a rail stretched between them – a communal wardrobe with no coat-hangers. Flora kicked her two suitcases under the bed.

One of the girls pointed to a bundle of cloth tied to the rafters directly above her bed, and asked what it was. They all looked at the orderly, still standing beside the door, and repeated the question, each pointing to a similar parcel above their heads. He smiled and made a buzzing sound.

Flora frowned, then looked over to the orderly and asked where one washed, pronouncing each word with precision, much louder than necessary. He looked blank so she rubbed her hands together then moved them in a circular motion on each side of her face. He smiled and nodded then stepped outside and beckoned.

They followed him along a rough path to a more substantial building. Flora describes the sanitation as: *exceptionally primitive and for such a camp I think this should have definitely been improved before having so many people in one place. There were baths and showers, but when they tested the water it was cold.*

Pat raised her hands above her head and wriggled her fingers, then clasped both arms around her body and shivered. The orderly stared at her for a moment then nodded and ushered the party to the rear of the building, where he showed them the boiler. He picked up a bucket, held it under a tap near the bottom, then staggered back round to the entrance of the building.

A path ran alongside the barbed-wire perimeter fence outside the compound. When the Wrens got back to their *banda*, a group of children had gathered and were peering through the wire. Flora shooed them away. When she emerged later, two local men walking along the same path stopped and stared. She changed her towel and washbag to the other hand, so they were partly concealed by her body, and quickened her pace.

Meals were served in the mess hut by stewards, local boys wearing the same long, white *kanzus* with white *kiofias* as the orderly. They all spoke no

English, including the head steward, who wore a red *kiofia*, so when Flora asked if she could have potatoes instead of beans they just shrugged. She didn't like to think what animal the meat came from, but it tasted a bit like pork. She learned later it was camel.

In the afternoon, they explored every inch of the grounds. It didn't take long. They called in at Regulating to ask for passes to go into town, but were told that no shore leave would be granted until duties had been allocated. When they asked if there was any mail, the petty officer said with a sneer that air mail letters took two months, so they'd need to have been written before they left England.

Flora left the others to their petty squabbles and returned to the *banda*, lay on the bed and tried to sleep. At five o'clock, the orderly shouted hello then pushed the door open. He made the same buzzing sound he'd made earlier then walked over to the first bed, where he released the bundle from the rafters above. He demonstrated how they should first get into bed and then tuck all the edges of the mosquito net tightly beneath all four sides of the mattress, so the overall effect was that of a bell tent.

That night, Flora was relieved to have the protection of her mosquito net as she lay in her bed, watching and listening as creepy crawlies emerged from the dried palm leaves in the roof. Others flew in through gaps between shutters and windows to join them. She woke in the morning to find insects, both dead and alive, dotted all over the outside of her net.

At breakfast, Flora scraped out the last of the butter but still only managed to cover half her slice of toast. She asked if someone could pass the marmalade, then repeated her request a little louder. No one took any notice. When the jar finally arrived, it was empty. Flora wrote in her diary: *It is always the same in Service life, so far as food is concerned everyone is out for themselves and manners are forgotten.*

The Wrens reported for squad drill with renewed optimism: at least today they'd find out what they'd be doing, and at least they'd get outside the gate, even if it was only to work. Groups were marched off for duties, but no one knew what to do with the SDX Wrens. They hung about but no orders were forthcoming; they were sent away with instructions to come back in an hour, and so it went on. At four o'clock they were told not to report again until the following morning.

When they asked if they could go ashore, the officer shook her head, then, sensing impending mutiny, reconsidered and told them about a Swahili class that evening and said they could go to that if they wanted. The class was held in an Arab school not far from quarters. Several Wrens, including Flora, went along. Once outside the gate the feeling of freedom was marvellous. They realised for the first time that their camp was close to the sea – near the entrance to the old harbour, on top of the cliffs that the *Christiaan Huygens* had sailed alongside before turning in to the docks.

The Swahili lessons had been going for some weeks, so the newcomers were rather lost. Flora wrote down the words she thought might come in useful. But writing them down was one thing, pronouncing them quite another. The following morning at breakfast, when she asked the steward for *'sukari'* to sweeten her tea, he eventually brought her a dish of *'siagi'*, but by then she'd already eaten her dry toast.

After squad drill they reported for duty, and were repeatedly told to come back in an hour, just like the day before. There was nowhere to walk to, nowhere outside to sit without being gawped at. Flora was convinced that the traffic passing along the path beyond the barbed wire was increasing. It was hot and stuffy inside the *banda* and the lack of light made it difficult to read or to write. But Flora did manage to record in her diary: *To say we were "chocker" in naval language was putting it mildly.*

At lunch, all the girls eyed the meat with suspicion and groaned when beans again appeared on their plate – potatoes were still in short supply. In the afternoon, as they ambled across to report for duty yet again, they listed their grievances. However, the petty officer greeted them, for the first time, with a smile and the news that they'd be starting work the following day. She pointed to a chart on the noticeboard. The four-day rota was unfamiliar and difficult to interpret, until the Wrens realised that they'd no longer be working eight-hour shifts as they had at Bletchley, but four-hourly watches: four hours on, four hours off on Days 1 & 2, then night watches on Days 3 & 4.

As the girls tried to comprehend the complex schedule, the petty officer added another bit of good news: they'd been granted shore leave. Flora describes how they spent the afternoon, in her diary:

> *We went to explore the shopping centre, but apart from one chemist, a hairdressers and a drapers all the shops were owned by Indians who seemed to sell almost anything and I was surprised at the plentiful supply of cosmetics. The curio shops fascinated me in spite of the fact that most of the goods were imported but I enjoyed looking at all the carved trinkets, bracelets and figures. On the whole everything is expensive, now there are more Europeans here prices have definitely soared. Fruit was the cheapest thing and there were a number of stalls just off the main road… so although we had been without fruit for so long we could now buy unlimited supplies. Baskets of sisal could be bought for 50 cents and everyone seemed to carry these, even the sailors, the little native boys come up to you with them. A number of boys used to sit each day on the pavement selling packets of peanuts but trade must have been slack as no one appeared to buy them. The majority of shops were shoemakers and to look into the shops and see them sitting cross-legged on the floor stitching away surrounded by various types of shoes and sandals was quite a picture.*
>
> *The population of Mombasa is a study in itself, the African natives wearing the most unusual apparel, some of them in absolute rags or hardly dressed at all and wearing any shape of hat or head covering they get hold of at most amusing angles, an artist would certainly find plenty of studies here. The Indians are a different type altogether wearing very colourful clothes, most of the women and children being very attractive and wearing saris of very fine materials, sometimes very vividly coloured and others in dainty pastel shades, always looking attractive. The Moslem women always dress in black looking very*

sinister usually also having their faces covered. The Arabs are the ones who drape themselves in any vividly coloured materials, sometimes checks of greens and reds, others in stripes often with a bright pink or orange shirt over the skirt, never tucked in but always hanging loose.

As they headed home they heard the rhythmic clink of china. A man in a flowing robe and a red fez walked by. Between his fingers he carried two tiny china bowls, which he was clicking together. In the other hand he held a tall brass coffee pot with a spout which curved up from the bulbous base like the neck of a swan. They watched as he was hailed by passers-by. After taking their money, he poured the thick black coffee into the bowls. He waited while his customers drank, then, retrieving his bowls to advertise his mobile beverage service, continued to thread his way past potential patrons.

The girls knew something was different when they arrived back at quarters, but they were outside the *banda* before they realised what it was. The barbed-wire fence was now covered in some kind of canvas. It exacerbated their feelings of confinement, but at least now the locals couldn't see in; the caged Wrens would no longer be the source of local amusement.

On Monday,12 April, Flora sent a letter home: just the words *With Love Flora* on a souvenir letter card of Mombasa. This concertina of photographs of Kilindini Road, Indian Quarter, Vasco da Gama Street, Fort Jesus, Salim Road and Old Harbour survived the postal service back to Halifax and has remained slipped inside Flora's diary ever since.

CHAPTER 10

HMS *Alidina*

We cursed the Arab dhows that came in from the sea beating drums so loud that we couldn't read signals at times.

– Joan Sprinks, wireless telegraphist, quoted in The Emperor's Codes *by Michael Smith*

Next morning, the Wrens on first watch arrived early at the pick-up point to await the 'liberty boat'. The battered charabanc arrived late and they drove at speed, the local driver honking his horn down Salim Road, past Mackinnon Market. On the other side of the old town they headed down a narrow and less-crowded road and came to a halt at a gate guarded by sentries from the King's African Rifles.

After boarding the bus and checking its occupants, the sentries waved them through. At the top of the drive was a two-storey stone building with shuttered windows and a tiled roof, the rear façade made up of two wings with a wrought-iron gate between them. The bus didn't stop there, but continued round the side and drew up at the front entrance. The Wrens stared at the stone columns and archways, the decorative cornices, the walls adorned with plaster bows and scrolls. Was this where they were going to work? They couldn't believe their luck.

The petty officer led the way up the steps, in through the front door, across a lobby, then outside again and around a raised walkway behind the arches and balustrades that surrounded a central quadrangle. Leading off this outside corridor were a series of doors to the ex-classrooms.

***

30 April 2008

'Jambo,' says Omar, who is waiting for us when we get off the bus outside Fort Jesus.

We smile and return his greeting.

He takes out his mobile phone and rings Ahmed, the taxi driver who drove us around yesterday. My research has revealed that when FECB withdrew to Mombasa, they requisitioned a boys' school on the rocky northern shore of the island. The word 'Alidina' is written on the luggage label that I found attached to the parcel containing Aunt Flora's diaries, so today they are taking us to Allidina Visram High School.

We take Digo Road, which Omar tells us was once called Salim Road, then Abel Nasser Road, which once led to the Nyali Pontoon Bridge. This floating link with the northern mainland that Aunt Flora mentions in her diaries was closed in the late '70s and replaced by the New Nyali Bridge further up Tudor Creek. As a result, the later part of Abel Nasser Road is now pitted with potholes, but nevertheless, crowded with people milling around stalls selling vegetables, fabric and bric-a-brac. I wonder what kind of school can be at the end of this rough track.

I expect just to look over a fence or wall, but no – Ahmed drives straight in through the gates, alongside the pristine playing field, right up to the rear of the school. Surrounded by tall poplar trees, the walls of this two-storey building are freshly painted in magnolia, the many windows have louvred wooden shutters to keep out the heat of the sun. The stone arches above them are picked out in sky blue.

Omar gets out of the taxi, beckons us to follow him through wrought-iron gates into a courtyard wrapped round on three sides by the building. The architecture surrounding us is not African, but a relic of colonialism, more reminiscent of a two-tiered cloister with walkways behind colonnades and stone balustrades. Leading off these open-air corridors are stout wooden doors; I guess they open into the classrooms, as one of them is labelled 4W.

A well-tended garden, boasting an abundance of large, shiny tropical leaves, sits in the centre of the courtyard. We skirt around the edges, hearing only the faint drone of insects. Omar leads the way up a few steps at the far end, across a lobby and out again through the double front doors. We turn and survey the front façade of the building.

Allidina Visram High School

The school is on a cliff top overlooking Tudor Creek. I remember reading a quote from Joan Sprinks, a wireless telegraphist stationed in Mombasa, about how when the Arab dhows came into harbour the boatmen beat their drums so loudly that at times they couldn't read the signals. It all falls into place: Alidina in Aunt Flora's handwriting, a requisitioned school, and now the boatmen beating their drums. This must have been the Bletchley Park outstation where they intercepted messages from the Imperial Japanese Navy and Army: from admirals to their fleets in the Pacific, from generals to their forces occupying South East Asia. Here, behind the closed doors of one of these classrooms, Aunt Flora operated the Hollerith and played her part in decoding those messages.

We walk back around the other side of the building. I admire the perfect creamy-white flowers of the frangipani trees and inhale their heady scent. A boy gazing out of a classroom window gives us a puzzled look. It is hard to believe that the four of us are just wandering around this school and no one has challenged us. As we get back into the taxi, two adults, probably teachers, just smile and say, '*Jambo.*'

***

The Hollerith was never used to its full potential until FECB settled in Mombasa. In Singapore they only had one and, although it survived shipment to Ceylon, it arrived with an essential part missing. By the time a replacement arrived, the Japanese were heading for Colombo, so the codebreakers had to withdraw westward once more. When more machines were shipped out to Mombasa, a young lieutenant came with them. He wasn't true navy; he knew little of the sea. Before the war he'd been employed as a data-handler by the Letchworth company that manufactured Hollerith. When the codebreaking potential of these tabulating machines had been realised, he was fast-tracked to lieutenant.

The Wrens surveyed the young lieutenant: he wasn't much older than they were and seemed a bit overawed to be in charge of so many females. He said that they'd be the first Wrens to operate Hollerith. The Admiralty and the Americans had said they couldn't do it. He'd said they could, so he hoped they wouldn't let him down.

To their surprise, he allowed the Wrens to choose whether they wanted to punch the cards or operate the machines. Flora remembered the chronic boredom of punching the cards and decided anything would be better than that, so she volunteered to work on the machines.

The lieutenant led the way along the walkway around the courtyard and into the ex-classrooms that housed the Hollerith. Flora was surprised to find that these machines were much smaller than the Bombe, the shape and height of an upright piano, but half the width. They stood on bow legs similar to the ones on the occasional table back home, but made of metal, not wood.

The lieutenant showed them how to locate the cards they required from the boxes that occupied the whole of one wall, from floor to ceiling. When they had a batch piled up ready and waiting, he drew the girls' attention to the day's instructions, and pointed to a series of numbers and typed them into a keypad. Then he fed in the cards and flicked a switch. They waited: the lieutenant's eyes on the Hollerith, the Wrens' eyes on the lieutenant.

Hollerith tabulating machines.
Reproduced by courtesy of the Bletchley Park Trust

The punched cards began to drop into slings suspended below the machine, and the lieutenant pointed to where all the cards that had the code group they'd just entered would end up. When the machine came to a stop, he lifted them out and gave the pile a tap to ensure they were all lined up, before pushing a metal skewer through the holes to check that a rogue card without a hole in the correct position hadn't sneaked its way in.

With a click and clatter, paper began to concertina out of another, smaller machine. The lieutenant explained that it was a printer and the complete coded message on all the cards with the code-groups they were looking for would be listed on the printout. This provided all the information the codebreakers needed, so all the cards could now be filed away. He pointed to the wall of boxes.

When the watch ended and they headed for the 'liberty boat', one of the

Wrens said that at least the lieutenant had promised to be around to help with any problems. One of the smitten replied that he could help with hers anytime.

In true Bletchley fashion, the Wrens kept their mouths shut. But the ominous warnings couldn't stop them from wondering. As the bus jolted its way back to quarters, Flora asked herself: what did they do with the strings of numbers the printers produced? How did they help crack the Japanese codes? The Japanese didn't even write in the same alphabet. They used a brush, not a pen, to draw their complicated pictorial characters called *kanji*.

***

Not again, thought Flora, as the punch-cards cascaded to the floor. No need to call the lieutenant; she was perfectly capable of fixing it herself. She knelt down beside machine No. 2, lifted the sling back into position, then took off her shoe and gave the clip that was supposed to keep everything in place a sharp whack with the heel. After checking that everything was now working correctly, she crawled around to retrieve the stray cards, placed them on the pile awaiting refiling and glanced across at machine No. 1. The feed tray was empty and there was still a load to go in. There wasn't even time to spend a penny.

After No. 1 had been fed, she turned to No. 3. That was fine, not hungry and it had only just started disgorging. But the printer was running out of paper. She fetched another batch and fitted the holes on the outer margins onto the sprockets. The filing could wait. Flora made for the door.

As she crossed the quadrangle, she could feel the guards' eyes on her back, so embarrassing. Flora opened the door to the toilet. At least the facilities at HMS *Alidina* were better than back at quarters. When she returned to the Hollerith room, cards from machine No. 2 were cascading to the floor. Flora took off her shoe.

A pile of cards was still waiting to be returned to their slots in the wall of boxes, when the next watch arrived, but Flora couldn't stay to put them away.

She couldn't risk missing the 'liberty boat': the Wrens had been invited aboard HMS *Hawkins* for tea.

> *They provided an excellent tea for us while the Royal Marine band played light music on deck. Afterwards we were shown round the ship which was exceptionally interesting. I had never been on a cruiser. It was a shame we had not more time there was so much to see. On the way round we stopped to talk to one sailor who was just opening a huge pile of mail he had just received, some of them were Xmas cards which had only just caught up with him. In the course of conversation I found he came from West Vale and so we were well away and soon discussing all the places round about. He insisted on giving me a* Courier & Guardian *which he had just received and it did seem strange to be reading the local news so far away.*

CHAPTER 11

Here Today Gone Tomorrow

It seems a very strange life sometimes you are always meeting people and making friends then after a short while they are sent away and it is very doubtful if you will ever meet again. Anyway I was very pleased to have known them.

– *Diary entry, April 1943*

One invitation led to another. The following Sunday, their half day, Flora and Pat joined five officers from HMS *Hawkins* for an afternoon's sailing:

It was a glorious day and we left from the Flag Staff steps. She was a fine boat, a 32ft cutter & there were four chiefs, a PO & [Pat] *& I. We did our best to learn a little about sailing although several times when I took over I think they thought she would capsize & were all making remarks about being ready to swim.*

We sailed along to a very pretty beach where we dropped anchor. They rigged up a tent for us in the boat from sails so that we could change for bathing and in spite of the pole collapsing every so often we managed fine. The water was warmer than I ever imagined it could be, but exceptionally salty. We then climbed once more into the boat and had tea, they really had done well for us as far as food was concerned, the bread was white and also new and there was peaches and cream and lime juice to drink. Did we enjoy it, it was just what we needed.

The boat had to be back before sunset so we had to leave soon after tea as the wind had dropped considerably. A very good beginning was made when we were driven onto fishing nets and for quite a while we were not able to get away. In the end some native boys who were swimming near by came along and pushed us off at the same time chanting a very attractive song. Earlier in the afternoon we had given them some white bread and butter much to their delight and to watch them swimming to the shore holding it aloft with one hand was a work of art, one of them had almost reached the shore when, much to the amusement of the others, he suddenly went under a wave and the bread floated away.

Going back the wind dropped altogether until we were hardly moving at all and when eventually we did sight the "Hawkins" they sent a signal for us to go in at once and much to our disgust, especially [Pat's], *they sent a launch to tow us back. We had thoroughly enjoyed ourselves & left them with a promise of more sailing lessons when they returned.*

We went back to quarters with a huge loaf of white bread, two tins of cream, a tin of syrup & a tin of peaches. The white bread we took along to sick bay & heard afterwards how much it had been appreciated as our bread was brown & very dry & had a most peculiar flavour.

HMS *Hawkins* sailed. The officers promised to invite the girls on another picnic when they returned, although no one knew when that would be. Others, however, were waiting to entertain them. Flora and Pat met two merchant seamen who had been docking at Mombasa for years and knew all the best places to go. They invited the girls to dinner at the Nelson Hotel, but there was a problem.

Not only did the Wrens have to wear their uniform white skirts and blouses when they went out in the evening but, as it was the rainy season, after 7 p.m. they had to cover their arms and legs as a protection against malaria. The gaiters, made of a stiff material, started above the knees and extended down over the foot. Fortunately, supplies of these had run out so they had to wear two pairs of white stockings instead. The sleeve extensions were threaded with elastic to keep them in place around the upper arm. Goodness knows what their escort thought when they came to pick them up from quarters. As soon as they arrived at the Nelson, the girls headed straight for the Ladies to remove these white balloons from their arms, and swap the two pairs of lisle stockings for one pair of silk.

Joe came from Rochdale so he and Flora had plenty to talk about, and at the end of the evening he asked if they could meet again. He took her to Kumalys, a draper's shop on Salim Road, where he negotiated a discount of 1/6*d* a yard on some very pretty cotton material that took her eye. When he found out that her birthday was coming up he persuaded the ship's cook to make her a cake. He gave it to her the night before his ship sailed and apologised that there hadn't been time to have it iced. Flora was touched by his thoughtfulness, and kept the un-iced cake for the two weeks under her bed in a tin, borrowed from the mess, and hoped the ants wouldn't get it.

Then it was Easter Sunday. Service personnel swelled the congregation at Mombasa Cathedral to such an extent that extra chairs were lined up down the aisles and the Wrens had to sit on extra benches at the front. The walls and central pillars were decorated with palm leaves and crimson bougainvillea. The fragrance of white frangipani flowers on the altar drifted back through the nave. Flora's thoughts strayed back home. Were her mother and sisters also singing 'There is a green hill far away' at St John's in Halifax? She describes the bishop's address as *very good and well worth hearing*. At the end of the service, the bishop remarked that never before had such singing been heard in Mombasa Cathedral.

The cake survived in its airtight tin under her bed and on 28 April, her 27th birthday, Flora shared it with the other Wrens. It was impossible to buy proper cakes in Mombasa; what a shame she couldn't tell Joe how much she appreciated it, how they all enjoyed it. She had no idea where he was.

In the evening, a South African Air Force corporal took her to dinner at the Palm Court Hotel. Another SDX Wren was also there, celebrating her 21st. After dinner they asked if the floor could be cleared for dancing. The waiters unearthed a gramophone and some dated records and the evening was a great success. In the taxi home they donned sleeves and stockings; the petty officer on duty always checked they were wearing two pairs!

A few days later, the South African corporal invited Flora to a cabaret dance held at the Goan Institute to raise money for the Aid to Russia Fund. She accepted, but then a note was left in Regulating to say his unit was being drafted and he couldn't make it. She never saw him again.

***

Some past acquaintances, however, did return.

On Monday, 3 May, on the way back from Alidina, Flora and Pat got off the duty bus in Salim Road to do some shopping in town. It was almost six o'clock when they arrived back at quarters, content with their purchases but absolutely exhausted. When Flora checked the mail box, there was a letter from John, the second lieutenant she'd met on the *Christiaan Huygens*, whom she'd assumed was now well on his way to a posting in Abyssinia. The message said if she was free, he'd pick her up at six-thirty.

Exhaustion forgotten, she rushed back to the *banda*, then across to the ablution block. She contemplated sneaking round the back to the boiler, but there wasn't time. Anyway, someone was bound to spot her and there'd be a protest – it wasn't her *banda's* day for hot water.

John was waiting at Regulating, along with his friend, who'd arranged to meet Anna, another of the SDX Wrens. The foursome went for dinner at the Nelson. The evening was cut short because there hadn't been time to get late passes. They arrived back in time for the ten o'clock curfew, having decided to meet up for a trip to the north mainland:

> *...we arranged to go to Shanso on the Tuesday afternoon if they could hire a car. We all had a jolly good laugh before we started off, the only one they could hire was very rickety one with a dicky seat. When you stretched out your legs you pushed & moved the front seat, how we ever*

managed to get there & back in it is a wonder, the engine also made a terrific rattle & whenever we stopped to enquire the way the engine stopped as well.

We got as far as Nyali Bridge but no one appeared to know where Shanso was, but one driver of an army lorry said White Sands was a very pretty beach and directed us there. We went through some very interesting country passing plantations of banana palms, this was the first time I had seen them growing and expected much higher palms. We also passed native villages with the small dark thatched houses clustered together and there seemed to be hundreds of children running about, looking quite attractive with their short black curly hair, dark eyes and white teeth.

At last we came to a sign pointing the way to White Sands, it was a very narrow track off the main road and we bounced along, it really was a wonder we were not thrown out of the back, however we clung on, we thought we were coming to the end of the world, it was such a long way. Eventually the road opened out and we found ourselves almost on the beach, there were a number of small white thatched bandas, *situated amongst palm trees & then a stretch of sand & the blue sea.*

White Sands

It was a picture I shall never forget, a perfect spot, I just wanted a long holiday there. You could see along the beach for miles with a headland jutting out and the sea rolling up the beach. It was a place one reads about but can hardly believe it exists, it was so peaceful

& miles away from any signs of civilization. We had a marvellous afternoon there, the time passed much too quickly as we had to be back by 7pm to change into uniform & don stockings & sleeves, also we were not allowed on the mainland after 7pm.

We had tea on the balcony of one of the bandas *overlooking the sandhills & sea, we were rather dubious of the small buttered pancakes they brought us but they tasted much better than they looked. We had to laugh when we discovered the old car had a puncture, we were sure something would go wrong with it, luckily there was a spare wheel otherwise I dread to think of the ride back on a flat tyre.*

On the way back, Anna wanted to pick a bunch of bananas to take back to the *banda*. Flora, all too aware of the consequences – suspension of late passes, cancellation of leave, stoppage of pay or extra duties – if they didn't make it in time, didn't want to stop. The men, however, insisted and presented the girls with two huge bunches of hard, green bananas. They crossed the Nyali Bridge and arrived back on the mainland with just minutes to spare.

***

30 April 2008

The New Nyali Bridge was completed in 1980. A concrete, six-lane highway, it spans Tudor Creek half a mile further up and, unlike its predecessor, is supported on firmly-embedded piles. We cross it in Ahmed's taxi on our way to visit White Sands.

On the north mainland the road is lined with buildings made of coral, thatch or corrugated iron – anything, in fact. They house a nursery school called Little Graduates, a beauty salon named Pretty Woman. A shack no bigger than a garage has a hand-painted sign saying *Nectar Pub*; a similar-sized shop displays a picture of a mobile phone and the words *Top up here.* There is a hoarding with the words *Support the Fight against Corruption.* On open land, Masai people stand next to their traditional homes and watch us pass by.

Further along the road, a garden centre displays palms and other tropical plants in plastic pots at the roadside, a modern supermarket advertises its special offers. Then the houses become grander, protected by electric fences. Ahmed brings his taxi to a halt outside the White Sands Hotel.

Back in the 1940s, White Sands was a public beach, but now it is private, access restricted to the residents of the upmarket hotels that border the shore. We invite Omar and Ahmed to join us for lunch. A five-star hotel, and for four of us it costs much less than a pub lunch for two back home. And the hotel itself is pure luxury: gleaming marble floors, shimmering chandeliers, a veranda overlooking a pond. Lily pads float on the surface, tall, sword-shaped leaves pierce the crystal-clear water and circular stepping stones lead across it to a path between palm trees to the beach.

I leave the men to their coffee and follow the path to the shore. Palm trees bow out towards the sea, casting frond-shadows over a great sweep of white sand that stretches for miles between green headlands way, way in the distance. Where the sea gently laps the shore, it is transparent; further out, it turns to turquoise with deep cobalt-blue patches in the distance. A white line of surf marks the coral reef. A few wispy clouds drift across the horizon. I now know why Aunt Flora wrote in her diary that it was a picture she would never forget.

A camel is being led along the beach, but no riders today. The jet skis are drawn up at the water's edge. The season is over; not only that, but with the troubles in Kenya the tourists have stopped coming.

It is time to leave. On the way back we pass the grand houses, then the rubbish tip where locals scavenge for scraps. Four or five cows graze the dry, dusty grass at the roadside. In Mombasa, Ahmed takes the back streets to avoid the traffic. A man is driving his herd of goats down the middle of the road.

***

It was a few minutes before seven when they arrived back at quarters carrying two huge bunches of bananas. The men waited while the Wrens changed into uniform, protective sleeves and two pairs of stockings, then the foursome went on to the Palace Hotel. After dinner they relaxed in armchairs in the lounge, while Anna sat at the piano and entertained them, playing a selection of popular songs. Flora's favourite, 'Jealousy', brought back memories of home and her time at Crawley Grange and Wavendon. The men escorted the girls back to quarters and John arranged to call for Flora the following afternoon.

Three weeks later, two bunches of bananas still hung either side of the door to the *banda*. Flora broke one off and peeled back the skin; inside it was rotten. When the orderly came on duty she'd ask him to throw them away. She didn't need any reminders. As she'd walked down to Regulating the day after their trip to White Sands, she'd had a feeling that the rumours would be true and John wouldn't be there. She was right – his ship had already sailed.

The other Wrens in her *banda* were either on watch or had gone to the weekly Fleet dance at the Goan Institute. Flora had been twice – each time she'd spent ages setting her hair, accessorising her white uniform with beads, a brooch, bracelet or belt, only to arrive at the dance and wish she hadn't bothered. It could only be described as a *smash and grab raid*. Never in England could she remember an evening out being spoiled by too many men. Most of the dances were an 'excuse me' and there was only the opportunity for a few steps with one partner before you were grabbed by another – manners were forgotten altogether. The last time, despite having passes until eleven-thirty, the Wrens had left early. Even worse had been the dance given by the merchant navy – again a surplus of men, whose main purpose was drinking, not dancing.

Had tonight's event been the fortnightly Kipanga Club dance, she might have gone. It was held at the Railway Club in a good-sized room, not too crowded, with tables for two outside under palm trees bedecked with coloured lights. The patrons were almost exclusively Royal Navy, but then again most of them were due to sail any day.

The orderly came in to release the mosquito nets then left with the unwanted bananas. Flora swatted the flies hovering around her head, then gave up and climbed into bed, tucking the net securely around her. More insects rustled in the thatch, then crept from their crevices and joined in the buzzing.

As she lay on her hard, prickly mattress, Flora thought that although the social life might be frivolous and fleeting, at least the work they did at HMS *Alidina* was beginning to make sense. At Bletchley she'd never known how the part she played fitted into the whole, but here in this small outstation, although no one spoke of their work, she'd seen what they did.

The German Enigma was an alphabetical cipher, every individual letter of every word being replaced by a different letter, but obviously this wouldn't work with the mysterious Japanese pictorial characters. Therefore, they used a numerical code: groups of four, or more frequently five, digits stood for words, phrases or complete sentences made up of the *kanji* characters, plus the seventy-odd *kana* phonetic symbols. Two code books were needed: one for encoding, where the *kanji* and *kana* were arranged in a way only the fluent Japanese reader understood; the other for decoding, where the groups of digits were arranged in numerical order. One of the tasks at HMS *Alidina* was to try to work out the 30,000 entries, a process commonly known as 'book building'.

But the problem didn't end there. To add a further layer of security, before the coded message was sent it was super-enciphered and this involved another book. Called an additive table, it contained random numbers arranged in ten columns and ten rows on a hundred pages, 10,000 numbers in all. A starting point anywhere in the book was chosen and this number added to the first digit group of the message, the next number was added to the second, and so on. The recipient of the message obviously needed to know which page, row and column had been used as the starting point so he could subtract it and begin the process of 'stripping the additive'. This vital piece of information, referred to as the 'indicator', was embedded at some prearranged position in the message.

Flora considered the seemingly impossible task of unscrambling a coded message that was subsequently enciphered. At HMS *Alidina* they didn't have the code book or the additive table, and even if they did, without the 'indicator' they wouldn't know where to start. Yet somehow they were managing to create these books, never finishing them because every few months, when the Japanese introduced new editions, they would have to start all over again. The main code they worked on was the Navy General Operational Code named JN25 by the British. Each new code book or additive table was designated by a consecutive letter and number. When Flora arrived in Mombasa, they were already on JN25e11. Still pondering how the long lists of numbers on the paper that concertinaed out of her Hollerith provided the clue to deciphering the code, she fell asleep.

***

On 1 June 1943, Flora was promoted to leading Wren or, as it was more commonly referred to, 'got her hook', a badge – a rope entwined around an anchor embroidered in pale blue. With tiny, neat stitches she sewed it exactly five inches below the point of the shoulder on the left sleeve of her uniform jacket.

The Wrens had now been in Mombasa for two months. The contingent at HMS *Alidina* was small and Flora knew everyone by sight, and many of them by name. The unit was headed by Lieutenant Commander Bruce Keith. Intercept operators picked up the signals and the young lieutenant and his flock of fifteen Wrens were responsible for Hollerith. The codebreakers worked on JN11, JN40 and JN25, assisted with routine and repetitive tasks by pensioner clerks and expatriate wives and daughters called Temporary Women Assistants – TWAs for short. The linguists translated the *kanji* and *kana* into English.

Alidina wasn't the only establishment working on Japanese codes; the Americans had units in Hawaii, Melbourne and Washington. It was the Americans who picked up and decoded the signal that led to the death of Admiral Yamamoto, Commander of the Imperial Japanese Navy. The JN25 message detailed the itinerary of his tour of inspection of airbases on the Solomon Islands, and US fighters were waiting when he crossed the Bougainville coast.

It would be many years, however, before Flora heard of this US codebreaking success. On 5 June 1943, the day of Yamamoto's funeral, she was more concerned about whether the 'liberty boat' would be back in time for her to catch the transport for that afternoon's sailing party. At dances, sailors competed for partners, but when ships in port arranged sailing parties, there was no shortage of female crew. She arrived at Regulating with a few minutes to spare, only to discover that so many Wrens had turned up that the transport had taken the first six and left early. Flora and the other disgruntled Wrens who'd also missed the boat went to see the petty officer on duty, and for once their complaint was taken seriously. The following day it was decreed that invitations were not to be passed on by word of mouth; all those who wanted to go sailing had to put their name in the sailing book and wait their turn.

Anxious not to waste their half day, Flora and another disappointed girl decided and go for a bathe instead. They set off through the old town, between the buff, ochre and rose-coloured coral houses of Vasco de Gamma Street, where intricately carved front doors opened onto doorsteps jutting out onto the cobbles, and balconies enclosed in fine wooden fretwork overhung the narrow street.

As they waited beneath the pinkish-brown battlements of Fort Jesus for the ferry to take them across Tudor Creek to the north mainland, Flora looked out over the harbour. Here, unlike the south side, the water was too shallow for warships. Instead, the dhows sailed in and out of the creek, just as they had a century ago, to barter beads, wooden chests and cloth for ivory and rhino horn.

The dhow-ferry dropped them off at a small sandy cove sheltered by

English Point, the headland that curves round to protect the entrance to the creek from the ocean. Flora's diary takes up the story:

English Point

It was a glorious afternoon & the beach was not too crowded. We were just thinking how lovely it would be to have some tea (there is nowhere at English Point to buy any) when we saw a chief we knew & he invited us up the mess for tea. It was just at the top of the cliff, a marvellous view across to the Island, the Indian quarter all clustered together, most of the houses having red roofs, the dhows moored alongside and tiny sailing boats just gliding along in the breeze, then the headland jutting out into the sea with palm trees down to the water's edge.

They told us they had built the mess themselves and they might well be proud of it, and the position was perfect. There was quite a party of us for tea as several POs brought their friends along and they provided us with huge slices of fruit cake which tasted exceptionally good. After tea they brought us back to quarters in their van to save us waiting for the ferry which only comes across occasionally so the afternoon which had been very disappointing in the beginning turned out to be a most enjoyable half day.

***

30 April 2008

On our way back from White Sands, as we approach the New Nyali Bridge to cross over to Mombasa, I ask Omar about English Point.

'It is where the English lived in their grand houses,' answers Ahmed. 'You would like to go there?'

Without waiting for an answer, he swings the car round and takes us on a detour down the road on the northern side of Tudor Creek. As we approach the headland, our way is barred by a stone wall built right across the road.

Omar gets out of the taxi and walks up to the wall. He puts his hands on the top and levers himself up to look over it. Then he lowers himself down, turns to us and shrugs his shoulders.

Ahmed points to the headland on the other side of the wall. 'You see the red roof in the trees. That house belonged to Jomo Kenyatta. This place is not called English Point any more.'

'My aunt came across the creek on a ferry from the old town… to a beach. Where would that be?'

We can see the blue waters of Tudor Creek, but access to it is barred by a modern house and next to it a fenced-off plot. Omar and Ahmed disappear down the narrow space between them. As we wait for them to come back I notice a discarded, non-matching pair of flip-flops.

When they return, Ahmed is most insistent that I go back with him.

'If you will come in three months you will not get here.' He points to the wire fencing: a sign says *Sold for Development.*

Ahmed and I have to edge our way sidewise down this rough, unofficial path. I see another non-matching pair of flip-flops – how odd. When we reach the beach, all is explained. Among the seaweed on the tidelines are hundreds of these rubber beach sandals of all colours and sizes.

'Why?' I ask Ahmed.

'The sea bring them here.'

But there are so many. Then I remember White Sands and other hotels up the coast, and imagine tourists going swimming, jet skiing, coming back to find the tide has washed their beach accessories away. That explains the flip-flops and the heaps of plastic water bottles. This has become the final resting place of the mislaid and discarded, so different now from the small sandy cove Aunt Flora described in her diary.

CHAPTER 12

Parties, Shopping and Sailing

Somehow it made you feel very sorry for them [the Dutch naval officers] when they spoke about their country and the people whom they never heard from. Their one wish was to return & what they would do, it made me realise how lucky we in England have been, in spite of everything, one cannot realise what it must feel like to know your country is in the hands of Germany & not know what has happened to your family and friends.

– Diary entry, June 1943

The party was held at the home of a Mombasa businessman who, as a young man, had moved down from the White Highlands where his Dutch family had been among the European settlers that arrived to grow coffee at the beginning of the century. Most of the male guests were Dutch naval officers. The ladies wore evening dresses, all except Flora, Pat and Anna, the only servicewomen present.

It was the first time since they left England that the Wrens had been inside a proper house. The room, cooled by fans, lit by subdued table lights, had chairs around the edge leaving an area in the centre for dancing. French doors extended the length of one wall and opened out onto the balcony where more easy chairs were arranged around small tables with shallow bowls of white flowers, their petals so perfect they could have been wax. After the utilitarian furniture of the *banda*, to relax into a comfortable armchair was pure bliss.

Flora spent most of the evening with a third lieutenant called Johannes. They waltzed to gramophone records then sat out on the veranda, where the heady fragrance of frangipani drifted on the evening breeze and fireflies danced among the crimson bougainvillea. He spoke excellent English; she fell in love with his accent. His eyes misted over as he spoke of his country in the hands of the Germans, of the friends and relations who no longer wrote letters. His one wish was to return home; he clenched his hand into a tight fist as he contemplated what he'd do when he got there.

When one of the Wrens caught her eye, Flora looked down at her watch and wished that they'd put in for late passes. Their hosts enlisted the help of the Dutch consul, who was only too pleased to ring the petty officer back at Regulating to ask that they be granted an extension. Even his influence, however, wasn't sufficient to persuade the ugly sister on duty that the three Cinderellas could stay out until eleven-thirty.

At the party they'd heard about Shelly, a beach on the southern mainland, ideal for a bathe. On their next half day, they boarded the Likoni ferry. During the crossing, Flora scrutinised the grey ships in Kilindini Harbour. With all their markings painted out and no flags, it was impossible to say which were Dutch. The one she was looking for probably wasn't there anyway; Johannes had told her they were due to sail any day. As they walked up the ramp from the ferry, Pat and Flora tried to recall the directions they'd been given.

The road from the Likoni Ferry, South Mainland

Somehow, we took the wrong turning and found ourselves wandering through a native village on what appeared to be market day. All along the road was a continuous stream of natives many of them carrying large bundles of goods on their heads & the African women with their babies strapped to their backs all making for the village where there were a few shops in the small huts and others had opened stalls on the ground and the people were sitting about in groups or by the side of the road and they made a most unusual picture.

Most of the houses are built of mud & the roofs thatched with palm leaves, many of them have no windows at all & those that have are exceptionally small, scarcely allowing any light or air into the rooms. They are built very closely together and the hens, goats just wander in & out. There are always donkeys about as these seem to be the beasts of burden and you often see six or eight of them laden, following one after another along the road.

It was an exceptionally interesting sight but we could not fully enjoy it owing to the fact that we were rather anxious to get back to the service club we had seen on the road as we came along, as there did not appear to be any other Europeans in this particular place, although we were only a few minutes' walk from the ferry we seemed to have had a peep into Africa…

They retraced their steps to the service club, and Flora vowed to postpone a bathe on Shelly Beach until the next time their Dutch friends were in port and able to show them the way.

***

While out shopping, Flora and Pat became braver, now venturing down the narrow alleys in the old town. The two girls peered into tiny shops and eventually found the one they'd been told about, and bent their heads to enter through the low doorway. The interior was dark and smelled of boot polish and leather.

The price that the shoemaker quoted for a pair of white buckskin shoes was much more than they'd been led to expect, so they mentioned the names of the

English merchant seamen now well on their way back to England. Eventually, they struck a bargain, and Flora later wrote in her diary: *it was quite a new experience to have the shape of one's foot drawn on a piece of paper & then the instep measurements etc. taken, the shoes are beautifully made here and although they are 45/-d they look worth it & are at least a good fit.*

The following week, they collected their shoes and, with the cost only a few pence less than two weeks' pay for a leading Wren, they had little money left for shopping. Nevertheless, they couldn't go back to quarters without visiting the fruit stall off Salim Road. The stallholder, an Arab, wearing a green checked *kikoi* round his waist, a long shirt hanging loose over the top and a red fez, saw them coming and smiled. He knew from previous bargaining that the girls would pay no more than a shilling for twenty-four bananas and he had their regular order waiting – and, for goodwill, dropped two oranges in Flora's basket as well. A boy of no more than 6 had been watching; he ran over, tugged at Flora's sleeve and pointed at her sisal basket. He looked far too frail to carry it, so she shook her head and offered him a copper. He beamed, seized the basket, hoisted it onto his shoulder and walked ahead, looking so pleased with himself that they hadn't the heart to protest.

With little money left for shopping, on their next off duty, instead of turning right outside St Joseph's and heading into the town, Flora and Pat turned left. Their billet was on the cliffs, near the golf course they had seen as they sailed into Mombasa. An idyllic place to live; such a shame they were confined inside a compound surrounded by a barbed-wire fence draped in canvas.

The scent of new-mown grass, as they walked across the fairway, was swept away by the salt-tang of the sea as they reached the cliff top. If it wasn't for the odd palm tree they could easily have been in England. The course grass and scattered boulders, the steep tumble of granite down to where waves crashed against the rocks that time had compacted into lopsided layers, reminded Flora of Clodgy Point. For a moment it was before the war and she was visiting her sister, Louie, in St Ives. Back then, in the 1930s, they had no idea what the future would bring. At least Louie and her family were out of the way of the bombs down there in Cornwall, but what of Vera and Jessie and her mother up there in the industrial north? Since she'd arrived in Mombasa, Flora had heard little of how the war was going back in Europe. The only news that had filtered through had been about North Africa, where German and Italian troops had surrendered to the British and Americans last month. Hopefully that was a good sign.

A large white ship sailed through the gap in the coral reef and brought her back to the present. She watched it follow a course between the buoys directly towards them, then turn, revealing a red cross on its funnel – a hospital ship. It sailed parallel to the shoreline, so close that they could see the people on deck. Both girls fell silent as they thought of the ill and injured aboard. Was there anyone they knew among them? They'd never know. In wartime, you just learnt to accept that those you said goodbye to… you may never see again… or ever find out what happened to them.

***

A long list of names in the sailing book meant it was the beginning of July before Flora and Pat's turn came around again. Arriving late at the jetty, they were relieved to find three other Wrens waiting, which meant the boat hadn't left without them. As time passed they scanned the ships in the harbour, fearing that they were waiting in vain. Then a cutter appeared from behind HMS *Sussex* and rowed towards them.

The six officers aboard apologised for being late, but then, as is often the case with first meetings, there was an embarrassed silence when no one knew quite what to say. The sail billowed out in the wind as they skimmed across the water, and by the time they reached the beach everyone had begun to relax. They dropped anchor then all dived off the boat and swam ashore.

Hermit crabs, enormous shell-homes on their backs, scuttled over the rocks. The sand itself appeared to be on the move, and closer inspection revealed that every inch of the beach was covered by an army of tiny crabs on manoeuvres, one large, red pincer weapon raised at the ready. At the approach of human footsteps, they broke ranks and scurried away to take cover in rock crevices or bury themselves in the sand.

The Wrens and their hosts all agreed that, while they didn't mind sharing their picnic with the cowardly crabs, the airborne division was another matter entirely. Squadrons of sand-flies and other fearless flying forces droned around, diving and attacking exposed skin. This was no place for a picnic.

Back aboard, the sailors brought out a large, wooden box; inside were tins of fruit, jam tarts, bread and butter and bottles of tea – but no cutlery or cups. Someone suggested they spread the jam from the tarts on the bread and use the pastry cases as spoons. The men ate bread and jam and watched the girls scoop up the grapefruit segments, sliced pears and apricot halves. They grinned when the makeshift spoons disintegrated into a soggy mess, and the hungry Wrens resorted to using their fingers to catch the slippery fruit portions. When they'd drained the last dregs of juice, the empty cans served as cups for the girls, who preferred not to drink tea from bottles.

When the time came to weigh anchor, the sails hung limp from the mast, the cutter lay becalmed on the tranquil sea. The sound of an outboard motor broke the silence; an RAF launch was speeding towards them. The crew exchanged sheepish glances and watched as the powerboat drew closer and a man in air-force blue rose to his feet. He raised a megaphone to his lips and hailed, 'Keep Clear. Catalina flying boat coming in.' As the boat roared off, the men took to the oars. Flora saw the relief on their faces and guessed that if they had been towed in by the RAF, they would never have lived it down.

Flora never expected to see Johannes again. Then, in mid-July, a note arrived to say his ship had just docked and inviting her to join him for lunch at the newly-opened Merchant Navy Officers' Club.

The checked cloths, a different colour on each of the six tables, gave the dining room a cheerful atmosphere. After they'd eaten, they relaxed in easy chairs in the lounge, then played table tennis in the games room. Flora beat Johannes by two points; a return match would have to wait, as she was on the afternoon watch and had no more half days due before his ship sailed. This time the Dutch warship would be at sea until mid-September.

But would the Wrens still be in Mombasa in September? At HMS *Alidina* rumours were rife that, now the Japanese were no longer a threat in the Indian Ocean, FECB would move back east to Ceylon. Flora resigned herself to never seeing Johannes again and put her name in the sailing book.

While the Wrens waited for news of their posting, Flora's name reached the top of the list and so, along with Pat and four other Wrens, she joined six 'subbies' (sub lieutenant engineers) from the RMS *Carthage* for an afternoon's sailing and another similar outing two days later. They should have passed this second invitation on to the Wrens whose names appeared below theirs in the sailing book, but didn't: the list of names was several pages long, and as they would shortly be leaving Mombasa a chance like this was unlikely to come again.

It was a perfect day with quite a good breeze and it seemed to take us no time to reach our usual beach. The tide was rather low & when we jumped out of the boat we just sank in the mud, it was terrible – horrible black mud, my ideas of bathing very soon disappeared and instead we went a walk along the beach…

The captain had put money into the "kitty" when he heard they were taking us sailing and the tea was a lovely surprise when we unpacked the eats, which on a picnic, are the most important item – or so it seems. All the sandwiches, egg, lettuce, cucumber were daintily wrapped in serviettes and we were also given them – what a luxury. For drinks we had orange squash but the best part of it was they had brought along a flask of ice just to complete things.

We were very sorry when it was time for us to leave, but it drops dark so very quickly. On the way back we had quite an adventure when we had a slight argument with a battleship!!! Somehow we suddenly lost the wind and were carried with the tide at quite a speed right up against her. There seemed to be thousands of faces peering at us from the decks and portholes. I think everyone on the ship must have gathered – the men worked exceptionally hard for a few minutes, pulling ropes, sails etc, while all the girls had to sit there helplessly getting more in the way than anything. However, I must say they managed the boat exceptionally well although at one time I had my doubts as to whether we should capsize, we seemed pretty near. When we were clear once more there was such a cheer went up as we sailed away.

Just to finish up the afternoon we met three destroyers coming into harbour and as we wanted no more "arguments" we had to go rather out of our way. It did look a picture to see them coming in one behind the other.

On deck, dwarfed beside torpedo tubes and gun housings, white-uniformed naval officers and ratings stood to attention, their right hands raised to the navy peaks of their white-topped hats, as the ships sailed through the narrow channel and into Kilindini docks – a reminder to the Wrens of why they were in Mombasa and of their imminent departure.

CHAPTER 13

Leaving Mombasa

There were about 46 of us going altogether in the first flight & we were very glad we were going with them. We piled into two naval vans and were soon at the docks and embarking on the Carthage. *It was quite a thrill to once more be on a ship but I liked Mombasa (apart from our camp which was very depressing) especially the various small beaches & we had had such very happy times there, in many ways I was sorry to leave.*

– Diary entry, 25 August 1943

Mombasa was only ever meant to be a temporary haven. The Far Eastern Fleet and the FECB arrived at the beginning of May 1942, having left Trincomalee and Colombo shortly after the thwarted Japanese attack on Ceylon on Easter Sunday. There were fears that they would try again. The Japanese, however, never did follow through with their plans to extend the Land of the Rising Sun into the Indian Ocean. Instead, they set their sights on Australia and America, and the theatre of war moved back into the Pacific.

In fact, the aircraft carriers *Soryu* and *Hiryu* were already on their way to islands north-east of Australia. The codebreakers, however, tipped off the US Navy, and so the USS *Lexington* and USS *Yorktown* were ready and waiting. Although the *Lexington* was lost in the Battle of the Coral Sea, the US Navy prevented the Japanese from landing on the south-eastern coast of New Guinea to set up an airbase at Port Moresby, from where they planned to threaten Australia.

In June 1942, the Japanese turned their attention to the tiny mid-Pacific base at Midway Atoll, a stepping stone to the USA. The American codebreakers, however, warned Admiral Nimitz of the Japanese plans and the attack came as no surprise to his forces. For the first time in the six months since Pearl Harbour, the tide was turning.

When Flora and the other SDX Wrens arrived in April 1943, the Far Eastern Fleet and FECB had been in Mombasa for almost a year. By the time the Wrens left at the end of August, the US Army had launched Operation Cartwheel to recapture Japanese-controlled islands in the South Pacific, and landed on New Guinea and controlled New Georgia in the Solomon Islands. The Japanese still occupied Burma, Malaya, the Philippines, French Indo-China and Sumatra, Java, Borneo and other islands of the Dutch East Indies. In the west, however, their tentacles only reached as far as the Andaman and Nicobar Islands in the Bay of Bengal.

With the Indian Ocean no longer under threat, it was time for the fleet to move back to their bases in Ceylon. The codebreakers, anxious to be closer to the action where it would be much easier to intercept the Japanese signals, would go with them.

The SDX Wrens were in the first flight to Ceylon. All materials had to be packed in advance and so, with no Hollerith machines to operate, they had three days of complete freedom before they sailed. This was Flora's last opportunity to take the ferries and explore more of the mainland of Kenya. Johanne and the other Dutch officers were now out at sea, and since her eventful, but unsuccessful, attempt to find Shelly Beach, she was reluctant to venture off the island without a male escort. Tom, one of the 'subbies' from the *Carthage* who'd taken them sailing, volunteered to be her guide, and together they made the most of their last days in Mombasa.

Tom met Flora at the gates of Fort St Joseph. They walked past the golf course, round the breezy, cliff-top promenade on the seaward edge of the island to the south side, where they waited for the ferry in the shade of the baobab trees. Flora takes up the story:

It was an exceptionally hot day so we went across to the mainland by Likoni ferry and decided to explore a little. After keeping to the main road for quite a while and passing the local Police station, consisting of a very small thatched mud hut in the centre of a compound, they certainly could not keep anyone in there very long, we saw rather an interesting path branching to the left and decided to go along here in the hope that we could work round in a circle and eventually be back on the beach.

Once off the main road you felt to be miles from civilization, there was nothing to be seen but palm trees in all directions with hills in the distance, there were several narrow paths leading in all direction some to small native houses, very primitive with a small garden in front and several goats and hens round about. What a simple life they must lead but they certainly look quite contented and the little black kiddies just fascinate me with their curly hair & usually such beaming smiles.

After walking quite a distance we came to the end of the path, it just faded out and as we had already done a little cross-country which was very unpleasant, the grass being very high and prickly, we retraced our steps and tried another with the same result. Finally we had once more to find our way to the main road and go back the same way.

By this time we were exceptionally thirsty what a terrible death it must be!! I had heard there was a house called "Sea Breezes" where one could buy tea so we wended our way to the one and only house up on the cliffs, just hoping!! What a pleasant relief when we were sitting on a verandah overlooking the sea drinking tea, it was a lovely view right across to the island. We felt much better for our refreshment so wandered down to the ferry & so back once more.

***

30 April 2008

We sit in the taxi in the queue for the Likoni ferry. The baobab trees are still there; they look just like Aunt Flora described them to me, their stout trunks topped off with a tuft of root-like branches as if they'd been uprooted and turned upside down. Omar tells us that they are hundreds of years old, and legend has it that the bones of Portuguese sailors are buried beneath them.

Sea Breeze at Shelly Beach is mentioned in our Kenyan guidebook. While we wait, I ask Omar and Ahmed if they know of a house or a café of that name. They look at each other and shake their heads.

The ferry docks. The metal ramp clanks onto the concrete and foot passengers stream off and head for the waiting *matatus*. These privately-owned white minibuses will stop anywhere to pick up passengers, the driver's mate crams in as many fares as he can, before sliding the door shut and the driver speeds off on a route spontaneously planned to drop everyone off wherever they want to go.

For the five-minute crossing, Ahmed warns us not to get out of the taxi, to keep the doors locked and the windows closed: in the crush aboard the ferry, pickpockets are on the lookout for unguarded cameras and jewellery.

The guidebook also says that the lack of a bridge has deterred property developers on the south mainland. When we drive off the ferry, I am amazed by the number of small shops and stalls jammed together on either side of the road, by the hustle and bustle, the noise. Then I notice that all the people are locals. We are the only tourists around. Ahmed turns left into an unmade road and zigzags between potholes. Between the road and the sea is a single-storey building. Today, a sign outside says YWCA, but I wonder if back in 1943 this was the service club Aunt Flora mentioned on her first visit to Shelley Beach.

There's no sign of a police station but I'm amazed by the number of homes for disabled and underprivileged children. Ahmed explains that in Kenya there are many orphans; their parents have died of AIDS.

Omar points out the fern-like leaves and the brilliant orange flowers of the flamboyant trees, and the deep purple and magenta bougainvillea, but we see very few palm trees. Instead, the land has been cleared and there are houses: next to the sea, large mansions protected by electric fences; on the other side of the road, a variety of more modest homes constructed of breeze-blocks and corrugated iron, many with only two rows of blocks to mark the foundations and lay claim to the plot.

In 1943, anyone could visit Shelly Beach, if they could find it! Not so today. Omar explains that it is not possible to get to the beach without going through the grounds of the big houses and hotels that border the shore. We pull up outside the Shelly Beach Hotel; it is surrounded by an electric fence and a barrier blocks the driveway. Ahmed goes to speak to the four security guards and comes back to tell us that the hotel has been closed since 2004, because the company is bankrupt. He has, however, somehow persuaded them to let us in. One of the guards escorts us around what must once have been an idyllic holiday paradise. Now, the thatched roofs of the holiday villas are in tatters – some have slipped and are hanging off at alarming angles – weeds grow in the guttering, and the concrete walls are smudged with black and green mould. The tiles on the side of the swimming pool are cracked and just a puddle of rusty water remains at the deep end. The palm trees, however, still stand proud, notices warning tourists to beware of falling coconuts still nailed to their trunks.

Shelly gets its name because it is a beach with an abundance of seashells. Through the crystal-clear sea water we can see many varieties of conch shells and coral from the reef way in the distance. The fine white sand is marred only by seaweed strewn on the tideline. Considering how difficult it was for us to get here, I am surprised to see other people wandering along the beach. Omar says they probably live in the grand houses we passed on the way. Now the hotel has closed, the beach is theirs and theirs alone.

***

At ten-thirty on Wednesday, 25 August 1943, the Wrens of the first flight mustered outside Regulating for roll call; of the original sixteen in the SDX section, two were missing: one remained in Durban recovering from yellow jaundice, the other had gone on three months' leave to join her fiancé in Alexandria and get married. The remaining fourteen piled aboard two naval vans and headed for the docks. On the quayside they surveyed the ships in port, trying to decide which one was to carry them on their seven-day voyage across the Indian Ocean to Ceylon. Eventually, one of the girls spotted their green canvas cases and they all watched as their possessions, bundled together in a net, swung from the arm of a crane to be deposited on the deck of a ship some of the Wrens recognised. Until they were marched up the gangplank, Flora didn't dare believe their good fortune – their ship was the RMS *Carthage*.

P. & O. R.M.S. "CARTHAGE" 15,000 TONS.
INDIA AND FAR EASTERN MAIL AND PASSENGER SERVICE.

Carthage was one of two P&O ocean liners known as the Far East Sisters. Built in 1931, initially to carry the Royal Mail, it was later converted into a floating luxury hotel to accommodate a maximum of 400 first- and second-class passengers travelling from Britain to its far eastern colonies. At the beginning of the war it was requisitioned as a troopship, and carried very many more servicemen and women in far less comfort.

As they left the quayside, forty-six Wrens stood to attention on deck alongside the ship's company, their right arms raised in salute. The smile on their faces, bronzed by five months' sunshine, mirrored their pride. This was the first time in history that women in the Royal Navy had manned ship as a vessel put to sea.

When they reached open water, the petty officer gave the command: 'Stand easy. Dismiss.'

Flora glanced across to where Tom stood among the other sub-lieutenant engineers, their hosts on the sailing picnics during their last weeks in Mombasa, and she still couldn't believe their good luck.

Several hours later, when they opened the door to their cabin, Flora reconsidered – perhaps they weren't quite so lucky after all. Inside, with only the minimum of space between them, were rows of low camp beds – thirty-six in all.

Sleeping on canvas stretched on a wooden frame a foot from the deck proved more comfortable than the thin, lumpy mattress over hard wooden slats back at the *banda*. However, since one of the selection criteria for the SDX Wrens had been height, the camp beds could have done with being a good few inches longer.

***

Flora was woken by a loud hammering on the cabin door. She looked at her watch. It was 6 a.m. A male voice outside shouted 'tea', and the Wren nearest opened the door. One of the two sailors who pushed the trolley conveying the urn told the girls that they'd have to come out and fetch it themselves. With sleep in their eyes and tousled hair, the Wrens picked their way between beds and out into the passageway, where they accepted the steaming tin mugs. As the sailors trundled off with the trolley, one of them remarked that not one of those lovely ladies dare look them in the face first thing in the morning.

Not everyone had slept as well as Flora, and there were complaints about the heat and cramped conditions of the cabin. The following night, permission was granted to sleep up on deck. Flora watched as some of her cabinmates rolled up their bedding, dismantled their camp beds and carried the folded the canvas and wooden poles up to A deck. When they'd gone, the Wrens who preferred to stay put moved their beds so they were in line with the draught of cool air from the ventilator. During the evening they shared orange crush they'd bought from the canteen, diluted with iced water in flasks provided by the ship's engineers.

The sun was barely over the horizon when the cabin door swung open. Raised voices and the clatter of wooden poles heralded the return of those who had departed eight hours earlier with visions of an enchanting night under the stars. Flora turned over in her camp bed to face the bulkhead, to stop herself saying, 'Surely you knew they swabbed the decks at five?' Then she covered her ears with the pillow: it was still another three hours until breakfast.

Meals, not up to the standard of the *Christiaan Huygens* but a definite improvement on the suspect meat and potato-less offerings of Mombasa, were served in a small mess reserved just for the Wrens. Even so, some of their number still protested that it wasn't fair. The TWAs weren't even in the services, but they ate in the officers' mess and had use of the ward room. Flora pointed out that most of them were officers' wives or daughters, but she had to admit that she found the children they had tagging along rather annoying.

One of the onboard films, *Hellzapoppin'*, must have been shown with these young passengers in mind. The children were, for once, seated in one spot, not running around and getting underfoot. They laughed and screamed in delight while Flora couldn't make sense of the plot and described the whole ninety minutes as utter rubbish. A film later in the voyage, *Yankee Doodle Dandy*, was more to her liking.

Four dances were also arranged, one each for the red, white and blue watches and one for officers and civilians. Flora declined invitations, preferring to read in the shade rather than perspire on the dance floor. Anyway, there was no need for male company when they already had the undivided attention of the ship's engineers. The little clique had claimed a shady spot on the crew deck as their own. They whiled away the time chatting or playing cards, and even on one occasion reading poetry, which all but one of the engineers found highly amusing. The seven days passed all too quickly.

RMS *Carthage* sailed into Colombo Harbour on Wednesday, 1 September 1943. As they passed through the small gap in the breakwater, two air force officers stood at the top of the round watchtower. Flora couldn't help wondering what they thought when they noticed that some of the naval contingent standing to attention on deck wore skirts, rather than bell-bottoms, and held their hand in salute alongside wide-brimmed, pudding-basin hats.

***

4 January 2014

I stand on deck as we sail out of Colombo Harbour at the end of our five-day stay on the island that, since independence in 1948, has thrown off the colonial name of Ceylon and become Sri Lanka once more. The watchtower Aunt Flora described is still there at the end of the breakwater, still the same more than seventy years later. This white, circular building, the shape of an upturned mushroom, has two storeys decorated with arched windows topped with a single tall pillar.

I remember the glow of pride on Aunt Flora's face as she told me how air force officers stood at the top of this watchtower and saluted as RMS *Carthage* entered port, how proud she was to be among the Wrens making history by being the first women to man ship alongside the men. She wrote in her diary: *It certainly made us feel to be definitely part of the Navy.*

PART 4: CEYLON

Ceylon, the dewdrop that glistens at the southernmost tip of India.

An island colonised in the nineteenth century by the British, their eyes dazzled by the rubies, sapphires and amethysts buried in the red earth, their expensive tastes tempted by the potential profit of taming the fertile upland soil to grow coffee and later, when coffee rust devastated the crops, to plant tea.

An island where sudden, short-lived monsoons drench the south-west coast around Colombo from April to October, and the north-east coast up to the port of Trincomalee from November to January.

An island where the thermometer registers 80°F all the year round; the only escape is to travel inland, where mountains rise to 8,000 feet and the temperature falls into the 60s.

CHAPTER 14

Colombo

After disembarking we were taken from the docks in naval vans to our Quarters and there were many guesses to what these would be like. We went through streets of very small shops and were very interested to see the bullock carts with canopies over, something we had not seen in Mombasa. After passing through the centre of the town we appeared to be going miles away, but eventually the vans turned off the main road at Alfred Place, The "Durdans"... There had apparently been a very nice garden attached to the house but when we arrived this was in complete disorder owing to building of kadjan *huts (or* bandas *as we called them in East Africa).*

– Diary entry, 1 September 1943

As the Wrens stood to attention on deck, the patches of white cloth they'd sewn over the crowns of their hats did little to deflect the sun's rays. Perspiration coalesced into pools beneath their detachable collars and formed into rivulets flowing beneath their cotton shirts.

They disembarked at one o'clock. As she stood outside the harbour buildings, waiting for naval vans to take them to their new quarters, Flora thought their new posting didn't look too bad. Directly opposite was a white, four-storey building with the name Grand Oriental Hotel over the entrance. Cars, not that different to those her father once owned, were parked either side of the wide streets; rickshaws wove their way through the traffic. Women in saris or sunhats and day dresses strolled along the covered walkways or stood gazing in shop windows.

Once out of the centre of town, the shops became smaller, the roads narrower. The Wrens saw their first bullock cart: two poor beasts, their ribs and joints clearly visible beneath their sunken hides, yoked together and pulling a wagon with large wheels and a Wild West-style canopy made of woven palm leaves.

The van turned off the main road into Alfred Place and came to a halt outside a colonial-style residence called The Durdans. The Wrens sighed with relief when they were led past the *kadjan* huts in the grounds and in through the front door of the mansion. Flora and nine others were shown to their cabin, a large airy room: green curtains hung either side of the louvered doors, which opened out onto a wide, tiled veranda. Furniture included the usual bunk beds and dressing tables with drawers for their folded white blouses and underwear, but no wardrobes, so they suspended cord from the picture rail and hung their uniform and civilian dresses round the walls.

Down the hallway was a proper bathroom, but no one could pluck up the courage to take a bath. It would be several days before the others, their fingers crossed, looked on while Flora struck a match and crept up to the awesome geyser and with a *whoosh* the rusty contraption sprang into life. After five months of carrying buckets, they could now enjoy the luxury of a long soak, with hot water on tap.

On their first evening in Colombo the Wrens were only allowed out until seven o'clock, but by the time Flora and her friends were able to leave it was already after five. They set off down Colpetty Road, following the map on the servicemen's leaflet. Apparently, all the leading shops, hotels and restaurants were in Fort, an area within easy walking distance. As it was right next to the harbour, they'd be able to meet up with the 'subbies' from the *Carthage*. Although the sun was low in the sky, the heat of the day still hung in a haze. They stopped to rest and decided that the leaflet must have been written for sailors aboard ships berthed in the docks, not Wrens billeted down the coast at Colpetty,

They hailed a passing taxi. As they drove past a vast area of grass next to the sea, the taxi driver called out, 'Galle Face Green'. They crossed the causeway into Fort, then slowed as they approached a road junction. A beacon flashed at the top of a tall tower with a clockface on all four sides. 'Clocktower and lighthouse… in town… very famous,' the driver said as he drove round it. On Queen's Street, he pointed to red-uniformed guards outside a white mansion, Queen's House.

The taxi dropped them off at the harbour outside the Grand Oriental Hotel. The Wrens peeked through the revolving doors into the foyer and marvelled at the sparkling chandeliers, the marble floors, the polished teak, and speculated about whether there was a chance that the 'subbies' might invite them to the hotel for dinner. Not then, as they had to be back at The Durdans before the seven o'clock curfew, but maybe the following night.

***

It took a while to get the Hollerith machines up and running, so, unlike the other newly-arrived Wrens, SDX section had a couple of days to do as they pleased. Flora arranged to meet Tom, the 'subby' she'd spent time with during their last days in Mombasa.

They began their explorations in Fort. Either side of the wide streets, colonnades sheltered the pavement, above them ornate buildings rose several storeys high. On the corner of York Street and Prince Street there was even a department store: below the rooftop balustrades and the plaster mouldings of the horns of plenty, the name *CARGILLS (CEYLON) LIMITED* in large white letters stood out against the puce sandstone façade. From the classical architecture, Flora could easily believe she was back home in Britain. However, the all-enveloping heat, the constant caw of crows and the rickshaw drivers calling out in Sinhalese told her she wasn't.

The servicemen's leaflet included the warning: *Make your purchases from shops of standing. Special precautions should be taken in purchasing Jewellery and Stones. Beware of spurious imitations offered at tempting prices.* But Flora and Tom were only window shopping. She admired the blue-pink sapphires, the blue moonstone, the orange fire of the garnet, the gleaming green-yellow of chrysoberyl, and could see why it was commonly called cat's eye. They marvelled at the filigree gold-work of the gem-studded armlets.

On Canal Row, they were enticed into The Curio Elephant Manufactory. The elephants, carved out of ebony, mahogany, palm wood or *kadura* ranged in price and size – from less than an inch in height to those too heavy to lift. There were carved bookends, pipe racks, ashtrays and table lamps. Flora ran her finger over the smooth ebony polished to gleam like her father's Sunday boots.

As they walked along Chatham Street towards the clocktower they passed the Ceylon Products Shop. It was mentioned in the servicemen's leaflet as a shop where: Arrangements have been made to supply visiting troops with goods produced in Ceylon at special prices. They didn't bother to go in.

During lunch at the Chinese Hotel, Tom presented her with a package. She unwrapped the brown paper: inside was a trio of ebony elephants, the largest the size of a cigarette packet, the smallest no bigger than a matchbox. Flora thanked him, but the smile on her face flickered when he said it would be something to remember him by; his ship sailed the following day.

***

2 January 2011

The ebony elephants are now in a display cabinet back home in Britain. We are in Colombo, walking along Galle Face Green where Flora and Tom came after lunch at the Chinese Hotel.

On the parched, patchy grass, families picnic, children fly kites and couples stroll hand in hand. We descend the steps to the promenade above the sea wall and look down at the waves as they crash onto the narrow strip of sand.

I understand why Aunt Flora wrote in her diary: *this was no place for swimming.*

The Green stretches from Fort along the seafront to the Galle Face Hotel; a misnomer, perhaps, as this hotel, built at right angles to the shore, has its back towards the ancient port of Galle, 70 miles further down the coast. The hotel was built in 1864 and the outside has changed little since my aunt was here. The architect must have been influenced by Buckingham Palace when he designed the three interconnected square blocks, the row upon row of identical windows. Here, however, the similarity ends as all three blocks have pagoda-style roofs, each corner turned up in a smile. Instead of standing to peer in through the railings, hoping to catch a glimpse of a royal, here the tourists, like ourselves, sit on the hotel terrace and gaze out through the archways and over the Green.

The skyline of Fort is dominated by the forty-storey Twin Towers. Lego-like hotels and office blocks loom over the red pan-tiled roofs of the older buildings. This morning we were surprised to discover that it is no longer a fort; it has retained its name despite the fact that its Dutch fortifications were torn down by the conquering British. Some of the landmarks of Aunt Flora's day are still here. Red-uniformed guards still stand outside the white mansion now called, not Queen's House, but President's House, and enclosed within a high-security area surrounded by wire-mesh fences. The clocktower-lighthouse no longer serves as a warning to shipping, its beam now obscured by the buildings which rose around it in the latter half of the twentieth century. It withstood a bomb blast during the 1983–2009 civil war and still tells the correct time. The Grand Oriental Hotel still waits at the harbour gates with a bed on dry land for weary passengers.

On York Street, the original signs offering DISPENSING, DRUGS, TOILET REQUISITES, PERFUMERY, OPTICAL GOODS or advertising GROCERIES WINES TOBACCO FANCY GOODS still swing from the arches over the pavement outside the department store. Beneath them, women now sell mangoes, limes and star apples. A man sits on the cracked paving slabs mending an umbrella.

Ornate gilt plaques bear the name CARGILLS beneath the now-empty shop windows. Most of the entrances are boarded up; we venture in through the only one that remains open. Inside, most of the store's colonial history has been stripped away. Supermarket checkouts and rows of steel shelving have replaced perfume and haberdashery counters. All that remains of the old days are teak shelves fixed to the far wall and some glass-fronted teak counters and drawers salvaged to sell children's toys, books and souvenirs. Abandoned, almost hidden, near the door is the wooden booth where a cashier once sat behind a grille. The lift is still there, but going nowhere as the stairs are roped off, the upper floors out of bounds.

We leave Galle Face Green and walk along Galle Road (formerly Colpetty Road) to look for The Durdans. On Alfred Place, ornate white pillars stand either side of a wrought-iron gate. Beyond them, just visible behind palm trees, thick foliage and a wire fence is a large mansion that might be where Aunt Flora was once billeted. If we are right, then the grounds where the *kadjun* huts once stood have long gone to make way for the Durdans Private Hospital.

***

Flora and Tom spent their last evening together with another three couples who'd also met on the voyage from Mombasa. The four Wrens wrote their names in the signing-out book, then their escorts filled in their name and rank – sub lieutenant engineers – their number and their base – RMS *Carthage* – and noted where they were going. For the whole time they were in Colombo, no Wren would be allowed out after seven o'clock in the evening without an identifiable man to collect her and a known and approved destination, in this case the Grand Oriental Hotel.

Flora takes up the story:

It is a very large hotel, but also very sleepy and one could only have a drink when having dinner… as this was the case we had dinner fairly early and afterwards coffee was served in the lounge, which was in fact a very large dance hall – it really would have been a good place for a dance. During the evening an orchestra played light music but the people sitting round looked as though they wanted waking up, we were forced to laugh at them, absolute characters most of them just having a few minutes before turning in for the night.

One felt as though it was only correct to speak in whispers!! There were several parties from the "Carthage" there & I am sure they must all have felt as we did. Eventually we left the GOH to its meditations & after arriving back at Alfred Place just had time for a short walk. It was a perfect evening & fireflies were darting around the trees like tiny stars. We had to be in by 11pm & the "Carthage" was sailing the following day. We were all sorry when goodbyes had to be said and wondered when once more we should meet again.

The SDX Wrens' duties in Colombo were much the same as in Mombasa, but the atmosphere was different: the first-name familiarity of *Alidina* was gone. The watches were even more complicated than before. The rota covered four days – the first two were the killers. On Day 1, transport picked them up at seven-thirty for an eight o'clock start, then collected them at noon and brought them back to The Durdans. There was just time for lunch and a doze through the afternoon heat before they were back aboard the transport to start again at four o'clock and work through until eight in the evening. At least on Day 2 they could lie in and try to sleep, while the Sinhalese orderlies swept the floors. Then an early lunch so they could leave in time to be on duty at noon. Off again at four, home for tea, then back to work the night watch from eight o'clock until two the following morning.

From two o'clock in the morning, Day 3 was free, but they needed to catch up on their sleep – difficult when Wrens on other watches kept coming and going. Then on Day 4, in the early hours, a Sinhalese rating would be standing beside the bed demanding they sign the knocking-up book to certify he'd done his job and woken them up in time for the two-to-eight-o'clock watch. Then there was a twenty-four-hour respite, before they started again on Day 1 at eight in the morning.

And so it went on…

CHAPTER 15

Up Country

I travelled the rest of the way alone and eventually I arrived at Haputale. It was rather a queer sensation wondering where I was staying & what the people would be like.

– Diary entry, 27 September 1943

No. 20124

Telegrams: PAT, COLOMBO.

Telephone: 2078, COLOMBO.

THE SAILORS' ENTERTAINMENT COMMITTEE

H. M. NAVAL OFFICE,
COLOMBO.

To Estate. Up-country Express.

FROM Captain Owen ESTATE Haputale STATION Haputale

DISTRICT Haputale TEA Yes RUBBER No.

TO THE CHAIRMAN, SAILORS' ENTERTAINMENT COMMITTEE, COLOMBO.

We would like to have as our guest on the estate:

Name Miss Crossley Home Town

Name Home Town

The following arrangements have been made by this Committee :—

OUTWARD JOURNEY

Boat will be alongside your ship at ... a.m. and convey you to Jetty.

~~Bus or~~ car will be at ~~Dock Gate/Passenger Jetty~~ Durbans at 5 30 a.m.

Your train leaves Fort Station 6. 25 a.m. from No. 1 Platform. Date 27. 9. 43 Front of Train

You will change trains at — Station at —

On arrival at Haputale Station at 5 33 PM there will be someone to meet you.

RETURN JOURNEY

Your train leaves Haputale Station at 9 12 AM. Date 4. 10. 43.

Your train arrives ~~Maradana~~/Fort Station at 6. 10. p.m. Platform No. 5

Car ~~or bus~~ will meet your train and take you to ~~Dock or Jetty~~ Durbans

Dinner will be provided on board for you.

Boat will leave Passenger Jetty at — for your ship.

INVITATION Kindly handy our invitation to your host or hostess at Station.

CLOTHES You should take warm clothes, including a raincoat.

...KE A MEAL FOR THE TRAIN

'Invitation' Up Country

The invitation to spend her week's leave as a guest on a tea estate up country arrived, along with travel warrants, just a month after Flora arrived in Colombo. The front of the single sheet of foolscap is more like a printed form than an invitation, the blanks filled in with a fountain pen and signed by Mr O'Shaughnessy, Organiser of the Sailors' Entertainment Committee. On the back is further printed information about this organisation, established in 1939 to arrange for naval officers and ratings to spend their leave on Ceylon's rubber and tea estates. This document has remained preserved inside the diary for more than seventy years.

Flora stood outside the front door of The Durdans and peered into the grey light of morning – no sign of a car. Last night she'd put her name in the knocking-up book, and this morning the guard had shone a torch in her face at four-thirty. She'd tiptoed to the bathroom then back to the cabin to grope around for her clothes, careful not to wake the night watch who had arrived back two hours earlier, or the morning watch who wouldn't be knocked-up for a couple of hours. She'd opened the veranda doors and stepped out to retrieve the bag of rations she'd hung outside overnight to keep cool, then crept back inside, fitted them in the space she'd left in her suitcase and fastened the catches.

The car was fifteen minutes late. That left just over half an hour to get to the station. Flora couldn't abide being late. She'd need to find the guard; he was probably next door, whiling away the time with the other Royal Marine on guard outside the officers' billet. When she got there, a car was parked in the drive, but no one else was around.

It was hard to understand what the local driver said, but she decided this must be her car and got into the back seat. They headed for Fort, calling first at the Grand Oriental Hotel where a man in naval uniform was waiting. He walked over, handed his suitcase to the driver and got into the back seat. He nodded to Flora and asked, in an Australian drawl, if she was going up country too.

Flora's travelling companion was a midshipman. When the driver dropped them off at the station, they searched in vain for their reserved first-class compartment. In the end they settled themselves instead in one already occupied by an Indian gentleman in European dress, who welcomed them in perfect public-school English. He asked where they were going, and when Flora replied Haputale, he nodded and said that, although it wasn't that far, only 160 miles, it would take all day because it was uphill all the way and they stopped at every station.

That was a good thing because the only way to get to the restaurant car was to wait until the train stopped, get out of the carriage and walk along the platform. Flora and the Australian went for breakfast together and were quite surprised to be served bacon and eggs. When the train stopped at Mirigama, they returned to their compartment.

They had now left the palm plantations around Colombo behind and were entering rice country. Waterfalls cascaded down from the thickly-wooded hills to the paddy fields terraced out of the hillside, or sewn into a haphazard patchwork on the valley floor. Each plot was enclosed within banks of red-brown clay, breached by shallow drains, to allow water to flow from one patch down to the next. Buffaloes pulled ploughs, workers in conical, straw hats and up to their calves in watery mud planted single blades of paddy, or gathered the ripe crop and tied it into bunches. Children on the trackside waved as the train chugged on and snaked its way upwards.

At Rambukkana an extra engine was added to the rear of the train to push them up the steep climb. The track rose to 6,000 feet, before descending back down to Haputale at 4,800 feet. Flora shook her head when asked if she'd like to sit next to the window. She was all too aware of the squeaking wheels, the lurching train and the sheer drop only inches away from the track.

The Australian midshipman left the train at Hatton, announcing his intention to climb Adam's Peak to watch the sunrise the following day. He shook her hand with great gusto and wished her 'g'day'.

It was then Flora realised that since leaving Colombo, she'd only seen one other white woman. She shivered; the fresh breeze, a welcome change as they'd left the coast behind and climbed higher up country, was now decidedly chilly. The train entered Poolbank Tunnel and she put on her coat.

Haputale was just a dot on the map; Flora had no idea what to expect when she got there. Her host was supposed to meet her at the station, but how would she recognise him?

She didn't need to. As she was the only Wren, he recognised her as soon as she got off the train. He strode down the platform to meet her, removed the pipe from the corner of his mouth and introduced himself, adding that everyone called him Capt'n.

His military bearing marked him out as ex-army: his grey hair trimmed short, his commanding officer expression mellowed by weather-worn tanned skin. He was of her father's generation and wore flannels, an open-necked shirt and a Harris tweed jacket.

He talked and joked on the drive from the station. By the time they arrived, Flora knew that he managed the tea estate for Liptons, he lived alone with Vanda, an Alsatian; Chips, a spaniel; and a black cat called Tom Satan. But the war had provided him with company; now rarely a week went by without house guests. At present he was host to two nursing sisters, two RAF sergeants, a South African sub lieutenant… and now a Wren.

They turned off the main road into a driveway, negotiated a series of hairpin bends, and came to a halt outside a white bungalow perched on the hillside. It was a long building just the width of one room with a low-pitched roof. Tacked on at the front was the lounge, a circular extension with a wall of windows around the circumference. On that first day, when Flora joined the other guests for tea, served in bone china cups, with home-made cake, the panoramic view was obscured by a thick veil of mist.

The Bungalow, Haputale

One of the sergeants suggested a few games of table tennis before dinner and Flora rose to follow, then remembered the instructions below the journey details on the 'invitation':

RATIONS

Now that civilians are unable to obtain all the foodstuffs they desire, it would be advisable to take some of the following: Flour, sugar, coffee, baking powder, cheese, marmalade, jam, sauces, oats, fish, corn-beef, pepper, mustard, dripping etc....

The petrol coupons supplied to your host or hostess is to transfer you to and from Estate-Station.

She found her host in the kitchen talking to the houseboy. As she handed over the rations and coupons, Capt'n smiled and said that at times they did find it hard to get supplies, but thanks to all these gifts from his guests they never went short.

His words were borne out at dinner that evening and every other meal they ate at the bungalow: variety never seen at the Wrennery, served in style at a table laid out with dainty table mats, napkins and flowers – fresh every day. A succession of courses was savoured at leisure, while Capt'n and his guests chatted and laughed.

No doubt, during these nightly dinner parties, conversation would turn to the progress of the war back home in Europe. Were the RAF lieutenants still talking about the bombing of Hamburg that had begun before Flora left Mombasa at the end of July and continued on into August? How RAF and US bombers had reduced shipyards and factories, and seven square miles of Germany's second city, to rubble? Maybe it was here that Flora first heard about the unconditional surrender of Italy, and how on 8 September 1943 the new Italian prime minister had signed a military armistice with the Allies.

Flora never mentions the progress of the war in her diaries, but she does record how much she appreciated the hospitality she experienced up country:

Afterwards we went into the lounge where there was a large brick open fireplace & a lovely log fire – what a treat to see a fire once more & it was really needed as it was quite cool. All the chairs and settees were exceptionally comfortable and the room was lit with standard lamps and table lamps, there was such a restful atmosphere you did not want to move once you were settled but about 10.45pm I went to bed feeling very tired but quite sure I should enjoy my leave. The bed was absolute

> *luxury after our hard mattresses, just to be able to sink into it and also have a hot water bottle.*
>
> *I was asleep very quickly, the next thing I knew being woken up by the sunshine (or very bright light) & also having morning tea brought in. When I sat up in bed the view from my window was almost breathtaking. The hills rose up one behind the other in various shades of browns, greens, purples, the summits being covered with fleecy white clouds, which kept drifting across the valley then lifting. There was a huge lawn & garden, tennis court, bowling green & deck tennis & wherever one looked there were trees of all descriptions, many of them flowering trees with vividly shaded flowers. It was an absolute picture & you could see for such a distance.*

Flora took her time deciding between the three cotton dresses she'd brought with her, relishing the thought that for a whole week she'd wear nothing but civvies. She chose the tiny floral print button-through with the wide lapels and puffed sleeves.

The others were already seated at breakfast. Capt'n rose to pull out a chair for Flora. The two dogs didn't move from their post at his feet. Not until the meal was over did she discover why they waited in anticipation. When their master rose, they bounded down the hall and out of the front door. Everyone followed, so Flora did the same. Outside, the dogs stood in wait, ears raised, eyes alert, either side of the path across the lawn. First Capt'n, then each of his guests, threw pieces of toast, which Vanda, the Alsatian, leapt high in the air to catch. Chips, the spaniel, too lazy to jump, still got his share. This ritual was repeated every morning, so by the third day Flora was also helping herself to an extra slice of toast before leaving the table.

Capt'n assured his guests that the views from higher up were even more spectacular, and to prove it on the first morning of Flora's stay he led them all on an expedition to 6,000 feet. He drove the ladies part of the way on a narrow track, which wound its way up through the hillside tea estate. The men had set out earlier and were waiting where the track petered out.

From the boot of the car, Capt'n produced stout staffs for the men, walking sticks for the girls, which proved very useful on the next stage as it involved climbing flight after flight of steps chiselled into the red earth between the terraces of tea bushes. They arrived at the top puffing and panting, their calves aching, but disappointment awaited them. A mist had descended into the valley and visibility was down to a few feet.

Capt'n removed the pipe from his mouth and, holding it by the bowl, pointed the stem through the enveloping fug as he told them what they should have been able to see: down the valley to the village of Diyatalawa, and the naval rest camp, up and over the hills to the coast and the sea. Then he shook his head and said that in these conditions it was best not to hang around.

The cold and damp didn't appear to bother the tea pickers they passed on the way down. The Tamil women chatted and sang as, with lightning speed, they plucked the tender shoots from the bushes and tossed them into wicker baskets, held in place on their backs by a hessian strap around their foreheads.

***

21 March 2016

Tea pickers still toss the young shoots over their shoulders, but not into baskets. Instead, they are now collected in nylon sacks, still carried in the same way, on their backs supported by nylon straps around the worker's head.

We are on a short tour up country and our guide, Sidath, is driving us up through the tea plantations. Our car climbs the zigzag road, slowing to negotiate the hairpin bends and inch past traffic coming down. For tea pickers and the more energetic tourist, steep stone steps lead straight up, dividing the neat terraces of tea bushes into squares of rich emerald highlighted with lime green.

Sidath, Terry and I squeeze into the back of a tuk-tuk – a car-moped hybrid, the two-stroke engine's answer to the rickshaw – decorated with plastic flowers, fringes and gold tassels, for the last leg of the journey up a narrow track. The engine of this tiny vehicle falters several times as it negotiates the even steeper incline with three passengers aboard. Where the road bends back on itself, plaques with a quote on a blue-bordered white tile are embedded into the dry-stone wall. We pause on a bend to allow the tuk-tuk coming down to pass; the tile here proclaims: *When the earth is sick and polluted, human health is impossible. To heal ourselves we must heal our planet and to heal our planet we must heal ourselves.* A truth more relevant in the industrialised world, rather than here where the air is unadulterated, and only the tea bushes and the more adventurous tourists encroach on nature.

The view below us becomes even more spectacular the higher up we go. As we near the top, a black and white pole extends across the track. A man comes out of a concrete hut – telephone box size with a corrugated-iron roof – and collects a 100 rupee vehicle fee, then swings back the barrier so the tuk-tuk can continue the rest of the way up to Lipton's Seat, as this famous beauty spot is now called.

We reach a platform surrounded by a parapet. Sitting on a bench, glass in hand surveying his tea empire, is Thomas Lipton's statue, the bronze worn smooth and shiny by the many hands of tourists who have sat next to him. A memorial stone chronicles the history of his tea estate and states that we are now: *Perched perilously at the edge of a sheer descent at over 6,000 feet* – which confirms that this must be the place Capt'n brought his house guests in September 1943.

Back then the 360-degree view was obscured by mist. Today, however, it is perfectly clear: we can see the road we have taken winding down through the tea estate to the valley below, the small town of Diyatalawa, and the army camp, which has replaced the wartime naval rest camp.

To find out what happens to the leaves we see the pickers carrying back down the slopes in their sacks, we visit the Dambatenne Tea Factory. A tour costs just 250 rupees and starts on the second floor in the withering room.

Here, leaves are spread out to dry until half the water content is removed, when they are dropped through a hole to the floor below where the rolling and cutting processes begin. At each stage of the process we are allowed to handle and feel how the tea leaves change from large, damp pieces to the familiar finer and drier tea leaves that we put in our teapots.

The fermentation process takes place on the floor: we have to be careful to avoid stepping on the neatly shaped 1m-square,10cm-high piles of leaves turning from brown to black. The tea is then fired before being sieved to remove any foreign material, then graded.

Aunt Flora records in her diary: *One tea bush produces 2oz of tea per year. It was exceptionally interesting and I had never before realized how many processes went into the manufacture of tea.* The tea factory Capt'n took her to visit was, most likely, Dambatenne, because the long, white, many-windowed, three-storey building was built in 1890.

***

The days up country began to fall into a pattern: a leisurely breakfast, a trip out in the morning, back in time for lunch, after which they'd retire to bed for an hour or so. Mid-afternoon they'd drift back into the lounge for tea and cakes, then challenge each other to a game of deck tennis or bowls. There was always time for a long soak in the bath before dinner, which lasted most of the evening, then coffee and a chat around the fire before bed.

By Wednesday, Flora and the South African sub lieutenant were the only two guests remaining and Capt'n took them on a tour of the tea plantation. When they heard the estate manager's car, tiny children would dash out of the palm-thatched houses with smiles from ear to ear, and shout *'Salame'*. On the weekly visit to the estate's school, a solitary thatched hut in the midst of tea bushes, Capt'n asked if the children were attending regularly. The teacher nodded and explained, for the benefit of his guests, that some of her pupils had to walk miles to get there.

***

Capt'n was going to visit his friend Sir Thomas Lester Villiers, and asked if they would like to go along with him. Flora was prepared to forgo her afternoon nap to see what her host described as an amazing house with a beautiful garden… and she wasn't disappointed:

> *The run there was through very beautiful country, in one particular part where we were at a height of 4500ft, we could look down on the lowlands 200ft & see for miles across. On a clear day you can see the sea over 40 miles away but there was a slight haze so we missed that.*
>
> *Eventually we turned off the road & up the drive to the house, on either side being beds of scarlet, pink and mauve flowers, just one blaze of colour but when we emerged at the house in front of which were spacious lawns it almost took our breath away. It was in the most perfect setting, surrounded by all the hills & a view across the valley to the hills beyond. It was so peaceful, not another house in sight & as the house itself was built of grey stone with small paned windows on the style of some very old English mansions one could almost feel to have jumped into a little of England for a while, it was so very unexpected to find a building of this description in Ceylon after the usual spacious bungalows so characteristic of out here – you absolutely felt to be once more back in England.*
>
> *Sir Thomas himself was very pleasant & just fitted in with the house & surroundings, his nephew who was there took us round the garden & for the first time I saw pineapples, grapefruit and breadfruit growing.*
>
> *We only went into the library which was just what one expected, the walls were panelled & there was a huge stone fireplace with two*

elephants carved on, but I shall never forget the garden, view & unexpected corner of England.

***

21 March 2016

Where was this unexpected corner of England? Sir Thomas Lester Villiers provides the clue. Before I left home, I googled his name. Born in 1869, the son of a vicar and the grandson of the British Prime Minister, Lord John Russell, he came to Ceylon in 1887, some say with just £10 in his pocket. He rose to become chairman of a trading and estate house in Colombo in 1928 and a year later began building his home, in the style of an English country mansion, and called it Adisham after the Kentish village where he was born. He died in 1959, and Adisham is now owned by the Catholic Church and has become a Benedictine monastery, which we are now on our way to visit.

A group of schoolchildren fill the narrow road, shadowed by trees on either side. We wait while their teacher shepherds them out of the way. They wave as we drive past. At the end of the road is a gate, and beyond it the words ST BENEDICT'S MONASTRY ADISHAM HAPUTALE etched into slate. To the left of the drive is a flower bed with bedding plants in various shades of red and pink arranged in neat rows, so similar to those Aunt Flora described in her diary. The closely-cropped lawns are broken up here and there with circular beds. We are both uplifted and amused by the words of wisdom – like *Lost time is never found again;* and *Optimism is the cheerful frame of mind that enables the tea kettle to sing through in hot water up to its nose* – painted on numerous smooth stones and wooden signs.

The house is as I'd imagined it: two storeys, walls of square granite blocks, and a high-pitched roof, but larger and more rambling than I'd expected. 1931 is carved over the main door, which is at the back, as the house itself stands at the cliff edge with views over the valley.

Only two rooms are open to the public, the rest make up the monastery. We enter by a side entrance; in the first room, schoolchildren are watching a DVD, the commentary in Sinhala. We move on into the next and I find it hard to believe that I am standing in the same room where Aunt Flora met Sir Thomas in 1943. It must be, because carved into the top corners of the stone fireplace are elephants! Maybe they sat on this same settee and in these armchairs, because the leather is sagging and I guess they have been on display, roped off and not used, for years. The ceiling still has its original plaster cornice and central rose, but a brownish damp patch is beginning to seep through. All around the room are glass-fronted bookshelves; the books are all hardbacks, their titles in English – every one! The ones I remember are several volumes of a naval manual and a biography of Sir Francis Drake.

Before we leave, I look up at this large, sprawling house with its six chimneys, its stone archways and mullioned windows, then down at green-covered terraces, the tiny bungalows in the valley, the hills in the distance. It is as if one night this country manor house had been spirited away from the cornfields of Kent, to materialize in the morning mist halfway across the world among the tea bushes of Ceylon.

***

On the morning of 4 October 1943, Flora put on her white drill dress, lisle stockings and white canvas shoes for the first time in seven days. She sighed; back in Colombo, this is what she would have to wear every day both on and off duty, except for three times a week when the Wrens could apply for civilian clothes permits. After breakfast, she threw a last piece of toast to Vanda and Chips waiting on the lawn, stroked Tom Satan, then put on her white-crowned, navy-brimmed hat.

Although a handwritten note at the end of the 'invitation' from the Sailors' Entertainment Committee suggested that she telephone the naval rest camp at Diyatalawa to arrange a lift back to Colombo by road, Flora had already collected her ticket. The train left Haputale station at 9.12 a.m., arriving at 5.10 p.m.

***

Back at the Wrennery, her cabin was buzzing with excitement: one of Flora's cabinmates was getting married. Not the first: one of the SDX Wrens had already been granted three months' leave to join her fiancé in Alexandria, and was due back soon. Now another wedding. The bride's and bridesmaid's dresses were to be made in Colombo; not only was it was easier to get hold of material, but also since leaving England both girls had lost weight, so it was sensible to have dresses made to measure by a local tailor. There was, however, still no guarantee that the bridegroom would be granted leave from his post in India. Then the letter arrived to say he'd be there in four days. Bride and bridesmaid went for a fitting, and Flora and the other Wrens in her cabin headed for Regulating to request civilian clothes permits.

Tuesday, 19 October arrived. The wedding guests managed to persuade the Wrens on the next watch to relieve them half an hour early, so there'd be time to change into civvies before naval transport arrived to take them to the church. The reception was held at the Galle Face Hotel. Photographs were taken outside on the Green, with palm trees, and the ancient cannons pointing out to sea in the background. There was a scuffle to catch the bride's bouquet. When the couple drove away, the Wrens called out their good wishes and 'see you after Christmas'. Only her closest friends knew she wasn't coming back.

CHAPTER 16

Kandy

Left on the 8pm train for Kandy where we were spending four days at the Queens Hotel – now the official leave centre for Wrens. Mr O'Shaughnessy happened to be going to Kandy at the same time so we travelled together &, as he is never short of words he entertained us all the way but, towards the end of the journey we were feeling so sleepy I am afraid he got very few intelligent remarks from us.

– Diary entry, 17 November 1943

Normally, leave came around every six months, but in Colombo the unrelenting heat meant that time off up country was granted more often. Flora and Irene, another SDX Wren, were sent up to Kandy for four days in the third week of November.

They left Fort station at eight in the evening. Despite the dark, the journey wasn't so daunting this time. It took a quarter of the time it had taken to get to Haputale, and they had the company of Mr O'Shaughnessy. There is no mention of what he talked about, but maybe he told them about his life, his various careers described in his biography on the back of the 'invitation' from the Sailors' Entertainment Committee:

WHO IS HE WHO MAKES YOUR ARRANGEMENTS FOR ESTATES

Pat. O'Shaughnessy, a member of the Comrades of the Great War. Wounded Ypres 1914. In German and British East Africa. Served in the British Army for a period of seventeen and a half years.

Mr. O'Shaughnessy has had the honour of catering for hundreds of distinguished visitors to Ceylon, many of whom have made valuable presents in token of their appreciation. He received a gold tie pin with Plumes of the House of Wales from the Prince of Wales, and among other gifts in his possession are: Cuff Links with the Royal Coat of arms from The Emperor of Japan; Medaillee [sic] *de la Maison de Roi from H.M. The King of the Belgians; an inscribed clock from Sir Hugh Clifford (when Governor of Ceylon); Suit Case from the members of the Donoughmore Commission and numerous other mementoes. Mr. O'Shaughnessy was at one time Catering Manager, Ceylon Railways (13 years); Manager, Grand Hotel, Mount Lavinia. He toured the whole of Australia in 1929 in an official capacity. Mr. O'Shaughnessy has worked with the Sailors' Entertainment Committee since 1939 to the present day and has been responsible for most of the 20,000 who have visited estates.*

As the train struggled up the Kadugannawa Pass to cross the circle of mountains that shelter the city of Kandy, even his lively Irish banter couldn't elicit more than a monosyllabic response from the two girls or prevent their eyelids from drooping.

On their first day in Kandy, Flora wrote in her diary:

Our impressions of The Queens [Hotel] *were not too good. It is not really a suitable place for Wrens unless you have friends going at the same time, we used to dread going into the lounge which seemed half dead & at night the lights were shaded in turquoise blue paper giving a very good impression of an aquarium which is what we christened it from the start. In the afternoon we were both tired & as there was nothing better to do we went up to our room & had a really good sing-song. We sang solidly for over 1½ hours & thoroughly enjoyed it afterwards plucking up courage to descend once more into the aquarium for tea.*

As the Queens Hotel was now the official leave centre for the Wrens, they were surprised and disappointed to find no other Wrens, or anyone else they knew, staying there. Normally this wouldn't have bothered Flora; she would have been happy to go for long walks and explore the area. Irene, however, was suffering from the painful, tropical fungus infection, 'Ceylon foot', so after a short walk in the mornings they usually finished up with coffee and cakes at the Elephant House café, not only for a rest but also because they never wanted to return to the hotel and have to wait in the 'aquarium' until the gong sounded for lunch.

Mr O'Shaughnessy was also staying at the Queens, and after lunch on the second day he introduced them to the owner of a local tobacco company. Knowing the girls would be at a loose end, he'd arranged for them to be shown around the factory. After the tour the company director offered the girls the use of his car and driver for the rest of the day.

The chauffeur took them to Peradeniya Botanical Gardens, about four miles out of Kandy. A gardener showed them around and boasted that the 147-acre site housed a specimen of every single species of tree in the world. To the girls' great amusement, he referred to all the plants in his care by their botanical names – as if they'd be able to pronounce, let alone remember, them.

The spice garden was full of memories of home: Easter and the aroma of cinnamon when hot cross buns came out of the oven; Mother grating nutmeg over the top of rice pudding; did the tiny red flower buds of *Syzygium aromaticum* really become the dried cloves that she used to flavour her apple pies?

The girls admired water lilies floating on the lake; towering trees, topped with a perfect semicircle of palm, lined up on either side of the wide avenues. As they left, Flora stopped to inhale the scent of hibiscus and jasmine, and the gardener asked if they'd like to take some home. Both girls arrived back at the car with quite a bouquet, Flora's prize exhibit a very tall candle from the candle tree, Irene's a flower called Napoleon's Crown.

***

4 January 2011

When the coach pulls up at the Peradeniya Botanical Gardens, it is, in the words of Giamini, our guide on the day trip up from Colombo, 'raining monkeys and elephants'. This elicits only a ripple of laughter as most of the passengers are by now very wet.

We began the day on a high, passing by paddy fields and coconut plantations. Giamini told us that the locals make use of every bit of the coconut palm, including the flowers to produce toddy, poor man's beer, which can be distilled to produce *arak*, now used in cocktails like Kandy Dance or Elephant's Kiss for tourists like us. Then, as we began to zigzag up the hills that surround Kandy, the skies darkened, and since we arrived it hasn't stopped raining.

That doesn't deter us. We don our cagoules, open our umbrella and walk down the Main Central Drive, but by the time we reach the Great Circle we are soaked. We take a photograph of Royal Palm Avenue like the one in Aunt Flora's album, then head back to the bus.

Royal Palm Avenue, Peradeniya Botanical Gardens, Kandy

As we drive away, I am disappointed not to have seen the spice gardens and the lily ponds, but most of all not to have been able to look for evidence of Peradeniya's secret wartime military establishment. When Aunt Flora visited in November 1943, little did she know that six months later, green, wooden huts would spring up on the pristine lawns and, in the hollow beside the almond, ebony and sandalwood trees, a brick building would rise and become the arena from which Lord Louis Mountbatten would address his chiefs of staff. Peradeniya would become the Military Headquarters of South East Asia Command.

***

For the rest of their stay in Kandy, the Wrens' room at the Queens Hotel was filled with the heady perfume from the bouquet they'd brought back from Peradeniya.

Mr O'Shaughnessy also arranged for the girls to visit a cocoa estate. Flora and Irene were waiting amongst the 'old trout in the aquarium' when at ten o'clock precisely the following day a bell-boy brought them a note and indicated a tanned, middle-aged man seated near the door. They'd seen him come in a few minutes earlier, and guessed he must be their host for the day.

Mr Cecil Rust's estate was about 12 miles outside Kandy. The sickly-sweet aroma of chocolate engulfed them as soon as they got out of the car. It was cool beneath the cacao trees; the leafy canopy filtered the sunlight to produce a dappled shade on the carpet of dried leaves which crunched beneath their feet. Cacao pods the size of rugby balls sprouted from the tall, branchless trunks; workers wielded cutlasses to sever those that had turned from green to golden yellow. The girls from Britain found it hard to believe that the slimy, white mass which emerged when the pods were sliced open would eventually become their most sought-after confection. They watched as the beans were scooped out then wrapped in banana leaves. These parcels were left to ferment, and when they were opened a week later their dark chocolate-coloured contents would be spread on bamboo tables to dry in the sun.

Their host was particularly keen to move on and show them the hospital, recently opened to take care of the estate workers' medical needs. It was a modern, brick building with a permanent staff of white-coated doctors and blue-uniformed nurses.

Mr Rust's bungalow commanded panoramic views of the valley below. In the garden there were forty-two varieties of hibiscus, and a swimming pool. He must have brought a souvenir back from every place he'd visited on his three trips around the world, because his home was adorned with tapestries, statues, carvings and a gallery of framed photographs on the walls. He drew their attention to one in particular. Flora knew who Ben Lyon was, as back home they always listened to *Life with the Lyons* on the wireless. Their host went on to say that he'd been a guest at Ben's mansion and could tell some tales about what those stars got up to, out there in Hollywood. On the drive back to Kandy he continued to come out with more titbits of scandal.

When he dropped them off outside the Queens Hotel, he invited the girls to stay with him the next time they were on leave. They had to explain that wouldn't be possible because of the new regulations: from now on, there had to be a woman in the house before Wrens were allowed to stay on the estates. A ridiculous rule, as after the surprise Japanese raid on Ceylon back in April 1942, most of the women had been evacuated. Not fair either, as this ruling applied only to ratings – not officers.

***

Every morning of their stay in Kandy, they woke to the rhythmic beat of drums – tom-toms from the Temple of the Tooth.

Temple of the Tooth, Kandy

Flora describes a visit to this Buddhist shrine:

> *Went to the Temple of the Tooth which was very interesting but we could not understand all the guide was saying. The tooth is only displayed once a year & it is supposed to be Buddha's but from all accounts the*

original relic was destroyed after being taken to India & a later king wishing to gain favour of the people sent an expedition to bring it back, finding it had been destroyed they brought in its place a bear's tooth, stating it was the original as they could not return empty handed.

The temple courtyards were very dirty & all the time they kept appearing with collection plates – luckily I had some change otherwise we should have been in a fix. It somehow did not seem right to be taken around sightseeing when all the time people were going in & out to worship – all who entered laid flowers of all descriptions on the different altars & the perfume from them absolutely filled the air.

***

4 January 2011

Giamini reminds us we will have to remove our shoes to enter the Temple of the Tooth and warns us that our feet may get wet, so only three of us get off the bus, leave our sandals on the shoe racks and paddle across the courtyard to the temple. The building is not as I'd imagined it would be from Aunt Flora's description. In some places, it appears that the original timbers have been replaced with smooth new wood. The damage caused by the 1998 bomb during the Sri Lankan civil war must have been more extensive than I imagined, and sections have had to be rebuilt.

The atmosphere, however, is the same: we are enveloped in the fragrance of jasmine, frangipani and gardenia. Buddhists come with their floral offerings and light coconut-oil lamps, the aroma mingling with incense to form an exotic, intoxicating mix. Despite the weather, the temple is thronged with people: in front of the altars Buddhists kneel in prayer and lay flowers: white lotus, pink water lilies, purple hibiscus – symbols of life, they bloom, wither and die.

The story of Buddha's Tooth is told in a series of plaques around the walls. The Tooth itself is encased in a golden lotus which is kept safely inside a series of seven caskets of increasing size. These caskets of beaten gold have remained firmly shut since 1815, so no one is sure whether the tooth inside belonged to Buddha or a bear. Nevertheless, visitors are already queuing up to file past the special room where this most-prized religious relic is kept. Viewing is restricted to three times a day, and they will have almost an hour to wait to peek through a small hole to catch a glimpse of the largest, outer casket.

We cannot wait that long, but we do manage to see the gold cage in which a replica of the Tooth – not the real thing, that stays within its many caskets – is transported every year during the Perahera. This festival lasts for twelve days in August when Kandy's streets resound with drums, pipes and trumpets while the town comes alive with processions of elephants, dancers and acrobats.

As we leave the temple, I look back at the flowers and remember the pressed flower petal, now fragile and brown with age. It is in Aunt Flora's diary, stuck down with the perforated border from postage stamps. Next to it is the original label made from rough fibrous card. In spidery writing is the date – *19 11 43* – and, in the curiously curly Sinhalese writing and illegible English, the name. Underneath my aunt has written: *From the Temple of the Tooth Kandy.*

***

At the end of their leave, Mr O'Shaughnessy arranged a lift with the tobacco tycoon in his chauffeur-driven Daimler. When they got back, Flora wrote in her diary:

> *...you could feel the heat meet you as we approached Colombo & after the meals at the Queens, wrenery* [sic] *food did not go down too well on our return. We seemed to have done a lot in the few days we had there but both agreed that unless you knew friends in Kandy or who were going, it was not a good place to go for leave as you had to rely on meeting people to get about at all & it was not a rest or complete change as staying on an estate.*

CHAPTER 17

St Peters and HMS *Anderson*

> *The house* [at Bagatelle Road] *had originally been taken over for officers & when a cadet course was due to commence we were turned out & sent to St Peters, about another two miles from the town, a new temporary Quarters that had been opened, the cabins being hospital wards with 28 in each and no privacy at all… When raining heavily a fine drizzle came through the roof which was thatched with palm leaves & not really watertight. However, as we were told they were only temporary quarters we were hoping each week we should hear of moving & that the next place would be more comfortable.*
>
> – *Diary entry, November 1943*

Flora and the other SDX Wrens had arrived in Colombo on 1 September, and by November they had lived in three different billets. From The Durdans, they'd moved to Bagatelle Road. They were pleasantly surprised when their new quarters turned out to be as good as, if not better than before: there was a recreation room and one cabin on the ground floor, then a further five cabins upstairs. Consequently, no more than half a dozen Wrens had to share. Flora and her cabinmates had their own bathroom with a geyser that worked.

Bagatelle Road was the next turning off Galle Road after Alfred Place, and it was only a short walk back to The Durdans, where they continued to have all their meals. Situated on the corner with the main road, at first it was difficult to sleep through the rumble of tyres and the clatter of bullock-cart wheels on their way in and out of Colombo. The nightly serenade of the flute player across the way was a novelty, until they realised that he had a repertoire of only four or five notes and at ten-thirty every evening he would begin playing them over and over for hours. Their stay there, however, only lasted a few weeks before they were moved on once again, this time to St Peters.

St Peters wasn't only a former convent, it had also been a hospital. The Wrens slept in rows down each side of the former wards: the walls were brick up to head height, then an open space about three feet high, interspersed with brick pillars which supported the overhanging *kadjan* roof. Flora lay on her bed and imagined black-clothed nuns gliding between the beds, and tried not to think of the patients who'd lain sick and dying within these whitewashed, but still grimy, walls.

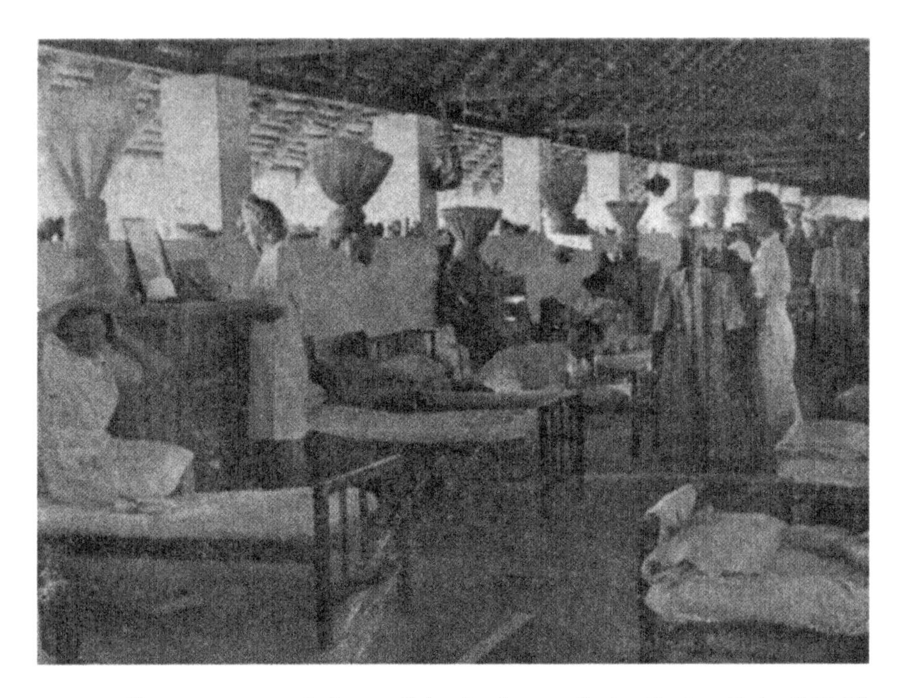

Sleeping quarters, St Peters, Colombo. Source: Ceylon Review (1 April 1944)

Flora ignored the first scream; they'd been told the showers would be cold and if they wanted hot water, it had to be collected from the galley. Another scream… then a crash.

The girls leapt off their beds and dashed down the ward to jostle in the doorway of the bathroom with no bath – just two showers and two washbasins. There, splayed out on the slimy, wet floor, was a naked Wren, not moving, just staring up at a water pipe on which sat the bile-green intruder, his thick, warty skin split by a broad grin extending beneath his bulging, black eyes. 'I'll swear I saw him wink!' one of the girls said later.

Despite all their attempts to remove him, Rupert the frog became the resident voyeur for the rest of their stay at St Peters.

The recreation room was in the old convent and much larger than the one back at Bagatelle Road. There were desks where they could write letters, a table tennis table and in the corner an upright piano, where Anna regularly played 'Jealousy'. The mess was the usual tabletops supported on trestles, but instead of benches there were chairs. No tablecloths, of course, but the heavy mugs were gone and they now had cups and saucers.

The cookhouse was the old hospital kitchen, but the food it produced was still the same naval fare. In a land of paddy fields they rarely had rice; even though mangoes, oranges and bananas grew in abundance, the fruits most commonly served were prunes and dried apricots; a stone's throw away from the sea, yet they ate canned sardines and pilchards. Central messing was given as the excuse: for reasons of economy, all naval rations were shipped out from Britain.

On their second night at St Peters it rained heavily and a fine drizzle came in through the palm-thatched roof. When they complained, the Wrens were told that they should count themselves lucky that it was now November – the monsoon season had ended in October.

A few days later they found that their uniforms and civilian dresses, which they'd hung on rails down the centre of the cabin, were still damp, and on closer inspection were covered in tiny black spots. In the humid climate, even Flora's leather belt and shoes were growing hairy, green mould. They complained again, only to be told that this was only a temporary arrangement: a new Wrennery was under construction.

Just as well. Anything that crawled or flew seemed to have found a home at St Peters: mosquitos had free access through the three-foot gap beneath the roof, grasshoppers chirped in the thatch, spiders spun their webs between the rafters and beetles scurried across the concrete floor. The final straw came when Flora opened her suitcase to find her underwear swarming with ants.

***

January 2011

A two-page article published in the 1 April 1944 issue of the *Ceylon Review* is pasted in Aunt Flora's diary. Entitled 'We Visit the Wrens', it describes their billet, but naval security doesn't allow the journalist to name it. I know what it was called because Aunt Flora has written above it in fountain pen: *St Peters Colombo*. The article describes it as somewhere on Galle Road with double gates and a sandy drive, so when we visit Colombo we think it will be fairly easy to find.

The library on Dharmapala Mawatha seems the best place to start. No one pays any attention to us as we walk in, so we take the stairs to the reference section on the second floor. I explain to the librarian, a lady in an orange sari, who speaks excellent English, that I am looking for information about the Second World War. She asks if I have a ticket, and when I say no she tells me to go back down to the ground floor and buy one for 50 rupees. I will need my passport. I don't have it with me, but the man at the desk accepts my UK library card instead!

Although the library is fairly modern, the books are all kept in old-style, glass-fronted, wooden bookcases. I find St Peters Place marked on a map and close to it St Peters College, but in the books the librarian finds for me there is no mention of a convent or hospital. Lack of time means we have to abandon our search, but after we return home I e-mail the college, to ask if they know where the convent hospital used to be. I receive no reply.

I do, however, have more luck with a second e-mail I send to Colombo, three years later...

January 2014

Aunt Flora's diaries include no mention of where she worked, but she does refer to Anderson transport. When I asked what that meant, a frown crossed her face before she answered, the wartime warning – never tell anyone where you work – still ingrained in her psyche. Eventually, she explained that they were the 'liberty boats' that took them back and forth to work at HMS *Anderson*.

I find references to HMS *Anderson* in several books: *Codebreakers* by Hinsley & Strip refers to it as being *on the south-east fringe of the town, a mile or so back from the sea.* In *We Kept the Secret* edited by Gwendoline Page, Margaret Sharman says it was *on a golf course a few miles from the centre of town*, and Irene Smith describes hurtling through the jungle in naval trucks to get there. *The Emperor's Codes* by Michael Smith states: *The intercept station and code-breaking operation had to be set up on the only available site at the Anderson Golf Course, just six miles from Colombo HQ. This was hardly the ideal site for intercepting radio traffic, stuck between a railway line and a main road, directly under the flightpath of aircraft flying into the Racecourse Aerodrome.* There is a picture of two Royal Marines standing in the middle of a track leading to a collection of single-storey huts. Propped up on the grass verge beside a tree, the lower part of its trunk protectively whitewashed, is a sign: HMS *Anderson*.

When I look at current maps of the area, the only golf course I can find is the Royal Colombo Golf Course and Ridgeway Links. I wonder if they were at one time called Anderson. I visit www.rcgcsl.com to find out. I click on general enquires and send an e-mail asking if the golf club once used to be called Anderson, or if they could put me in touch with someone who remembers another golf course of that name back in the 1940s. Four days later, I receive a reply from Priath Fernando, a former President of the Royal Colombo Golf Club.

He tells me that Anderson Links was opened in 1917 and closed down in 1942. His late father lived opposite the links and played there as a student member. When we visit Sri Lanka, Priath offers to show us the site, now acquired by the government. We arrange to meet up at the golf club when we arrive in Colombo the following month.

5 February 2014

Somehow, Colombo seems brighter, more spruced-up since we were last here. Even though it is the rush hour and we sit for ages in traffic jams, we arrive early at the Royal Colombo Golf Course. The links are immaculate – the caddies wear brilliant white baseball caps and T-shirts a similar shade of lime green as the lush, freshly-mown grass. We are in the centre of a bustling city, surrounded by trees; the only sound is birdsong, and sometimes the hoot of the train that runs through the middle of the sixth green.

It is Prakrama Fernando who arrives first. He has thick, dark hair only just beginning to turn to grey; it is hard to believe he is 88 years old. Priath has told us that his uncle will be joining us, because now, out of all those who used to live in the family home opposite Anderson Golf Links, Praky is the only one left. Priath arrives soon after and shows us around the clubhouse: first the original colonial building with the portrait of his father, the first Ceylonese captain of the club, and then the modern extensions of entrance hall and veranda, where we sit and drink tea. Uncle Praky remembers when Anderson Links was taken over by the British. He always thought it was a prisoner-of-war camp because, as a child, he remembers Italian prisoners coming across the road to visit his father's house.

Priath tell us that his grandparent's home is still there and points out Park Road in Havelock Town on our map. Praky says Anderson flats have now been built on the site of the golf links. Everything begins to fall into place: Galle Road, the main route out of Colombo, is to one side, a railway line on the other. I'm not sure it would be under the flightpath in to the racecourse, requisitioned to serve as an aerodrome during the war. Then Priath tells me there is another airport just to the south at Ratmalana, which was also there in 1942 and more likely to be where the planes were heading when they flew over the huts at HMS *Anderson*.

We leave the quiet green sanctuary for the bustle of Colombo traffic and head for Havelock Town. In Park Road, Priath points out the house his grandparents once owned, but my eyes are on the other side of the road, searching for any signs of the old golf course and HMS *Anderson*. There are none. I would like to stop, get out, stand where Aunt Flora worked all those years ago, but the road is narrow, there is nowhere to park and local inhabitants have turned to stare at Priath's pristine, white, chauffeur-driven car.

History has disappeared beneath post-war public housing. I try to imagine how it was seventy years ago: the wooden huts, the naval transport bringing the Wrens in from their billets, to work the four-hourly, day and night watches. How did they feel? Exhausted by the heat, bored with punching cards and feeding them into the Hollerith machine, wondering how this could possibly help to create copies of current Japanese code books so the Allies could read the enemy's messages.

All intercepted messages were stored on punch-cards. The Hollerith searched through them for those with a series of five-digit groups which matched the ones the Wrens typed in… but why those particular numbers?

They were often parts of messages where the codebreakers suspected they knew what the numbers meant. Perhaps it was messages with a stereotyped preamble like: 'I have the honour to report to Your Excellency that…' or they were routine signals which stated that there was nothing to report. They could be enemy sightings or convoy schedules, which always followed the same format, or weather reports, often also transmitted in other codes which were easier to crack. What the Hollerith was searching for was 'depth', several messages with the same sequence of numbers.

When the Hollerith came up with a 'depth' of perhaps half a dozen, a printout of these messages was passed on to another hut at HMS *Anderson*. Inside, other workers, often civilians, temporary women assistants (TWAs), or pensioner clerks, leaned over a large table and copied these figures onto an equally large sheet of paper while the codebreakers stared in deep concentration at the rows of numbers. The messages had to be carefully aligned so that the same number groups were all beneath each other in the same column. Then subtracting a known code-group would give a possible 'additive', and maybe indicate the starting point, in the book of 10,000 random numbers, selected by the Japanese sender. This process was known as 'stripping the additive' and those involved were known as 'strippers'.

When the numerical code for the Japanese plaintext had been confirmed five times, it could be used to construct the Allies' own copy of a code book, a process known as 'book building'. When a run of random numbers was similarly ratified it could be used to fill in the blanks in the additive books.

It was like a giant jigsaw puzzle, one number slotting into place gave rise to more possibilities which could be tried and accepted or rejected. But the jigsaws they did at HMS *Anderson* had most of the bits missing, there was no picture on the lid of the box, and the scene was just sea and sky. They had to look long and hard for subtle shades of blue, for faint ripples on the water to discover where all the pieces went.

I wonder if the Wrens knew how their work contributed to winning the war in the Pacific. Did they know that by now, the latter part of 1943, the Americans were liberating the islands overrun by the Japanese two years before? Lae was now under American control, and US Marines together with the Australians were moving across the eastern side of New Guinea and the small islands around it.

All this depended on intercepting millions of signals and accumulating a wealth of data; the British had no hope of accomplishing this mammoth task on their own. The Americans, with their listening posts in the Pacific and on the north coast of Australia, were much better placed for picking up whispers through the ether. Since moving back to Ceylon, however, the British were much closer to the action, could intercept a much larger share of the enemy signals. There was plenty of work for the SDX Wrens and the Holleriths.

CHAPTER 18

Thoughts of Home

I could not believe that the following day he would be starting on his way back for England & Halifax. It just made me realize how far away I was, & how much I should have loved to have popped in & surprised everyone as he was expecting to do.

– Diary entry, 12 December 1943

When Fred, an RAF sergeant stationed in Colombo, heard that Flora also came from Halifax, he invited her to dinner at the Metropole. There hadn't been time to get a civilian-clothes permit so as soon as she arrived at the hotel, Flora headed for the Ladies. She removed the metal rings which held buttons in place on the front reveres of her white uniform dress and replaced the boring white horn with a red, flower-shaped alternative, pinning a matching brooch on the lapel.

It turned out that Fred had visited his uncle and aunt, who lived across the road from her family home on Milton Place, many times as a child. Although this made her feel closer to home, she also ached to be back among familiar surroundings. Together they listed all the shops in Commercial Street, they named all the villages round about – Southowram, Mytholmroyd, Sowerby Bridge – compared rambles they'd taken over the moors. The only landmarks he knew, but she didn't, were the pubs and the dance halls.

They were still asking 'Do you know…?' and 'Can you remember…?' at the party he took her to later. It was held in a bungalow belonging to his friends. Another meal was laid on, but having already eaten they were forced to decline. However, when the cook brought on the final course and their host held a lighted match to the brandy and a haze of blue flames drifted over the shiny dark brown mound of dried fruit and treacle, Flora couldn't resist. As she savoured the pudding she'd not tasted for almost a year, she realised that here, beneath the cloudless blue skies, in less than a month it would be Christmas – the first Christmas that she'd spent away from home.

Fred had been overseas for four years and was expecting to go home on leave. Clothes and dressmaking material were still on ration back in England, and he had promised to take several dress lengths back with him. Flora was very happy to help out. The only day when their time off coincided was when Flora was on 'dog watch', with only four hours from the time they came off at noon until she went back at four.

He was waiting when Flora arrived back at St Peters and they took rickshaws straight to the pettah. They had to fight their way through the crowds in the criss-crossing narrow lanes, past a chaotic collection of stalls and shops, avoiding the open sacks of rice, beans and spices displayed on the ground beside them. Fred grabbed Flora's arm to pull her out of the way of a porter's barrow; two eight-foot-long planks supported on just a pair of cart wheels in the centre, these seesaw-like vehicles had no brakes. They found Second Cross Street. Shopkeepers waited for customers at the entrances to their dark, narrow premises, lengths of fine silk and voile, rich satin and brocade displayed all around them, bolts of cotton and linen piled high on tables outside. Flora wrote about this shopping trip with Fred in her diary:

> *What a list he had, there were five dress lengths for his requirements & his friend also asked me to get something suitable for his mother & sister so we had quite a time selecting all these but it was rather fun. I only hoped they all were suitable, when choosing for people one has not met it's rather difficult but we had quite a selection & between them we hoped they would be suitable… I've never bought so much material in such a short time but it was lovely just seeing them all & just picking out the ones I fancied. I had a Xmas present bought at the same time a lovely dress length in powder blue linen, something I had wanted for*

> *a while & I managed to get just the shade I fancied & it should make up very well…*
>
> *I wanted some currants and raisins to put in my parcel which he was taking for me, but we had not much time so* [Fred] *said he would get them for me. The morning after he brought me 2lbs of each which just fitted into a tin I had sent from home so I was well away & so pleased with them.*

The invitation on thick card with frilly bevelled edges, still preserved in Flora's diary, came out of the blue. Printed in silver was the name of a couple she'd never heard of. Below r*equest the company of*, in copperplate handwriting, was her name, then *at the Wedding of* and two names she didn't recognise either. The only clue was in the words *Queensland Australia* in brackets beneath the would-be bride's name. Fred had told her about an officer in his squadron, who'd been waiting for weeks for his fiancée to arrive so they could set the date.

But why was she invited? Then Flora remembered telling Fred how her sister, Vera, was soon to be married. Perhaps he'd noticed her knuckle away a tear when she'd said there was no chance of getting home for the wedding.

The service was held at St Andrews Scots Kirk, on Colpetty Road. When she looked back, Flora realised that Fred must have known then that he was in the next draft home, but he didn't tell her. Perhaps just as well, because if he had, as the couple drove away, a *Just Married* label stuck on the back window and large tin cans clattering behind, she would surely have cried. As it was, she joined in with the dancing and community singing at the bungalow and went on in a foursome for a bite to eat and a nightcap at the Metropole.

***

5 February 2014

Priath doesn't remember the Metropole, but he says that some of the other places that Aunt Flora mentions in her diary are still there. We are driving down Galle Road on our way to see them. The traffic is three abreast, but no one keeps in lane: tuk-tuks and cars compete to weave their way into the smallest of spaces. People cling to the outsides of buses, arms and heads protrude through unglazed windows. The high-pitched beep of the tuk-tuks and the deep growl of the trucks never stop.

We pass the Majestic cinema. It is now extended beyond recognition, hidden beneath red-painted cement rendering and renamed Majestic City, a multiplex, a far cry from the single-screen picture house where Fred took Aunt Flora. Afterwards, they went on to the Chinese Hotel for dinner. Priath is not sure where that was, but as we pass a terrace of grey colonial buildings with iron verandas on Union Place, he says it might have been there.

***

It was after they'd seen the film *Enemy Agent* at the Majestic and were at dinner in the Chinese Hotel that Fred told Flora that he was leaving for home the following day. She attempted a smile, and asked if he had been able to let his family know he was coming. He shook his head; he was just going to turn up, walk in and surprise them.

Flora imagined what it would be like if she arrived home unannounced: she could see her mother looking up from her baking, hear her gasp, see her flour-caked hands fluttering to her mouth before she wiped them on her apron and bustled to the bottom of the stairs to summon her other two daughters.

When he dropped her off at St Peters, Flora gave Fred the tin box he was to take back to Halifax; inside were the two pounds of currants and two pounds of raisins that her mother needed to make her sister's wedding cake.

In her diary, Flora describes the days leading up to Christmas:

Saturday December 18th 1943

Invited to a services Christmas Party at the International Club… It was built in a very large garden on bungalow lines with a beautiful room for dancing & verandah outside, also tables & chairs in the garden & a floor there for dancing also. At one end of the main room was a long table absolutely laden with food, all the cakes one could think of, it really did look like a party & at each end of the table were small decorated Christmas trees. To start the party off everyone collected in the dance room & the platform curtains were drawn back revealing a huge Christmas tree all decorated with tinsel and fairy lights & everyone sang "Hark the Herald Angels Sing" & "The First Noel", it absolutely resounded and made everyone feel it was getting on towards Christmas, which was difficult to imagine in such a climate & being so separated from everyone.

All the men had been invited by special invitation and were from all three services but [Irene] *and I were the only two Wrens, all the others being civilians, people who help with the club & friends & many of them were wearing very attractive saris of beautiful shades and materials. I happened to meet someone in the RAF I had previously met at a Toc H dance soon after arriving in Colombo and we were very soon in with a party and had a very good evening. It was so lovely and cool outside, although as the floor inside was much better than the one laid in the garden, we danced inside most of the time. All the men were given presents during the evening & at the end we sang "Auld Lang Syne", "Oh Come All Ye Faithful" & "God Save the King". It was an exceptionally good party with such a happy spirit from the start & it certainly gave a touch of Xmas to things.*

Sunday 19th December 1943

Went along to the carol service at Christchurch Galle Face arriving about 5.45pm to find it absolutely crowded & many waiting outside.

However, eventually seats were put down the aisle so we were able to remain & it was a very inspiring service. Before each carol was a short reading from the Bible by various service personnel and Sinhalese referring to the following carol. The choir sang several by themselves, but the majority were for the congregation & all the well-known ones were sung with such feeling it was really uplifting & a service one will always remember.

In Flora's diary there is no entry for Christmas Day 1943, just a small chit of paper glued onto a page:

This is to certify that
L/Wren Crossley
is entitled to wear plain
clothes from 1900 - 25.12.43

OFFICER-IN-CHARGE
Date...............
QUARTERS

Civilian Clothes Permit

The next diary entry is on 3 January 1944. Flora is in hospital.

CHAPTER 19

Convalescent Leave

...the door opened and all of us (even the lieutenant) were a little taken aback by the figure in the doorway. We certainly hadn't imagined Mrs P to be such a character – she was dressed in breeches, a huge yellow pullover, very untidy hair surrounding a round sunburned face, on her feet were long rubber boots, split at the sides, a revolver at her hip!!

– Diary entry, 12 January 1944

Swallowing the pills made her head throb even more. But the nurse said they were M&B and she must take them. It still hurt to open her eyes. Flora slid her hand down between the bedclothes – yes, the swelling in her groin was still there. They'd diagnosed dengue.

It could have been worse, much worse. Before Christmas one of the Wrens at St Peters – fortunately not one from their cabin – had also been taken to the naval hospital. She had polio and was now in an iron lung.

Flora remembered the painful walk to sickbay, the nurse examining her. During the bumpy ride in the ambulance she'd struggled to sit upright. After she'd vomited, they'd allowed her to lie down. What a relief to arrive at the hospital and find someone she knew already there. With difficulty, Flora turned her head to the side and lifted her eyelids a fraction. There in the next bed was Pat.

A VAD arrived with a cup of tea, which she placed on the locker before unhooking a chart from the end of the bed. As the volunteer nurse made an entry under 'input', she asked Flora if she'd been collecting her output. Pat explained that everything she drank had to be recorded, then when she spent a penny they'd measure what was in the bedpan.

On the second day, Flora could keep her eyes open without pain for a few moments. Lunch was white fish. For breakfast there'd been boiled eggs and fresh milk in her tea. Last night there'd been chicken, but she'd managed only a morsel. An ayah helped her into a bath-chair and pushed her onto the veranda for some fresh air. Half an hour later, her back was so sore she asked to be put back to bed.

By the fourth day, her temperature was normal – when she'd come in, it had been 104°F. Flora was beginning to feel much better. But she was warned. With dengue it was always the same. In a day or so there'd be a relapse. Her gaze travelled to the next bed, where Pat now lay motionless, eyes closed, face flushed. Yesterday her friend had been telling everyone she was just fine.

By day seven, neither of the girls needed a bath-chair; they could walk the length of the ward unaided. The doctor decided they were both fit to be discharged, but not to go back to work; they were given a week's sick leave.

By eleven-thirty transport still hadn't arrived, so they took rickshaws back to St Peters. The petty officer handed them their leave passes. Their destination was Haputale; their host wasn't Capt'n, but a married couple. They were to depart from Fort station at seven in the evening, leaving only a few hours to go into town, collect the tickets, go shopping for flour, sugar, coffee, bacon, cheese, jam, tins of corned beef, whatever they could find to take for their hosts, then come back and start packing.

Mr O'Shaughnessy had managed to get us sleepers. We were both so tired we could have gone to bed before the train left the station at 8pm. but thought it better to wait until we were on the way, but as soon as we left, we turned in & settled down for the night. Neither of us actually slept but it was much more comfortable to be lying down & have a soft pillow. About 12.30pm I was dozing off when to my surprise I heard a man's voice saying "It's alright it's only the R.A.F." & when I peered out of the top bunk which was so high I had a step ladder to get in, there was this man trying to open the door into the corridor – he had apparently been left behind on the platform and as our window was open managed to climb in.

They awoke shivering; outside it was light, but a grey mist lay over the hills and torrential rain beat on the windows – a typical Yorkshire day. They both put on their coats and Pat went to order morning tea. The train drew in at Haputale at seven-thirty. The girls hung out of the window and searched the platform for the couple who would be their hosts for the next week. The man who approached them wore sandals, shorts and an Aertex shirt. He was on his own. He introduced himself as D'urques and raised his straw panama to reveal a balding head with two tufts of white hair above his ears. His eyebrows, above dark, deep-set eyes, were almost black.

With their luggage in the boot of his car they set off on the two-mile journey. The route was the same as Flora had taken with Capt'n on her last visit to Haputale, except that they passed the lower road and climbed even higher. Blackwood Arms, named after D'urques's favourite pub back in England, was at the top of a steep, winding drive. A cliff towered behind it and the front garden was a series of tiered rockeries. The front of the bungalow was dominated by a row of white, stone pillars.

D'urques led the way up the steps onto a wide veranda, and as he opened the French doors a fox terrier leapt up at his chest. Their host put out his hand to prevent another similar black and white dog from doing the same to Flora, and explained that Jose and Pym both got very excited when visitors arrived. A cairn sat on his haunches in the hall, aloof from the whole proceedings. His name was Nobby, and the three dogs were collectively known as 'the children'.

The spoilt 'children' were also present at dinner. Nobby heralded the arrival of the soup by trotting from the kitchen into the lounge. All three dogs then took their places on the floor next to the dining chairs. Joseph, an elderly Sinhalese servant with a drooping, white moustache, ladled consommé from the tureen, then took up his post by the door while they ate. Jose looked up at her master with limpid eyes and D'urques broke a piece off his bread roll and held it out to the dog, who leapt up and swallowed it whole. Pym made a similar appeal to Pat. After looking across to her host for approval, she did the same. Flora looked down at Nobby, who still maintained an air of detachment, then held out a crust which he ate with decorum. From over by the door came the faint sound of tut-tutting.

When Flora asked when his wife would join them, D'urques leant back in his chair, roared with laughter and said that there'd never been one, that he knew about. Joseph, who stood with one subservient hand across the front of his white robes as he waited to clear away the plates, also thought it was funny.

They found out later that pretending that planters' wives were still around, hadn't been evacuated in '42, and that bachelors, like D'urques, were married, was Mr O'Shaughnessy's way of getting around the new rule that decreed that Wrens were not to stay on estates unless there was a woman in the house.

Flora and Pat spent their first day's convalescence on the veranda, lazing in the easy chairs, flicking through the large selection of magazines. When the mist rolled away they gazed at the view across the valley and over the hills to a glimmer of sea in the distance. After lunch they took an extended afternoon nap, and then a long luxurious bath before dinner.

They left Joseph to clear the dinner table and moved to the snug, where they sat round the log fire. When the Sinhalese servant had finished his chores, he appeared in the doorway and announced it was time for bed. The Wrens started to rise but D'urques gestured that they should sit back down. It was just the 'children's' bedtime. Jose and Nobby trotted towards the door, but not Pym. He made a beeline for the settee and lay there with his legs in the air, refusing to budge. Joseph clicked his tongue with disapproval just as he had during dinner, picked up the spoilt pet and carried him out of the room – a ritual that would be repeated every night the Wrens stayed at the Blackwood Arms.

The phone rang. It was an American naval lieutenant on leave at a neighbouring estate who'd heard that two Wrens were staying with D'urques, and wanted to know if they'd like to join him on a trip to Horton Plains the following day. D'urques warned them that it was no gentle stroll – several miles through very rough country – not a good idea, so soon after dengue. But Flora and Pat insisted they were much better and arranged to meet the lieutenant in the morning, weather permitting.

At breakfast, the weather didn't look too promising: cloud had settled in the valley below and drizzle hung in the air. D'urques tried to persuade his guests to cancel their expedition and looked to his servant for support. Joseph put a tray of scrambled egg, bacon and sausage down in the centre of the table, then straightened up, shrugged his shoulders and gave his usual non-committal answer: 'What to do?'

The American lieutenant phoned to say he would meet them at the station at nine-thirty. D'urques was going to visit part of his estate, so he came with them on the train then got off at the first stop. He looked up at the leaden sky and shook his head.

When the lieutenant and the two Wrens alighted at Patapola, the mist was even thicker and it was teeming with rain. They put on their macs and went to ask directions from the stationmaster, who seemed absolutely astounded and kept saying that Horton Plains was a long way. Reluctantly, he directed them down a narrow track to one side of the railway line then stared after them, shaking his head.

With hair dripping into their eyes and water streaming down their raincoats into their shoes, they trudged on. About a mile down the track, they came across a wooden notice with a surname painted in large letters: the same name that D'urques had casually mentioned before they left. He'd said that they might drop in on Mrs P as they were passing, so they decided this would be a good opportunity to ask for directions, as they were no longer quite sure which way to go.

The homestead was hidden amongst the trees, and in searching for a way through they found themselves round the back by the stables. No one was about apart from a number of dogs, that surprisingly didn't even bark as they approached. The lieutenant and the two Wrens retraced their steps through the dense undergrowth and found a small gate, which led into a yard surrounded by a collection of small thatched buildings. As they hesitated before venturing inside, a door opened and a woman emerged, her finger on the trigger of a revolver. Flora's diary takes up the story:

> *After enlightening her that we were hoping to go to the rest house on the Hortons we were told it was madness to continue & invited to stay there for lunch & later in the afternoon walk about 4 miles to Ohio the next station & catch the train back from there.*
>
> *Upon entering the room we were surprised to find a young Senhalese man there & we seemed to have interrupted their morning break for "horlicks" – we were soon drinking some out of soup bowls, which did taste good. The Senhalese we were informed was in the Police Force & staying there on leave as it was a good spot for hunting a sport of which he was very fond.*
>
> *We were disappointed at first when told it was unsafe to continue as we had set our minds on going, but as we heard one tale after another of the storms up there (8000ft) in bad weather, huge hail stones, bitterly cold, wild animals appearing in the mist, no definite track, people being found exhausted, our courage gradually dwindled & we decided it best to take advantage of the offer & stay to lunch.*
>
> *The room we were in was quite small with thatched roof & walls, around which were sketches and photographs of hunting scenes etc. We had the most entertaining lunch I've ever been to, we were still sitting round the table talking at 2pm & all the topics discussed whilst we were eating salted venison (cut with a dagger) we all had good appetites and certainly did justice to it, it tasted exceptionally good – the tea was drunk once more out of soup bowls & everybody seemed to talk at once & some good laughs were had.*
>
> *Mrs. P had apparently had a very eventful life & as there are so few visitors to that isolated bungalow thoroughly enjoyed telling us, stranded on an island 11 months, relying on the natives for food. Prairie Rose*

with her six cowboys, married on a battleship ([the lieutenant] *just could not get over this one)*

She had a soft spot for Americans & one tale led to another, it was three to one when the C. in. C.C(L) [Commander in Chief, Ceylon] *was mentioned, the poor lieutenant did his best to stick up for him, but* [Pat], *Mrs. P & I were in full agreement about him & his ears must have burned that afternoon.*

She was definitely entertaining & showed us leopard skins that were the record for Ceylon, the animals being trapped "just at the bottom of the garden". A bit too near for my fancy. [The lieutenant] kept exclaiming "Well, You don't say."

By the time they were ready to leave it had stopped raining. Wet leaves glistened in the sun now beginning to filter through the dispersing cloud. They followed the policeman on an almost non-existent track through the undergrowth, wet foliage springing back against their faces. The two girls struggled to keep up with the men as the path dipped then climbed round the hillside. After what he assured them was only four miles, their guide stopped, looked up at the sun and said there wasn't much time. He pointed to the railway line below and said they'd need to walk along the track until they got to Ohiya.

As they stumbled from sleeper to sleeper, a hooter sounded and a puff of smoke appeared in the distance. The threesome scattered either side of the rails as the train rounded a bend behind them. They thrashed through the long grass and when the last carriage had passed, scrambled back up onto the track. Then they were running after it – like the cast in a silent movie.

At the station, the engine driver watched them arrive panting on the platform, and saw them aboard before climbing back into his cab and raising steam.

When they arrived back at Haputale, hair windblown, faces glowing, they told D'urques what Mrs P had said: how they should never take the advice of the planters as they never got out of their cars to walk anywhere. Their host just laughed and asked how they had got on with Mrs P. He believed their implausible story, but the 'gold braid' he entertained later that evening at the Blackwood Arms didn't!

When they'd listened to the Wrens' tales of being sent out to certain death on the mountains, being threatened with a revolver, enormous hailstones, ferocious leopards, the naval officers exchanged glances and grinned. Flora and Pat were never quite sure why, for the whole evening, everyone was absolutely helpless with laughter. Maybe there was something they didn't know about Mrs P – she had said she was married on a battleship.

Flora took another sip of the rum punch, prepared according to the American lieutenant's special recipe. Rum was something she'd never really fancied, but it was really refreshing and she wrote in her diary that *it just went straight to the spot.*

It was eleven o'clock when they sat down to dinner and the early hours of the morning before they went to bed, with orders that there was no need to get up early, just ring for morning tea when they were ready. They fell asleep to the sound of raucous laughter.

***

On Friday, D'urques went to a planters' meeting at the Bow Club and Flora and Pat got up early to go along with him, so they could go shopping in Bandarawela. The shops had little to interest them – the jewellery was expensive and, Flora suspected, not genuine – but it did lead to an invitation. A lady hailed them and said how good it was to see women from England, and they must come to dinner on Saturday and bring D'urques with them. When they told him, he said they should go, but he would prefer a quiet night in.

Their hostess was quite put out when D'urques just dropped the girls at the door and drove off without saying hello, but her husband didn't seem bothered. He hardly spoke all evening; his wife, on the other hand, only stopped talking when she was out of the room, fetching some handiwork or recent purchase for the girls to admire.

They were relieved to hear D'urques's car arrive to collect them, and as they drove off Flora looked back at the woman standing alone on the veranda, still waving, and thought how lonely it must be for a planter's wife. When she got back to the Blackwood Arms she wrote in her diary: *It was a very queer evening… there was an atmosphere rather difficult to explain… They were very well meaning but we could quite understand D'urques disinterest at going.*

On their last evening, Flora and Pat went to the pictures in Diyatalawa to see Melvyn Douglas and Anne Southern in the comedy *Three Hearts for Julia.* They returned to the Blackwood Arms for a dinner of snipe, courtesy of two of D'urques's friends who were staying up country for the shooting.

***

This time, as there were two of them, Flora and Pat decided to take the handwritten advice on the back of the 'invitation' from The Sailors' Entertainment Committee. It suggested they ring the naval camp at Diyatalawa to ask if there was a truck going down to Colombo and, if so, could they cadge a lift.

Although it meant a five-hour journey as opposed to eleven hours by train, as they sat on boxes in the back of the open truck, they weren't sure they'd made the right decision. The continual rattle of a consignment of tins made conversation with the only other passenger, a lieutenant, almost impossible. As they screeched round hairpin bends the Wrens resorted to fastening their hat straps under their chins. Flora closed her eyes and prayed that the wheels weren't too close to the edge. The driver kept his foot firmly on the accelerator and chickens and dogs scattered in all directions as they roared through villages. With only a brief respite at Ratnapura rest-house, they arrived back in record time. At a naval depot in a suburb north of Colombo, the driver informed them that he'd completed the job and was signed off for the day. They'd have to find their own way back to the Wrennery.

They eventually arrived back at St Peters to be told that their annual leave, which should have been a continuation of their sick leave, had been cancelled. They decided to put in a request for another seven days at the earliest possible date.

CHAPTER 20

Down the Coast

There is something very attractive about Galle, we felt to be on holiday immediately, there is no rushing traffic & it appears such a peaceful place & what a change from Colombo. You have to enter the fort under the old archways, all the houses are on the Dutch style & the bazaar is outside the fort.

– *Diary entry, 16 February 1944*

Neither Flora nor Pat could face another eleven long hours by rail up to Haputale and a hair-raising five hours by road back down to Colombo so, when Mr O'Shaughnessy asked where they'd like to go for the leave they were owed, Flora said Galle. He sucked in his lips and said that might be difficult. The problem was that British service leave had to be taken in the cooler climate up country, not on the coast, but he'd see what he could do and let them know.

There was no sign of moving on from their temporary quarters at St Peters, where the insects were still swarming. It was now mid-February and the monsoon was looming. Drastic action was required if they were to avoid further wardrobe disasters, even more urgent now that permission had been granted for Wrens to have a suitable dress to wear when off duty if they didn't have a civilian clothes permit. They had to buy the material themselves – cotton, linen or rayon – silk if they could afford it – but it had to be white, and they had to pay a local tailor to make it up in regulation style. They became known as 'tidley dresses'.

Regulations also decreed that Wrens coming off duty at two in the morning weren't allowed out before noon. However, when, after only four hours' sleep,

Flora and Pat called at Regulating to sign out, nobody asked what shift they'd been on. They headed for Fort and Cargills department store. The luggage department had what they were looking for, but at a price way beyond a Wren's means, so they left and walked along Main Street to the pettah. They searched among the jumble of baggage in the succession of tiny shops in Front Street without success, so pushed their way through the crowds to First Cross Street, where they found a hardware shop that sold tin trunks. They haggled with the storekeeper, who finally agreed to a discount as they needed two each if they were to protect all their possessions. To get them back to St Peters they had to hire a taxi, which cost another four rupees. But it was worth it. Their clothes, albeit rather creased, remained dry and free from infestation for the rest of their stay in Colombo.

***

In her family home in Halifax, the wireless had usually been tuned in to the light programme, so it wasn't until Flora was stationed in Colombo that her taste became classical:

> *Every Wednesday gramophone recitals of classical music are held at the Y.M.C.A. for the services & are always very well attended & whenever possible we used to go along, they were well worth hearing and usually good recordings. The main snag was transport, this never arrived at St Peters until the concert was due to start with the result the Wrens must have had a very bad name for arriving late & the first time it arrived punctually was a shock to everyone.*
>
> *The Junior Fleet Club also had a trial musical evening and it was so successful more were arranged. The club itself is very restful & a very happy atmosphere & really comfortable with easy chairs & plenty of cushions. Originally intended as a club for naval personnel under 20yrs & run by civilians who said they tried to make it a little like home for them & as comfortable as possible.*

A programme for a musical evening at the Junior Fleet Club is pasted on the facing page of Flora's diary. Recordings included a soprano singing an aria from Verdi's *Rigoletto*, Brahms's *Hungarian Dances* played by The Boston Promenade Orchestra, and Tchaikovsky's *Nutcracker Suite* by the London Philharmonic. As she listened to Wagner's *Flying Dutchman*, did Flora's thoughts drift back to Mombasa and Johannes, the Dutch lieutenant she had met there the previous summer?

***

Mr O'Shaughnessy was true to his word. Less than a month after their conversation, an invitation arrived from the manageress of the New Oriental Hotel in Galle. The officer in charge said there was no way that Flora and Pat could go, as they'd only just come back off leave. When they reminded her that was sick leave and pointed out they were entitled to leave every three months, she replied that they'd have to get official approval, because the arrangements had not been made through normal WRNS channels. Permission was granted the day before they were due to travel.

Galle is an old port on the southernmost tip of Ceylon. It is only 72 miles from Colombo's Maradana station, but the journey took over four hours as the train meandered its way past tiny fishing villages along the coast. The girls were grateful for the cups of tea that two RAF sergeants bought for them when they stopped at one of the many stations. Flora unwrapped their delayed breakfast, then gasped, leapt to her feet and hurled the greaseproof paper package out of the train window – the sandwiches were crawling with St Peters' red ants.

The manageress of the New Oriental Hotel was away for the first couple of days of their stay but had arranged for a friend to meet them. He escorted the girls out of the station, along Esplanade Road and through an archway in the ancient ramparts. Once inside the ancient Fort of Galle, they passed the services club and turned down Church Street until they came to the New Oriental Hotel. Their escort inclined his head to indicate the girls should precede him up the steps onto the veranda, then held open one of the tall arched double doors into the large lobby, where chandeliers hung from the ceiling and old maps of Ceylon lined the walls.

The hotel had the usual slumbering lounge and smoke-filled billiard room. Many of its spacious bedrooms boasted four-poster beds, but the Wrens were shown to a much smaller room that was also used to store luggage. It had its compensations: an amazing view overlooking the old harbour, comfortable beds, and its own private bathroom with a bath – such a luxury after the lumpy mattresses and cold showers at St Peters. The manageress had left a message to say they were welcome to use her private sitting room.

Most mornings the girls slept late and ordered breakfast in bed. Then, perhaps, they would walk round the grass-covered ramparts, climb up the bastions or just sit on the stone benches and stare out to sea. Sometimes they wandered through the narrow streets between houses with their red pan-tiled roofs and distinctive Dutch architecture: ornate wooden gables and balconies, and wide *stoeps* (verandas) a few steps above street level. Or maybe they would walk through the archway beneath the ramparts, out of Fort and down past the cricket ground to the harbour, where the fishing boats were drawn up on the beach with the day's catch laid out on the sand.

When they were feeling more energetic, they continued right round the harbour and took the narrow track down the promontory to Closenberg. Here they strolled along the shore and scrambled among the rock pools to watch the striped and spotted fish, some yellow and black and others with quite a definite blue head. They bathed in the gentle sea, so different from the breakers that crashed onto the sea wall in Colombo.

Then they lay on the beach in the sun and watched the fishermen hauling on each end of a *ma-dela*, a large net which arced way out into the sea. In tug-of-war fashion, the men leant back and took backward steps through the waves. When the net closed in around their catch it became a boiling cauldron, as fish leapt into the air in a futile attempt to escape.

Most evenings they went to the service club. The clientele were both service personnel and civilians. There were the usual bridge foursomes and players leaning on cues around the snooker table, but at least here women were served alcohol, unlike in similar establishments in Colombo.

Two days after their arrival they met Clara, the lady responsible for their invitation. Enquiries had put the hotel manageress in her late 60s, so they expected a kind of dowager aunt, not the youthful woman they met playing snooker at the club, where she went every evening while in town and was well known for her expertise at the game. She introduced them to her gentleman friend, a very jolly Scottish air force officer.

At the club, Pat met the Sinhalese wife of a British civil servant and mentioned that they were planning to go shopping at the pettah; the local lady insisted on coming with them, to make sure they weren't swindled and to help them beat down the prices.

The following morning, they stood on the veranda of the New Oriental Hotel, leaning over the stone balustrade looking out through the archways, Pat with her eyes on the clock on top of Moon bastion, and Flora staring down Church Street for any sign of their shopping companion. Clara shook her head and said the locals were always late.

***

5 January 2011

We arrive in Galle unsure if the New Oriental Hotel will still be here. Situated at the southern tip of Sri Lanka, Galle was in the path of the 2004 tsunami, but as we drive around the harbour heading for the fort, we see that the flattened buildings of Galle have risen again. The day's catch is once more spread out on tarpaulins alongside the *oruva* outrigger canoes.

Fort was built on a peninsula to the north-west of Galle Harbour in the seventeenth century by the Portuguese to safeguard their trading interests, and completed in the nineteenth by the Dutch. Zon (Sun), Maan (Moon) and Ster (Star) bastions defended it against attack from inland. Nine other bastions and stout ramparts of rock and coral protected it from invasion by sea. It was these strong fortifications that saved the old colonial buildings inside Fort from the tsunami.

We drive into Fort through an archway in the ramparts, between Moon and Sun bastions, and make our way round the western side. Scores of schoolchildren, immaculate in their white uniforms, presumably on their morning break, play on a scuffed patch of grass leading up to the ramparts. Here the sea's constant pounding is beginning to take its toll on the ancient defences, and planks bridge gaps where the grey rocks and pink coral are falling into the sea.

The grassy banks on the other side of Fort have been mown and watered, the ramparts repaired for the tourists. Here women with brown, wrinkled faces wearing hand-embroidered clothes sell factory-made lace tablecloths. A bride in a flowing white dress and a groom in top hat and tails pose for photographs on Triton bastion; Galle has become the 'in' place for a honeymoon.

We stroll up Church Street, past the traditional Dutch houses with their elaborately carved front doors and wooden fretwork enclosing their flower-filled *stoeps*. At the junction with Middle Street stands a colonial-style, rectangular three-storey building. It is newly painted in pale grey but has no sign outside to indicate its purpose. We go inside to ask if this is the New Oriental Hotel. The receptionist nods and tells us its history: it was built in 1684 as the Dutch Governor's residence, and became a hotel in 1860. It has recently been restored to its former colonial glory by a Middle Eastern conglomerate and is now called The Amangalla.

We order tea on the veranda and sit on rattan chairs at a marble-topped table, a bowl of lotuses in the centre. As I drink my orange pekoe tea and look out through the stone archways, it's hard to believe that sixty-six years ago Aunt Flora waited on this same hotel veranda for the Sinhalese lady who was to escort them to the pettah. I wonder how much of the décor is original. Did

Aunt Flora once walk over the mosaic of hexagonal blue, cream and black tiles on the veranda, through into the lobby with its gleaming jack-wood floor, and sit on the teak and rattan chaises longues beneath the glittering chandeliers?

We pay the 650-rupee bill for our tea and make our way down Church Street to the archway between the Sun and Moon bastions. On top is the clocktower, built by the British in an unsuccessful attempt to instil punctuality into the locals.

***

Despite being married to a British civil servant, the Sinhalese lady was still half an hour late. She waved away the rickshaw drivers, who made a beeline for Flora and Pat every time they stepped out of the hotel, and together they walked down to the pettah. When the girls admired some very vivid patterned fabric she shook her head: the dyes weren't fast, the colours would run. She nodded her approval at a bolt of green linen, bargained with the stall holder and managed to get the price down to five rupees a yard. Her personal tailor would make it up. With only one fitting it was ready two days later, and Pat was delighted with the price and the fit, far superior to any dressmaking they'd commissioned in Colombo. The tortoiseshell goods were also much cheaper; Flora ordered a powder compact, Pat purchased a set of combs. Their escort bought two lengths of white voile which she presented to the two girls before negotiating them a cheap rickshaw ride back to the hotel.

On the Sunday, Clara and the Scottish air force officer invited the Wrens to join them on a trip to Elpitiya:

> *It was a very pretty run most of the way along the coast & took about an hour & a half. We were going to tea at* [Clara's] *son's, her old home, it was quite a way off the main road through the rubber estate & a beautiful bungalow with specially planned open veranda, flowers and comfortable chairs everywhere & so cool…*

Once a month servicemen from a camp several miles away are invited up to the Club for the day where they can play tennis, golf or have a lazy time, when we arrived they were in the middle of a game of Base Ball – what shouting & excitement & the effort they put into it, even the spectators got quite worked up – they were Canadians who were being entertained that week & one had a good laugh at all the expressions that were being used. After this everyone disappeared to the Club & during the evening a really tempting meal was provided – everyone queuing & helping themselves to cold meat, ham, salad, fruit salad & jam tarts – it really was a credit to the planters' wives who arranged this each month & it certainly disappeared very quickly.

Half the veranda was then cleared & a dance held, the pianist really made it go, he had been in a dance band previously & could he play!! What a dance, it was quite hard work considering the uneven numbers, there could not be more than ten [women] & [Pat] and I were the only two Wrens, the others being planters wives & "getting on". The floor was concrete & almost every dance was an "excuse me" and you changed partners about every two steps. When they announced a selection of Viennese waltzes this was just too much & [Pat] and I made for the cloakroom the only place of refuge until these came to an end. I just could not have faced that.

About midnight the dance came to an end… It was quite a relief to get into the car & sink back on the seat. It had been good fun but very tiring. The roads back were absolutely deserted except for occasional bullock carts with the tiny lamps swinging & of course dogs lying in the middle of the road not appearing at all worried as we approached.

Upon approaching one village we saw a crowd of people right across the road & when nearer discovered there was a devil dance in progress & as we had never seen one before & were very interested we stopped the car a few minutes to watch. It was very weird, in front of the tiny hut a small altar had been erected & lit with torches, in front of which a little girl was sitting cross legged & a boy – not very old, dancing

& waving aloft torches to the rhythm of beating drums. Although he seemed very interested in us when we stopped to watch he still kept dancing trying his best to look over his shoulder at the same time. [Clara] *was informed by some of the bystanders that if we stayed it would be coming on better – even the short while we were there the drums pepped up & beat louder. We just pitied the patient with all the noise going on.*

***

After they arrived back in Colombo on 22 February there are no entries in Flora's diary for a whole month, so there is no mention of the *Khedive Ismail.* Is that because the Wrens of Colombo never knew about it? But they must have known another draft of Wrens was due. Must have wondered why they didn't arrive. There must have been rumours. Most likely it was a subject no one wanted to discuss openly, let alone write about; to do so would be to admit what had actually happened.

By the end of 1943, the first flight of Wrens had been joined by other migrants, and now a whole flock worked watches at HMS *Anderson*. More were expected early the following year. On 12 February 1944, the British troopship *Khedive Ismail*, en route from Durban to Colombo, was spotted by a Japanese submarine just south of the Maldives. Most of the 1,200 British and US troops were below deck when two torpedoes struck and the ship sank within two minutes. There were just two Wrens among the four survivors.

Even if they didn't talk about it, the Wrens must have thought about it. What was the point of this wanton destruction of young lives? Now some of those girls would never see their 21st birthday. When would it all end?

In November 1942, Churchill had declared that the victory at El Alamein marked the 'end of the beginning'. But that meant the beginning of the war had lasted three years. Now, fifteen months later, the question remained: how long was the ending going to take? Granted, the Allies had driven Rommel out of North Africa and Mussolini had signed the Armistice last September, but Hitler still controlled France and the Low Countries, and at the beginning of the month London had been hit by the heaviest raids since 1941.

And out in the east, the Japanese were still creeping through Burma. The Americans had landed at Guadalcanal and moved on to invade the Gilbert and Marshall Isles… but on all these islands the enemy still lurked in the undergrowth; the jungle warfare continued.

CHAPTER 21

The Monsoon Season

At last, after hearing months previously that we should be moving to new quarters we were eventually told the date was fixed May 20th. It was quite unbelievable of course, being the Navy, we moved during the monsoon – it simply poured down, many of the lorries taking luggage etc. were open & many things were soaked… We had great expectations. so much had been promised but when we arrived what a dump. With the rains it was just a sea of red mud, there were no proper paths laid you just had to wade & hope for the best.

– Diary entry, 20 May 1944

With one eye on the door, Flora fed the next batch of punched cards into the machine. As soon as she glimpsed the Wren coming on watch, she grabbed her hat and ran. Aboard the 'liberty boat', she glanced at her watch and called *'pace pace'* to the local driver, who grinned and pressed his bare foot down on the accelerator.

When they arrived back at St Peters, Pat was waiting with the cases they'd packed the night before and sufficient sandwiches for both of them. For once, Flora was pleased that the transport was late, as there was time to dash back to the cabin to change into civvies. Flora's diary takes up the story:

As usual we were late starting but, eventually, after calling at various wrennerys [sic] *we were really on the way. It was an open bus very similar to the "locals" with canvas screens to roll down in case of rain. It was glorious when we left but the clouds gathered when we were well on the way & when the storm burst it just came down in a sheet, we were in rather a bad position being just behind the driver & there was no protection his side of the bus whatsoever & when the wind was in our direction we were just drenched.* [Pat] *had the bright idea of taking towels out of our case* [and] *draped these round me which did help to keep it off a little.*

Our bus had no lights on & a relief was expected at Chilaw, but this did not arrive so we carried on in the hope that we should meet it on the way, but no such luck. The last 20 miles or so was like a nightmare & however we arrived at all is still a wonder, the driver a P.O. deserved a medal.

The lightning helped a little but most of the way the driver was leaning out of the bus, at a very precarious angle holding a small torch which one of the Wrens happened to have brought along. What with bullock carts all over the road, also minus lights, ditches at the side, narrow bridges we were lucky to arrive after having only slightly knocked one bullock which was still standing in the middle of the road when we looked back, apparently no worse.

We were sleeping in what will sometime be Wrens quarters but what a primitive place, the ablution block had only one tap which ran into a huge concrete tank in the middle of the floor, the water from the tank running onto the floor where you had to stand & wash, so you were more or less paddling all the time.

It did not take us long to change into evening dresses & find our way across to the Ward Room where the dance was being held. Most of the evening we spent sitting outside where it was so much cooler, the floor was not too good being concrete & it was much too hot to dance often. There were quite a number of New Zealanders there and those we met were very good company & seemed full of life & kept us well supplied with things to eat, which we did justice to, not having had a proper meal since midday.

About 12.30 "The King" was played & Wrens were supposed to be in the cabins by 1am. The joke was, everyone being in evening dress one could not tell who was who & the poor 2/O made several mistakes by asking officers to go to bed that when she approached our table she did not know quite what to do, but a young Subby at the next table soon settled this by saying "They're officers too" so we were not troubled, but after a short while wandered back to the Quarters. That little incident just spoilt things, for once at a party of that description all should have been treated alike.

In the morning we had breakfast in the wardroom, the Wrens, of course, wearing civvies & looking much tidier than the officers who were in uniform very much the worse for wear after the hectic ride the evening before. We had a good breakfast bacon & eggs, fruit, coffee. The 2/0 who was at our table gave [Pat] *and myself a very queer look. I don't think she ever reckoned up who we were!*

Even during the monsoon season, temperatures in Colombo rarely fall below 80°F. During March and April, Flora and Pat sweltered both off duty at St Peters and on duty at HMS *Anderson*. Then, at the beginning of May, their passes for a week's leave in the cooler climate up country arrived. This time it was Pitakanda.

A white-haired lady, wearing a gingham blouse and grey slacks, was waiting for them at Matale station. Mrs B drove Flora and Pat the 12 miles back to the rubber plantation where she lived with her husband. Either side of the rough track, shafts of sunlight filtered through the leaves of the tall, spindly trees, their silvery-grey bark scored with diagonal gashes. The planter's home consisted of several interlinked single-storey buildings. A mass of flowers on a wooden pergola covered the walkway, which stretched right across the front of the extended bungalow. All this was surrounded by trees and set on a raised platform, with steps leading down to the lawn below. The only sound was birdsong.

Mr & Mrs B made us so very welcome we soon felt quite at home, there were plenty of books to read & for a whole week we thoroughly relaxed

> *& just did as we pleased. Most days we went a walk in the morning, our favourite being beyond "the gap", very high up the hillside with a marvellous view, we should have been content to sit there all day, except there was always the call of "food" and our beds in the afternoons!! We were always so thirsty with the climb by the time we arrived back we made straight for the home made lime juice, this was the only thing lacking when we reached the top of the hill.*
>
> *One morning when passing the estate school, there was such a chanting going on we looked in for a few moments to see what was happening. At one end of the room the tiny tots were sitting on the floor with sand spread in front of them in which they were forming letters of the Tamil alphabet at the same time repeating a little rhyme about each one in a sing song manner. A little boy, he looked about 8, was teaching them from a scroll on the wall & seemed to be doing the job pretty thoroughly. Some of the children were quite attractive, especially when they smiled & the majority wore bracelets, anklets & ear rings. At the other end of the room the older children were doing arithmetic under the supervision of a teacher. How they could concentrate at all with such a noise going on from the others I can't imagine.*

During an evening stroll around the rubber estate, they stopped to watch the tappers at work: they made diagonal slashes into the silver-grey bark on the trunks of the tall trees, so that overnight the milky-white fluid would ooze from the cut and drip down a metal spout into a small bowl suspended beneath it.

To find out what happened next, the following afternoon they visited the rubber factory. It wasn't hard to find: they just followed the peculiar smell, that could only be described as sucking a pear drop while wearing a gas mask. The foreman showed them how the latex that the tappers had collected that morning was poured into metal trays, where it was mixed with water and acetic acid. When it had settled, the latex was removed and then passed through a mangle to remove more water. The thin sheets that emerged from between the rollers looked just like lace curtains when they were hung up in the steam house. When dry, they were rolled into bundles ready for export to Britain to make tyres for military vehicles.

On the way back, the sky became very dark and they were lucky to reach the bungalow before the rain started in earnest.

> *Later in the evening there was quite a storm, both* [Pat] *& I were in the bedroom & were quite startled at small explosions which kept occurring round the room, eventually there was a worse one than previously & cackles in all directions, we both made a dive for the door at the same time & into the lounge as quickly as poss, trying to make ourselves look a little respectable on the way. Mr & Mrs B had been wondering when we would appear, apparently our room was well known for this during a storm, but it was quite terrifying at the time, although we saw the funny side afterwards – we came out of that room so quickly.*

The Gap was a small wireless station on the hillside above the estate, manned by a lone naval petty officer. Although Flora never realised it at the time, he was probably one of the operators who intercepted Japanese signals and passed them on to HMS *Anderson*. Being stationed in such a remote location, he was totally reliant on headquarters down in Colombo for his food rations, and Mr & Mrs B for company. He'd often pop down to the bungalow of an evening and on a couple of occasions played mah-jong with Flora, even though the rules had been lost and they had to make up their own.

He invited the Wrens to call in on their morning walk. They arrived during a transmission. When he'd finished speaking he handed the microphone to Flora and, to her surprise, asked her to say a few words. She later wrote in her diary: *I put the subby in Colombo completely off his stroke when I said Good Morning, he stuttered and stammered and was at such a loss for words we had to laugh. I quite upset his line of thought!!!*

***

On the return journey to Colombo, they had been asked to look out for an elderly British lady also taking the one-thirty train – they would recognise her by the amount of luggage she had with her. She was already waiting on the overcrowded platform amidst cases, baskets and parcels. In one hand she clutched a radio, with the other she was gesticulating to the porters who were loading a cage containing two rabbits into the guard's van.

Flora and Pat helped carry her belongings and look for a compartment. The train was crowded and the only three seats left were beside a family with a host of rowdy children, and opposite several men smoking. They'd only gone a short distance before it started to rain and the windows had to be closed, so children's chatter and screams ricocheted off the walls and the air was thick with cigarette smoke.

The train rattled through the lush greenery, past small houses and huts, every one hung with decorations. In the villages there were archways made of plaited palms, and colourful flags and lanterns strung through the trees. Their travelling companion explained that it was the Wesak festival, a national holiday to celebrate Buddha's birth – always the first full moon in May.

At Kandy station they became separated from the lady with the luggage, although once on the train down to Colombo they could hear her at the far end of the carriage, asking if anyone had seen her radio or her rabbits.

Back at St Peters, they were given the good news: they would be moving to their new quarters in ten days' time. After five months of waiting in what they had been told in January was temporary accommodation, they were finally going to leave the mosquitos, grasshoppers, spiders and Rupert the frog behind.

The new quarters were in Cinnamon Gardens, a very desirable residential area of Colombo, so the Wrens had high hopes. Guilford Crescent was a wide road lined with trees and flowering shrubs. The trucks came to a halt outside wrought-iron gates set in a high wall. The naval guards checked the driver's pass, then waved them on. They stopped just inside, in front of a small hut, the Regulating office. A long drive led up to Kent House, a white, neoclassical mansion with ornate pillars and archways, balconies and balustrades.

The house was set in extensive grounds and it was here, not in the house, that the Wrens would live. Lawns and flower beds had been torn up and huts were in various stages of construction. The cabins were named after ships: Flora and Pat were in Fury and two of their friends in Defiant, names which the Wrens thought quite appropriate as they reflected their anger and disappointment. After all they'd been promised, their new accommodation wasn't much different from the huts they'd just left behind at St Peters: the five-foot-high walls, built of brick and painted with whitewash, had a space above, and then a *kadjan*-thatched roof – so much for thinking that the constant war against insects would be a thing of the past.

Entrance to Kent House, Colombo

Four huts were grouped around a central ablution block, and each one consisted of two dormitories, each sleeping twelve Wrens, with twin-bedded units partitioned off at the gable ends. These were allocated to leading Wrens, and, for the first time, Flora and Pat were accorded a privilege of their new rank. They were delighted to have more privacy and space and light from a proper window. A connecting door led directly into one of the dormitories, but they preferred to keep this closed and use the door onto the veranda which ran along the front of the cabin. Now, at last, Flora and Pat could get away from the crowd, read as long as they pleased, and switch off the light and go to sleep whenever they wanted.

The furnishings were rather sparse when they first moved in, just two beds and a dressing table. At least the fitted hanging space was a good size and could accommodate all their clothes, and they'd been promised some curtains to transform it into a wardrobe. There was a shelf with room for all their knick-knacks. They went scavenging and helped themselves to two chairs, a linen basket, a towel rail and a box, as well as two quite presentable rush mats to cover the bare concrete floor, from an untidy heap of household goods dumped in a corner of the grounds. At the first opportunity they went shopping in the pettah. In Third Cross Street they found exactly what they were looking for: blue and white folk-weave bedspreads and appliqué mats for the dressing table.

It still rankled that the officers were billeted in Kent House itself. Not that the Wren ratings weren't allowed up the steps to the massive porch and in through the front door. But they were confined to the ground floor: to listen to the radio, read or write letters in the two hopelessly small recreation rooms, to visit the hairdressers, the laundry, or the room where the resident tailor sat on the floor. He would alter and repair Wren uniforms and, for a haggled price, make up the white material they bought at the pettah into 'tidley dresses'.

The officers ate in the house but their minions were relegated to two *kadjan*-thatched huts in the grounds: a small one for petty officers, a much larger one for all the rest. Outside the black crows cawed, ready to swoop in through the gap between the wall and the roof the moment any food was left unattended.

***

31 December 2010

The crows are scavenging downtown in Fort and along the Galle Road, but there are not so many here in Cinnamon Gardens. Guilford Crescent is still the same desirable residential area: a wide road separated from the pavement by grass verges dotted with shrubs. Large post-war houses, their walls and balconies painted brilliant white, are just visible through the abundant trees behind the high boundary walls. A few of the old colonial houses remain, their once extensive grounds sold off for development.

On the map of Colombo pasted into Aunt Flora's diary there is a cross on Guilford Crescent: the location of Kent House, I presume. We stand at the midpoint of the crescent, where I judge the cross to be, and look down a side road with new houses on each side and round the cul-de-sac at the end. Has Kent House been demolished to make way for this new housing? The only landmark which might have been here sixty-six years ago is a tree; parasitic plants thrive in crevices in its massive trunk and thick branches. I would like to think this is the tree the Wrens stood under, waiting for the 'liberty boat' to take them to HMS *Anderson*, but it isn't a banyan.

***

Some said the banyan tree in the grounds of Kent House was more than 100 years old, but no one was really sure. It could have been, because of its numerous extra trunks supporting the spreading branches. These additional supports form when seeds germinate while still on the tree, and grow aerial roots which reach down to obtain sustenance from the rich, red soil beneath. The tree's leaves, all shaped like a giant's multi-fingered hand, formed the canopy that provided the Wrens with a shady place to wait for the 'liberty boat' to take them to HMS *Anderson*.

It was 20 May 1944 when Flora recorded the move to Kent House, but after that, for all of June and most of July, there are no entries in her diary. There are, however, two theatre programmes: one for *Blithe Spirit*, an improbable farce written by Noel Coward performed at the Royal Air Force Theatre; the other for a joint NAAFI and ENSA production of *Love in a Mist*, a hilarious comedy by Kenneth Horne.

Maybe the hectic social life left little time for writing, or perhaps she was just homesick. After all, at that time the tide of war was turning. On 6 June

1944, an announcement from General Eisenhower's HQ told the world: *Allied naval forces, supported by strong air forces, began landing Allied armies this morning on the Northern Coast of France.* It was D-Day. The Americans reached Cherbourg fifteen days later, forcing the Germans into retreat. What the Wrens in Colombo didn't know was that Hitler had now ordered the launching of his Secret Weapon, the V-1: their target, the south of England. Londoners now lived in fear of the 'doodle-bug'. They listened to the drone of its engine above them; if they heard it stop, they knew the bomb was destined for them. The Wrens were so far away they only heard whispers about what was going on back home: the letters they received were censored, and anyway, to avoid the enemy hearing where their missiles had landed and fine-tuning this pilot-less flying bomb, no details of the damage were reported.

A more likely explanation for the lack of diary entries is that Flora was exhausted with the day and night rota of watches. During this time there was a significant increase in the number of Japanese signals deciphered at HMS *Anderson*; the Holleriths were in great demand. The navy were certainly grateful for the Wrens' hard work, because a VIP made a point of visiting HMS *Anderson*. The event took place on 17 July 1944 at St Joseph's barracks. A photograph of an admiral, knees visible below his tropical white shorts, and a line of Wrens, white drill dresses and a white covering to the crown of their navy-blue hats, appeared in the local newspaper.

Underneath is the caption:

To celebrate his birthday, Admiral Sir James Somerville, Commander-in-Chief of the Eastern Fleet, held an inspection of W.R.N.S serving in Colombo. Nearly 250 of them were on parade, and after the

Admiral Somerville inspects the Wrens in Colombo

inspection they marched past the saluting base to the strains of the Royal Marine Band. As the Admiral was leaving, the Wrens, casting aside their parade ground manner, broke into a musical birthday greeting. In his message to the Chief Officer W.R.N.S. congratulating them on the excellence of their drill, bearing, and appearance, Admiral Somerville added: "I noted with much surprise that the percentage of nightingales camouflaged as Wrens appeared to be remarkably high."

Maybe it was Admiral Somerville who was responsible for the Wrens' invitation to an afternoon dance organised by the crew of HMS *Victorious*. Flora wasn't bothered about going to a dance, but she'd never before had the chance to see over an aircraft carrier. She'd also learnt in a letter from home that a boy she'd known at school was serving aboard this Royal Navy carrier.

HMS *Victorious* was well known for her part in sinking the German battleship *Bismarck*. In 1943, she was loaned to the US Navy and sailed to Pearl Harbour to join the USS *Saratoga*, their only operational carrier at the time. Together, they provided support for the Allied landing on New Georgia in the Solomon Islands. When the other US carriers were repaired and back in service, HMS *Victorious* returned to Britain, leaving the war in the Pacific to the Americans while the Royal Navy continued its role in protecting shipping in the Indian Ocean.

The withdrawal of German U-boats, the Allied victory in North Africa and the surrender of Italy meant that in the summer of 1944 Royal Navy warships could be spared from duty in the Atlantic and the Mediterranean. They were sent out to join the much-depleted Eastern Fleet, which was then able to take a much more offensive role against the Japanese. HMS *Victorious* arrived back in Colombo on 5 July 1944, and during the next two months, together with other aircraft carriers, HMS *Indomitable* and HMS *Illustrious*, was involved in successful attacks on Japanese bases in Sumatra.

The dance was held below deck in the stifling heat of the aircraft hangers, where the fighter planes waited, their wings folded upwards like butterflies. Two petty officers who didn't want to dance were happy to take Flora on a guided tour of the vessel. They weren't sure if one of their fellow officers was from Halifax, but asked in the mess and eventually found him on deck. When he had recovered from his surprise and embarrassment, they talked of home and Flora promised to write to his wife to say she'd seen him, and tell her how well he looked.

***

When the promised curtains for their *banda* arrived, they were plain, cream calico – a sore disappointment. Even though it was the day before they were due to go up country on leave, Flora and Pat went down to the pettah to find something to brighten them up. They settled on some pretty braid, plaited from strands of blue, green, yellow and fuchsia, to sew across the width of each curtain.

As they headed back to Kent House to finish their packing, a group of Dutch naval officers was walking towards them. Flora couldn't believe it. She'd thought that she would never see that smile again, the smile that had remained with her as they'd sailed across the Indian Ocean from Mombasa and had been in her thoughts many times during the last year in Colombo.

Up until then, Flora had been looking forward to going on leave, but now she would have preferred to stay in Colombo, despite the heat. There was, however, no way that she could change her plans at this late stage; she had to decline Johannes's invitation to dinner the following evening. To her relief, he said that he was in Colombo on a course for several months and when she got back, he'd be waiting.

CHAPTER 22

So Near Yet So Far

> *We had been unable to get tickets previously owing to sleepers being on our warrant & the queue at the one & only booking office. I thought we would never make it, but luckily we had allowed plenty of time – they do not know what it is to hurry out here & the booking clerks are the last straw!!*
>
> *– Diary entry, 3 August 1944*

The words Flora wrote in her diary reflect her mood as she stood alongside Pat at Colombo's Fort station. The mounting excitement as she looked forward to their two weeks' leave had faded, leaving only concern that, in her absence up country, Johannes would find another Wren to show him the sights of Colombo.

Her spirits lifted a little as the train chugged its way through the countryside. An almost full moon silhouetted the trees against a dark blue sky. Hundreds of candles illuminated temples hidden amongst the palms alongside the track. August is the month for festivals and peraheras.

They decided against dinner on the train, and instead ordered coffee for nine o'clock and ate the sandwiches they'd brought with them. Then Flora climbed the ladder into the top bunk and eventually she fell asleep, only waking for a few moments with the jolt of the train as more carriages were added at various stages along the track. When the steward brought morning tea at six-thirty, it was decidedly chilly – a sure sign that they had climbed much higher during the night.

Flora's exasperation of the previous night resurfaced when they found no one waiting to meet them at Haputale station. The letter confirming their arrival date most probably hadn't arrived – not surprising, as the Wrens' letters were held up for several days as they were checked by the censor. Although they knew D'urques would still be in bed after a late night at the weekly Bandarawela Ball, they had no option but to ring the Blackwood Arms. In a voice thick with sleep, he said he'd send his chauffeur to collect them:

...after waiting about 20 minutes we were on our way to Blackwood Arms. It was a very fresh morning, just a cool breeze & the view did one good after the uninteresting flatness of Colombo. The "family" seemed very pleased to see us & made such a fuss, old Nobby toddling on behind, not wishing to be left out and Pym & Jose almost tripping us up...

D'urques made us very welcome & once we were inside the bungalow it was hard to realize that it was six months from our last visit. We had the same room our two large comfortable beds, white nets & on the dressing table two silver vases of roses, they were beautiful & for a change had some scent. The garden was one mass of flowers, more so than last time & the lilies in the pond were open & were a delicate blue. It was all so peaceful & quiet & to think we had 14days – almost too good to be true.

We were never up very early for breakfast, making the most of such luxurious beds, when we had our tea in bed this was the signal for the children to invade, it was always a dangerous time not knowing when either Pym or Jose would take a flying leap onto the bed. After the way food is served in a Wrennery & tables laid it was wonderful to feel civilized once more, be able to take your time without the usual mad rush (especially for breakfast) & no time limits and the freedom of wearing civvies all day.

We were not feeling very energetic the first few days & only went a short walk after tea, coming back we were not sure which path to take so decided to follow "the children", of course we might have known they would lead us a dance & one ended up by scrambling down the steep hillside almost on hands and knees clinging on to the tea bushes for support. It had been raining during the afternoon & as the soil is very red we looked rather worse for wear when we arrived back to find D'urques looking very smart & tidy. However, we were soon wallowing in hot baths (another luxury when you have not to carry buckets about for one & we always made the most of it) – I think D'urques often wondered if we would be there for the night, but we always turned up for dinner.

On the Sunday D as usual went to the tennis club at Haputale we waited & waited expecting him back about 2pm for lunch, but when it came to 3.30pm & he still had not returned, Joseph appeared & asked if we wanted our lunch – he seemed highly amused when we said we were waiting for master to come back & replied "sometimes he comes at 2pm, sometimes at 3pm and sometimes not at all!!"

The following Sunday, the girls accepted D'urques's invitation to go along with him. They discovered that the club was a regular meeting place for the planters, an opportunity for drinking and a chance to catch up on the week's local gossip; very few of the regulars had any intention of playing tennis.

One morning we decided to climb the hill, just behind the bungalow. It's about 1,800ft but until we started we did not realize quite how steep it was & deciding to take a short cut up some steps at the start of the walk did not help matters & we were soon out of breath and puffing and panting like two old ladies. The "children" were well away, miles in front of us, even old Nobby held his own with the other two until we were on the way back when he kept us company.

We were going merrily along one path & came to one of the many waterfalls down the hillside, forming a bridge across, were two tree trunks & not until we were almost on top of it did I notice a snake having a sunbathe in the middle. What a shock. I stopped dead & told [Pat] *to look. It was about 5' long & as thick as one's wrist. We had never seen one outside a zoo before. We stopped absolutely dead,*

> *clinging to one another our eyes glued to it – although they are so evil looking they have a fascination. We did not know whether it was harmful or not & the dogs would go and paddle and took no notice when we shouted for them to come back. We must have disturbed the snake with the noise for after a while it uncoiled & slithered under the trunks & out of sight… We were afterwards told it was only a rat snake & quite harmless, but even so it was too large for my fancy.*

On three evenings during their two-week stay, D'urques's chauffeur drove the girls down to the naval rest camp at Diyatalawa to the Wavel picture house. They saw the musical *Moonlight and Melody*, Deanna Durbin in the rather dated *That Certain Age*, and Loretta Young in *Ladies Courageous*, a glamorised portrayal of the Air Transport Corps. On Thursday, he took D'urques and his guests to the Bandarawela Ball.

***

21 March 2016

Sidath, the guide who has driven us up country, tells us that, although it would be possible to visit the small town of Diyatalawa, the Wavel cinema is now within an army camp, a restricted area. We can, however, visit the Bandarawela Hotel, the venue for the famous Thursday night ball.

Bandarawela Hotel circa 1940.

Wikipedia describes the Bandarawela Hotel as: *locked in time somewhere between the 1930s and 1950s.* Is that really true? Is it still exactly the same as when Aunt Flora danced there in 1944?

On the outside, the hotel looks like an extended version of a typical up-country bungalow. When we venture inside the decor is colonial: wood panelling, highly polished floors, gleaming brass fittings on windows and doors. The reception area is carved from solid teak and extends from floor to ceiling, with a flap in the counter to allow the receptionist to enter, and a roll-down shutter to close it up when he's not there.

On a small table opposite is information about local tourist spots and a book that chronicles the history of the hotel. It opened in 1894, the year that the railway reached Bandarawela, as a club and guest house exclusively for Europeans. This was still the case when Aunt Flora was here, as local people were not officially admitted until the 1950s, although there is a hint that they did manage to sneak into the public bar through a door at the back of the building. The hotel's history ends with a quote from a guest who stayed here in 1992: *Lovely, eccentric, worldly hotel, reminiscent of British days… The hotel is certainly a time capsule, we'll return in ten years' time to find it unchanged as it resists the modern temptations of the 1990s.*

The dining room, with its high-backed, solid-teak chairs is unchanged, but the menu has moved into the twenty-first century and is served on square plates. After lunch I take a wander around. The lounge is on the opposite side of the entrance and, like the dining room, has a continuous expanse of small-paned, teak-framed windows overlooking the front gardens. The chesterfields, mentioned in the guidebook, have now been replaced with box-shaped armchairs and sofas upholstered in geometric-patterned fabric, but two teak and rattan chairs have survived and the pendulum on the wall clock is still swinging.

The guest bedrooms are in similar single-storey buildings, tacked on at the back and arranged to completely surround three courtyard gardens. Guests step out onto an open-air walkway and can breakfast at tables just outside their bedroom doors while they admire the flowers and shrubs surrounding an immaculately-trimmed lawn, and listen to the chirp of birds that hop along the teak, trellised balustrade.

At the end of a narrow corridor a sign points to the pub and billiard room. Four lights are suspended on a brass pole above the billiard table and at the far end of the room, dimly lit by just one window, is a bar. I imagine D'urques sitting on one of the high stools, elbow on the bar counter, or leaning over the billiard table to pot the ball, while his female guests danced in the ballroom.

I don't manage to find the ballroom but I do spot two things that convince me it is here somewhere. After her first visit to the Bandarawela Hotel, Aunt Flora wrote in her diary: *... went in search of the dancing there was supposed to be. After a while they started to the strains of the gramophone. The room was rather small, especially as they also had tables round as well & there was a pillar right in the middle which one had to keep a watchful eye on.* In most of the rooms the roof is supported by a central pillar, and in the reception area there is a lovingly-preserved gramophone, complete with highly-polished brass horn.

Gramophone beside the reception desk at the Bandarawela Hotel

***

On Thursday, 19 August 1944, there was no need of a gramophone: the band at the Bandarawela Ball was composed entirely of servicemen – army, navy and air force – and included a kilted Scottish piper. They played waltzes, tangos, polkas and Scottish reels until midnight. Then, although Flora and Pat were ready to go home, D'urques wasn't, so they joined a party from the Dutch Fleet Air Arm and continued drinking and chatting into the early hours. Flora's mind, however, was elsewhere – would Johannes still be waiting when she got back to Colombo?

Two army staff sergeants at the ball persuaded Flora and Pat to join them the following day for a round of croquet, a game which Flora had never tried before, but found quite fun and managed better than she expected. This led to another invitation: a picnic at Diyaluma Falls the next day. Flora wrote in her diary: *It was a very pretty run there but the hairpin bends!!! Although I can ride in almost anything, anywhere, I was glad I was in the front of the car where you do not feel it quite so badly.*

***

20 March 2016

I know what Aunt Flora meant. We sit in the back seat as Sidath follows the same route to Diyaluma Falls. The narrow road curves out to circle the rocky outcrops, then sweeps inwards to bridges over water that rushes over a tumble of rocks down the hillside. Rising up on one side of the winding roadway are steep banks of red earth, colonised here and there by ferns and long grass and overhung by rubber tree branches from the plantations above. To the other side is a steep drop protected only by stumpy concrete posts, painted white.

Sidath gives a man carrying a bundle of sugar cane on his head a wide berth. As we approach every bend he pips the horn; just as well, because we meet the local bus coming the other way. We have to stop precariously close to the edge to allow it to pass by on the inside.

The height of the Diyaluma Falls is 628ft – the second-highest waterfall in Sri Lanka. We know this because it is written in Aunt Flora's diary and confirmed by a roadside sign where we get out of the car. The original bridge which spans the boulder-strewn river flowing on from the falls is still there, but now only strong enough to support pedestrians. A sturdy traffic bridge has been built alongside it.

On one side of the new bridge is a wooden shack; outside, beside a cauldron suspended over a fire made of sticks, an elderly couple sell coconuts. On the opposite side of the bridge is a shop built of corrugated iron; a blue and green sign outside advertises *Telecom Mobitel services available here.*

It is March, a few weeks before the monsoon season begins, so today the waterfall is just a thin ribbon of foam. Aunt Flora was here later in the year when the monsoon was almost over, so neither of us have seen the spectacular cascade, or heard the water thundering down the sheer cliff face, but nevertheless we both still feel insignificant as we stand here, just tiny specks at the foot of the falls.

I linger, and try to imagine two Wrens and two sergeants spreading out their picnic on the rug, boiling water on the primus stove and having to make tea in the kettle as they had forgotten a teapot. I search the rock pools for the *hundreds of brilliantly coloured dragonflies darting about the pools in the rocks, their wings black velvet with vivid splashes of emerald, turquoise and blue,* that Aunt Flora describes in her diary as *simply beautiful.* I catch only a fleeting glimpse of just two of these luminescent insects.

***

On the return journey, the Wrens told the two sergeants about the basic facilities and the uncomfortable beds back at Kent House:

> *They were astounded to learn that ours were wooden slats & said they had spare spring beds that they would send round for us on our return. When these arrive we shall be the envy of the Wrennery and when I'm on night watch think it will be a good idea to hire it out for so much a night!! It will be a great day when they arrive – my present one has bumps in all the wrong places. I shall be glad to see the end of it.*

Two days later, as they waited for a lift in a truck back to Colombo, they were still thinking of the spring beds and wondering if and when they'd receive them

– knowing that the two sergeants would be unlikely to forget to send them, but almost sure that army regulations would forbid it. Discomfort was something they were used to: even though they knew from experience what the journey they faced that day would be like, they still chose five uncomfortable hours by road as opposed to eleven long, tiring hours on the train.

The truck that arrived was fairly comfortable there being one seat in the front next to the driver who was so Scotch we could not understand a word he was saying & two seats in the back facing the wrong way – an army captain was travelling with us – also Scotch but I could understand him. We were in the back to begin with & luckily the seats had very good springs in – we just whizzed along and the dust – by the time we stopped at the rest house I was so covered in dust & was glad of a wash and some lime juice to refresh us. [Pat] wasn't too bad having had a little more protection in the front. We discovered the truck was a very old one, almost on its last legs & it kept refusing to go & whenever we stopped it was just luck whether it started again. They had visions of having to ring up for another one – however it managed & we eventually arrived. The steering was also strained & the swing round corners!!

For the next part of the journey to Ratnapura I was in the front – the dust not being so bad, but getting almost drenched when we ran into very heavy rain but it was quite refreshing. The lunch at the rest house was terrible, the soup watery, the fish he said was salmon turned out to be herrings, the meat I did not attempt looked very tough and the coffee – hardly recognisable.

As usual they did their best to sell us some jewels, Ceylon precious stones, it was rather like watching conjuring tricks the way they would produce from their pockets small parcels in tissue or hankies & display the stones – all the time you were having a meal they were hovering around far more interested in showing these than serving the meal.

***

21 March 2016

'Gem mines,' says Sidath, as he brings the car to a halt at the roadside.

We are on our way back to Colombo, just entering the town of Ratnapura. In what looks as if it might, at one time, have been a paddy-field, men stripped to the waist lean on the palm trunks which support a weather-worn canopy, the thatch now grey and brittle.

'They go down 500 metres,' says Sidath.

We cannot see the shaft as it is behind a bund of yellow earth, but above where we presume it must be a hook dangles from a chain, and a pipe, possibly part of a primitive pump, extends out to one side.

This is just the first of several gem mines that we pass as we continue into the town. Ratnapura is no longer the small hamlet it was in the 1940s; the streets are crowded as Buddhists decorate homes and temples with coloured lights, hang bunting and raise flags in preparation for Poya Day tomorrow. I tell myself that the rest-house where Aunt Flora went hungry, and might possibly have missed the chance to buy a genuine blue sapphire, is by now probably long gone. Horns blare as a baby calf darts out into the road, and by some miracle reaches the other side without being hit by the chaotic tangle of cars, trucks, motorbikes and tuk-tuks. A cow gazes forlornly across the road, unable to offer her offspring any help. Then there it is, a large yellow sign: RATNAPURA REST HOUSE. There is no place to stop; soon it will be dark and we still have a three-hour journey to Colombo.

***

At three-thirty, Flora and Pat were back in Colombo; if they had taken the train it would have been eight-thirty. Both Wrens had quite a pile of letters. Normally Flora would have been delighted, especially as there was also a parcel containing a film for her camera, but not this time: the one note she was waiting for wasn't there. There was no message from Johannes.

CHAPTER 23

Reunited

Queen Wilhelmina's birthday & Netherlands National Day:

[Pat] *and I were invited to make up a party with* [Johannes] *& a friend, a 2/O from the same ship, & we went along to a dance at the International Club given by the Netherlands Navy... we had a very happy time, tables and chairs were outside in the garden & the dance held inside. The band was very good.*

– Diary entry, 31 August 1944

Flora said it was ridiculous. No men allowed within 250 yards of Kent House. The rule had been introduced after a herd of drunken GIs had descended on the Wrennery. Rumour had it that there'd been some misunderstanding about the purpose of the knocking-up book. To the Wrens, it was the book the guards made you sign to prove they'd woken you up, so they weren't to blame if you missed the duty bus; to the Americans, it meant something quite different.

What would Johannes think? Flora wondered as they hurried down Guilford Crescent. In the few minutes she'd seen him before going on leave, there hadn't been time to explain this absurd new rule.

The note from Johannes had arrived ten days after their return from Haputale; by then, Flora had told herself he'd found someone else while she'd been away. It was an invitation to make up a foursome on 31 August to celebrate Queen Wilhelmina's birthday and Dutch National Day. The dance was organised by the Netherlands Navy and the venue was just a few hundred yards from Kent House, not far from where the two Dutch officers were waiting, but they couldn't go straight there. They all had to walk back to Kent House and into Regulating so the lieutenants could write their name, rank and number in the signing-out book.

When they eventually arrived at the party, they sat at a table in the garden and were joined by two other Dutch officers. There is no mention in the diary of what they talked about, but very likely it was about what was happening back in Europe: a week before, American and British troops had entered Paris – the Germans were leaving. How long would it be before the enemy was defeated, the Netherlands liberated and they could go home?

The official band finished at eleven, and a group of servicemen with a variety of instruments – including an accordion – took over and dancing went on until midnight. The Wrens had late passes until twelve-thirty and, for once, were the last to leave.

On her next evening off, Johannes took Flora to the New Olympia picture house to see an American war propaganda film, *Up in Arms*. Flora was not impressed:

> *There was very little story in it & it was far too American but we had a good laugh in one part. An American troopship was sailing with a number of Nurses on board. What a troopship, they were lounging over the decks on lilos in sun-suits, bathing costumes etc. Glamour & a luxury cruise was not in it & to hear the remarks of the audience who were mostly services was really funny and there were bursts of laughter when it showed two sergeants leaning over the rail looking at the sunbathing glamour girls and saying "there was nothing like this in the last war".*

When they came out of the pictures, Johannes suggested they go on to the Silver Fawn. Flora had heard of this new nightclub – the only one in Colombo – but to go there one needed to be in evening dress. She looked down at the day dress she'd had made up from the powder-blue linen bought from the pettah and shook her head. Johannes put his arm round her shoulders and said she looked beautiful.

At the entrance to the Silver Fawn a waiter, wearing a white tunic and dhoti with a tortoiseshell comb in his hair, greeted the couple and gave Flora a corsage to pin on her dress. He showed them to one of the tables under the arches around the sunken dance floor. Lights were dimmed; on a small dais at one end of the room a band played 'Smoke gets in your eyes', 'Deep Purple' and 'These foolish things'.

'I like to dance to these English tunes, but not that American dance. How do you call it?'

'The jitterbug,' said Flora. 'I hate it too.'

'We like the same things, I think.'

There were only half a dozen couples on the dance floor; Johannes held Flora close as they waltzed to 'All the things you are'.

***

Flora banged the still-cold iron down on the table. Why was it that whenever something broke, no one reported it? Everything was against her. She'd been looking forward to their day out for almost three weeks, then thought the weather might put an end to it, but yesterday there'd been no rain and it looked as if she needn't have worried. She'd washed her 'tidley dress' – it was either that or uniform: they were going out for the whole day and the Wrens weren't allowed to wear civvies in the morning. When she'd returned to collect her dress, there were black marks all down the front, so she'd washed it again and hung it up in the laundry overnight. This morning she was pleased to find her dress was dry and the spots had gone, but now the iron wouldn't work.

As they left to meet Johannes and his friend, Pat reassured Flora that as the material was pique, her dress wouldn't look too creased. They were off to the tiny fishing village of Negombo for the first of many pleasant days they spent on the beach:

It's only just about 30 miles from Colombo but takes almost two hours by train, we arrived at 10.45am & as there were only rickshaws & bullock carts for transport decided to walk to the rest house about 10 minutes away… some of the houses had wooden balconies outside & small porches painted pale blue and white – all carved woodwork, they looked rather attractive. The rest house is in a very good position, right on the beach & the first thing we required was something to drink.

We then changed out of uniform and went for a bathe. The sea was very warm but the current and waves were far too strong for me to do much swimming – each wave almost bowled one over & by the time we came out our legs were quite aching with trying to stand but it was good fun. As usual we had an audience. Whatever one does in this country the locals collect to watch.

We walked along the beach & for a while watched an old fisherman throwing & drawing in his net. It was fascinating to watch, the net was circular – very fine and weighted round the edge, he draped this over his right arm in folds &, as he cast it, it dropped on the sea in a perfect circle, the weights then drawing it down encasing any small fish there might be. Further along the beach were the katamarans [sic], *one of them with a huge red coloured sail – they wanted us to go out fishing in one but, as it would have meant for 2 or 3 hours, we declined. There are no seats in them you sit across the boat which is very narrow & looks extremely uncomfortable.*

By the time we got back it was time for lunch so we found a shady spot under the trees on the lawn of the rest house & unpacked the lunch… There were ham sandwiches, tomatoes, hard boiled eggs, chicken & biscuits – did we enjoy it, of course the crows all collected as soon as any food appeared & had a great time. It was funny to see them fight over a piece of chicken, the lucky one who managed to get it first was chased out to sea about 20 more following him & the noise!!

During the afternoon a conjurer came round – he was an Indian

& had a little boy with him. He was carrying a large bundle which he put down on the lawn & taking a basket from it, placed it before him then sitting down started to play on his pipe – out came a huge cobra swaying about – I was quite glad to see it safely back in the basket & the lid on once again. The next trick he started to dig up part of the lawn & planted a seed – this he watered & then placed over it a tablecloth several times he uncovered the seed and replaced the cloth all the time muttering some mumbo jumbo & waving his arms about – this continued for about five minutes & then he started to lift the cloth & underneath was a tree growing from the seed (about 15 inches high).

The plan was to get the 7 p.m. train from Negombo station, so there'd be time for a meal in Colombo before the Wrens' ten-thirty curfew. The train, however, was an hour late – engine failure, the stationmaster said – then stopped for ages to pick up or drop off goods wagons at every station, and by the time they arrived back at Fort it was after ten. So, that evening the two girls dined alone back in the cabin on two packets of biscuits and four hard boiled eggs left over from the picnic. Before getting into bed they covered their red, angry skin with liberal amounts of cold cream.

That night, both girls tossed and turned, and couldn't bear the touch of the bedclothes. The following day at HMS *Anderson*, as she reached up for the punch-cards and leant over to feed them into the machine, Flora's back was on fire. By the end of the watch her skin was beginning to peel. But there was no chance of reporting in sick: it was September 1944. They'd just been given another pep talk: everyone was told to keep up the good work, it was vital to the war effort, especially right now. No one ever explained why. The Wrens, however, obeyed without question.

***

It was mid-November before Johannes and Flora were able to return to Negombo:

> *The sky was perfectly blue with white fleecy clouds & the sea rolling in on the beach… A conjurer came round after lunch & did various tricks mostly making eggs & nuts disappear to reappear under three silver bells. To make the "magic" work he had a rag doll about 12" high which he waved round & round at intervals, talking continually, to everyone's amusement. He also did the usual tree growing trick & snake charming but the snake was a very frisky one & made a sudden dive out of his reach – was I glad when he just caught it in time by the tip of its tail & put it safely in the basket once more.*
>
> *We then went out for a couple of hours in a katamaran – as there are no seats in these boats we had been wondering where we would sit & found they had lashed a few bamboos across & we sat with our feet dangling above the sea. It was great fun & they go at quite a speed & just glide through the water. There was one very old fisherman & quite a young boy sailing the boat.*

A Katamaran at Negombo

As the wind ballooned the huge red sail and they sped across the sparkling water, beneath a perfect blue sky, the war must have seemed very far away. It was only after her return to England that Flora would find out that, in August, Winston Churchill and President Roosevelt had held talks in Quebec. It had been decided that, with Nazi Germany nearing collapse, the theatre of war should be shifted to the Far East. During the naval battle at Leyte Gulf in October 1944, the Imperial Japanese Navy lost three battleships, four carriers, ten cruisers and nine destroyers, and subsequently General MacArthur took control of the Philippines. In years to come, Flora would remember the pep talk back there in Colombo in the autumn of 1944, and think that perhaps her work on the Hollerith had contributed in some way to this turning point in the war with the Japan.

CHAPTER 24

Christmas and the New Year

Xmas eve we helped to decorate the bungalow with fir branches from the garden & red berries (a type of holly but the leaves have no prickles) & it did look effective and very festive. On Xmas morning when the boy brought in our tea there was a very interesting looking parcel on the tray for us. Travelling sets, gold pins, diary, scent and hankies from Mr & Mrs B & I also had Kandyan silver bracelets from [Pat] & hair shampoo. What a lucky day but we really felt they should not have given us presents. There were also tangerines.

– Diary entry, 25 December 1944

Flora and Pat were pleased to be leaving early. At this time of the morning, there were few people about and the station, with its fretwork wooden canopy and wrought-iron banisters, didn't look that much different from Halifax station – after all, it had been built by the British. They were going up country again – just to Pitakanda this time – but, even so, they couldn't face another train journey in a hot, smoke-filled, second-class compartment, so they had altered their travel documents to first class. They hadn't, however, had them authorised and signed by the RTO, so they were very relieved to be settled down in an uncrowded compartment without anyone querying their tickets.

Mrs B was waiting at Kandy to drive them back to the plantation, where they were to spend Christmas. It was only six months since their last visit, so they soon felt quite at home. Their hostess left a bowl of roses in their bedroom, then a few days later a vase of violets – their scent reminded them both of summer in England.

They took long walks up to the Gap, where two new naval petty officers had taken over the transmitting station. Flora stood there looking down over the rolling hills, covered with lush green leaves, not frost-covered bare branches, and found it hard to believe that it was December. Mr & Mrs B had invited another ten guests for Christmas dinner: six planters, a couple from Colombo and the two naval petty officers from the Gap. The table was decorated with candles, holly and crackers. Flora found the lucky ten-cent piece in her helping of Christmas pudding.

In the evening they sat in the lounge around a crackling log fire. Outside, a brilliant silver moon lit up the sky and there was quite a nip in the air, so it did feel a bit like Christmas. Mr B turned on the radio to listen to the king's speech. More than 5,000 miles separated Flora from her mother and sisters, and yet they were listening to the same words at the same time.

The king no doubt mentioned the war, but was it a subject everyone at the bungalow in Pitakanda avoided on this festive occasion? During the previous summer, when British and American troops were advancing rapidly across France, there were hopes that the war in Europe would be over by Christmas. But it wasn't: the Allies still hadn't succeeded in crossing the Rhine, and in December the Germans had launched a counteroffensive through the densely-forested Ardennes region of Belgium.

***

Two days after Christmas, it was back to the claustrophobic heat of Colombo – to Kent House, with its mattresses too thin to cushion the hard, wooden slats, and the sleep-depriving watches at HMS *Anderson*. Johannes invited Flora to the New Year's Eve dinner and dance at the Grand Oriental Hotel. She accepted before she realised that on Sunday, 31 December she was on Day 2 of the rota, and would be on watch from noon until four and then back on again from eight until two in the morning. It wasn't fair. Everyone would be celebrating the New Year. The TWAs could take a day off whenever they wanted, never had to do night duty. Flora wasn't the only one to complain. In the end, it was agreed that those on duty could work an eight-hour watch from noon until 8 p.m. Flora's diary continues the story:

> *...there was a rush round when we came off duty. I changed into my evening dress & wore my new white voile blouse with black skirt & was very pleased with the result. I met* [Johannes] *just turned 9pm (I think it was pretty good going) & we went along to dinner & dance at the GOH. It was very well arranged having both dining room & dance room for dancing with tables around, all brightly decorated with flowers & holly. By the band were two huge Xmas trees ablaze with fairy lights. We had a corner table but had quite a good view of the dancing. There was a very happy feeling all the time, a definite party spirit & everyone seemed to be enjoying themselves. We were all given paper hats which made it look very gay.*
>
> *At midnight the band stopped playing & all lights were put out while the hour struck then the lights were put on and the band started Auld Lang Syne and everyone joined in the singing. Afterwards the whole place went crazy the band played such a selection of well know known tunes & songs and everyone joined in singing & careering about & wishing Happy New Years until quite exhausted.* [Johannes] *met another Dutchman in the Navy who joined us towards the end of the evening. I really did enjoy it & could just have kept going when it was time to go. I had an extension until 1.30am which was not too bad but it would have been nice to not to have had to hurry back. The taxi we had ordered was not waiting so we eventually managed to join a party in an RAF brake going our way. We were rather held up in a traffic jam outside "Pembroke" & by the time we arrived at Kent House we were 5 minutes adrift but for a change no one worried – they must have had the New Year feeling!!*

***

31 December 2010

For the best views of Colombo Harbour, the guidebook suggests the Grand Oriental Hotel. In the lobby, a tiffin bar sells bagels to take out and speciality coffees in cardboard cups. GOH is leaded into the stained-glass window and the floors are still marble. The polished teak and burnished brass, however, have been concealed under sheets of white-painted MDF, to compete with the sleek modern lines of the new twenty-first-century high-rise hotels. In the foyer, models of Snow White and the seven dwarfs jerk their heads from side to side and lazily wave their plastic hands. Polystyrene reindeer pull Santa's sleigh across the ceiling above us.

We ask if we can have tea in the harbour room and are directed up to the fourth floor. Today, the tables are all laid for dinner, and at three in the afternoon we are the only two people there. A waiter ushers us over to the floor-to-ceiling windows where we have a good view of the old harbour building, with its clock over the entrance, ornate pillars and rooftop balustrades – so out of place against a backdrop of modern cranes and shipping containers. I wonder why there is a sign prohibiting photography, then I spot the grey naval vessels.

I would like to stay here and see in the new year just as Flora and Johannes did sixty-six years ago, but we already have a reservation at the hotel where we are staying. We hire a tuk-tuk to take us back there. I cling to the chrome rail that separates us from the driver as he weaves his tiny vehicle at speed through the undisciplined traffic on Galle Road. A man is riding a bicycle; the cakes he has for sale are displayed on shelves in a glass cabinet on the back. The tuk-tuk driver points out McDonald's and the President's residence with khaki-clad soldiers guarding the gates.

A few miles on, we turn right and follow Hotel Road down to the shore. Children look out from the doorways of small houses and shacks, women stand chatting at roadside stalls. At the end of the road, behind a red and white barrier, is the Mount Lavinia Hotel. A white vintage car is permanently parked outside the entrance. In the centre of the circular driveway is a fountain, and behind it a trio of silver-lit Christmas trees. A doorman in a white jacket with brass buttons and blue epaulettes, a metal spike on the top of his white helmet, opens the door for us.

That evening, three parties are going on at the hotel: one on the roof, one on the beach, and the one we are attending around the swimming pool on the governor's terrace. Victorian-style lampposts illuminate the dark night, and highlight the palm trees which grow on a patch of grass below the terrace and rise up behind the stone balustrade. I hear the sounds of the sea and look down to where the waves roll onto the sand. The skyline of Colombo twinkles in the distance.

The tall teak doors are folded back so partygoers can wander inside to the buffet: every starter you could imagine, Sri Lankan and English main courses, puddings from junket to profiteroles. It is almost midnight, yet out on the terrace the ladies have no need of a wrap over their strapless evening dresses, the men have discarded their dinner jackets.

We count down to midnight, and in the first moment of 2011 the band strikes the first note of 'Auld Lang Syne'. As the last words die away, they continue with the 'Hokey-cokey', 'Roll out the Barrel', 'Knees up Mother Brown' and 'The Conga'. As blue, orange and purple lights strobe around me, I travel back in time. These tunes of the '40s could have been playing as Aunt Flora welcomed in the New Year of 1945.

Sea surrounds the Mount Lavinia Hotel on three sides. Paradise Beach on the south side is for hotel patrons only, but early in the morning on New Year's Day only a couple of people lie on sunbeds beneath the palm-thatched umbrellas; the fish bar, where you can choose your freshly-caught fish and watch it being cooked, is closed.

To the north is the public beach. To get there, we have to go down back alleys and balance on the concrete sleepers to cross the railway line. Here, people just wander along the track, which explains the constant hooting we hear in our hotel room. We edge our way down a slope to the shore, and our feet sink into soft sand as we make our way between stalls selling ice cream and cola, and white plastic chairs and tables under canopies of coir matting. As it is New Year's Day the beach is crowded with locals sleeping, picnicking, playing on the sand or battling huge breakers in the sea.

Perched on a rocky outcrop, the original porticos and terraces of the Mount Lavinia Hotel overlook miles of palm-lined beach right up the city of Colombo, as they have for more than 200 years. Built in 1806, Mount Lavinia was the governor's house before it became a hotel in 1877. During the war a section was requisitioned as a military base and hospital.

***

Maybe this was the hospital where Flora was treated for dengue fever, but this is never mentioned in her diary. However, she does mention a trip to Mount Lavinia and calling in at the hotel on 7 January 1945:

> *We had a "watch" off very unexpectedly so went along to Mt Lavinia… We got a marvellous hitch from Bagatelle Road almost to the hotel so felt to be in luck for once. The sea was very rough & beyond the breakers one was out of one's depth so did not stay in very long it was far too exhausting, we were just knocked completely off our feet with every breaker until quite breathless. The other two being strong swimmers were well away. We all bought pineapples which were very welcome & refreshing, I certainly needed something after all the salt water I had swallowed.*
>
> *Not knowing the time, we wandered back to the Hotel as we thought just*

Mount Lavinia

right for tea & were astounded when we found it was 6 o'clock & all we could get was lemonade.

Wondering what kind of a "hitch" back we should get, we couldn't have arranged it better as an "Anderson" transport was just leaving so we all piled in & asked to be put down at the "Green Cabin" for tea. They are noted for their chocolate cake & it really is worth having. The first cake disappeared before the tea had arrived along with a whole plate of almond whirls much to the amusement of the "boy". We asked if they had any more & he produced a second whole cake & some more almond whirls & we thoroughly enjoyed our tea. We expected to have to walk back the rest of the way to the wrennery but when passing "Pembroke" the bus (Liberty 7pm) was just going so we sailed back in style.

***

5 February 2014

The Green Cabin Café is still there at 453 Galle Road. On display in a glass-fronted, stainless-steel cabinet is a large, square chocolate cake, but they don't have any almond whirls.

***

As World War II spilled over into yet another year, the Wrens' exhausting rota at HMS *Anderson* continued: Japanese signals were recorded on punch-cards to be sorted by the Hollerith and provide a means of building up copies of the enemy's current code books. The signals were now from an enemy in retreat, as US forces began to liberate the Pacific islands: the battle for Manila in the Philippines began in January, and would continue until April; the naval bombardment of the island of Iowa Jima, just 800 miles away from Japan, began on 19 February.

CHAPTER 25

Off Duty

...went to Town Hall to see the Indian Dancing by Ram Gopal & two of his pupils.

It was simply wonderful, I have never seen anything like it & how they can possibly move their neck, eyes, hands & fingers is just incredible. To watch their hands alone is a full time job & fascinating. Two outstanding dances by Ram Gopal (the most notable Indian dancer of today) were the Cobra Dance & a Creation Dance. The two pupils were also excellent, one doing dances of Northern India – a very different style from Southern.

– *Diary entry, 17 March 1945*

For the first three months of 1945, Flora's record of her time in Ceylon is more of a scrapbook than a diary. A clipping from a local newspaper reviews *The Stuff to Give the Troops*, produced by Gaylord Wayne and staring McDonald Hobley, as *'A Play Not To Be Missed'*. Above it, Flora has written a short note to explain that she went along to the RAF theatre with Johannes and, as the reviewer promised, *came away with aching sides caused by the non-stop laughs.*

Also pasted into the diary is a programme for an amateur production of *Housemaster* by Ian Hay, a comedy in three acts. A note beside it describes it as an all-naval show; many of the cast Flora knew by sight, as they worked at HMS *Anderson*.

The local talent, however, warranted a much longer entry:

…went along to an Indian Army Medical Corps mess at their invitation, along with about 12 other Wrens. Kotte where they were stationed was about 6 miles from our quarters & their mess was in a very attractive position, quite isolated from a town but by the side of a wide river & by the time we arrived about 7.30pm the sun was setting in a crimson glow reflected in the river. There was to be an Indian concert including Indian dances & we were very much looking forward to seeing them.

The stage was only small with crimson curtains with tassels round & the stage itself was decorated in crimson, royal blue & white, very colourful, with lamps hanging from the ceiling. As the stage was built under a lean-to, one side towards the river, was open so there was a fair amount of breeze. We had very good seats (rather hard towards the end of the performance) near the front so, of course, had an excellent view. Behind us were the Indian Army personnel of the camp several Indian women &, of course, children.

The announcer was a huge man with jet black curly hair who seemed very proud of his English & his important Job. The band were sitting cross-legged on forms on one side of the stage & all the way through seemed to thoroughly enjoy themselves. There was a fiddler, a man with a queer instrument similar to an accordion, but it rested on the ground, & the drummer who had three drums of different sizes, which he beat with his fingers, their rhythm was quite good & they kept together very well, but so much of this Indian music is repetition & the tunes never end.

Another item was Mohamed… who played the accordion instrument & sang at the same time, whilst the man with the drums also played an accompaniment. I think he would have gone on all night singing if left to his own devices & the two men who were drawing the curtains kept trying to attract his attention to make him stop, but he appeared not to hear. At last the announcer, who had a whistle for such occasions, blew about three times and the curtains were drawn as the man still continued to sing. With many of the items it did seem funny to hear the whistle blown when they had gone on long enough.

The dancers were four men & four girls & on such a small platform they were very cramped but it was a very interesting display. They all had bracelets of bells round their ankles, jingling all the time, especially as there is so much stamping, this mingled with the band & also about half a dozen people who were standing behind the band singing at the tops of their voices & what lungs they had!!

A conjurer was also very amusing with his various languages & patter & he did various odd tricks but one where he started to blow fire from his mouth was really alarming & we were sure he would set his whiskers alight, but all ended well. He also made us rather shudder when he hit his tummy, made revolting noises & out of his mouth came at least 12 marbles which he dropped on the platform just to show they were not fakes, he also produced two huge stones in the same way which only just came out of his mouth they were so large & these dropped to the platform with such a thud. We were near enough to see them so there was no trickery – he must have swallowed them before the performance.

Several sketches were given (all the speaking being in Tamil) & the Indian audience certainly appreciated the jokes – we even found them very amusing, they were so full of life & their queer mannerisms we had a good laugh as well. We gathered one dialogue referred to people in the audience in several places & they were all having a huge joke at our expense, knowing we did not understand.

The last item was the "Snake Charmer Dance" by two speciality dancers & they were exceptionally good & just to watch the movement of their hands & fingers is fascinating. There were also two "Filum stars" as the announcer insisted upon calling them. They were the weakest in the programme and sang duets both looking very embarrassed (we presumed they sang love songs)… the man seemed to more or less organise the company & for some unknown reason stayed on the platform throughout each performance usually chatting with the announcer or the man who was looking after the curtains – the latter was always wandering across the platform to have a chat with a pal in the band not bothering at all about the performers.

During the interval we were very surprised when we were given sandwiches, curry puff (very tasty) & cool drinks, they made quite a party for us. We had to be in by 10.30 & the concert ended about 10pm so once more we returned in the transport to Kent House after spending a very interesting & enjoyable evening.

The Snake Charmer Dance by the 'speciality' dancers was the highlight of the concert, for Flora, so a month later she bought tickets for a performance by the renowned Ram Gopal and two of his pupils at Colombo Town Hall.

***

Above another programme pasted into her diary, Flora wrote: *Wednesday March 21st saw play 'Home from Home' at RAF Theatre. Very good comedy and the cast were very well chosen, the evacuees especially were fine.* Flora knew all about evacuees.

Her mother often wrote about the family from London's East End that was billeted at her home back in Halifax: strangers sleeping in her room, eating her mother's Yorkshire pudding and jam roly-poly. How long would it be before she, herself, could go home? They'd left England in February 1943; it was now March 1945. The year had begun with the good news that, back in Europe, the Russians were advancing on Germany from the east; on 12 January they had invaded Poland. Then, in the west, Field Marshall Montgomery and General Patton had launched a two-pronged attack on the Rhine. Early in March, US troops had crossed the bridge at Remagen, and later in the month the British crossed at Oppenheim and Wesel. It was just a matter of time before British,

US and Russian armies converged, but, even if things went well for the Allies, it was still likely to be a while before Germany was defeated.

Flora's growing discontent is evident from the comments and crossings out on a cutting from a British newspaper sent by her mother. Entitled 'Wrens in Ceylon', it is an account of their glorious surroundings, pleasant working conditions and comfortable quarters. Flora has underlined the words No Wren is asked to serve more than two years abroad and on the facing page written: *We have already done 2 years & no sign yet of returning.* Other inaccuracies are also highlighted: About a hundred Wrens live in such quarters and a dozen share each hut. However, rough and ready their living accommodation was at first, their huts are now comfortable and as cool as possible with hot and cold running water. Flora has contradicted this: *Our quarters are for about 500. There is one ablution block for 4 cabins (112 girls) one geyser (often not working) & all hot water has to be carried from this in buckets either into the bathrooms or to the main washing place.*

The article also states (and Flora has underlined): The Wrens use their quarters just as they would their home. Friends are welcomed and at least once a fortnight there is an open night when invitations are eagerly sought after because the Wrens know how to give a good party. Flora, however, calls it a *'Closed Night' when you must stay in and attend a compulsory lecture or concert whether it interests you or not.*

Preparing the ground for laying the lawns around the bandas *at Kent House, Colombo*

Since the monsoon, some effort had been made to combat the mud at the Wrennery: cabins closest to Kent House were now linked by concrete paths. Defiant and Fury, however, being much further away, were still surrounded by bare earth. Then, towards the end of March, Sinhalese labourers began to lay lawns on either side of the main drive and plant zinnias alongside some of the paths. The reason for this was evident when it was announced that Lady Mountbatten, wife of Admiral Lord Louis Mountbatten, Supreme Commander of South East Asia Command, was coming to inspect Kent House.

When the visit occurred Flora was on watch, but as soon as she got off the 'liberty boat', the other Wrens told her about it. Lady Mountbatten had taken only a short walk on the paths across the newly-laid lawn to a specially spruced-up cabin, before being whisked off to the officers' quarters in Kent House.

All shore leave had been cancelled, and the Wrens not on duty had been ordered to assemble in full uniform and marched into the recreation room, where they sat in rows to listen to their important visitor's speech. With so many bodies crammed into the restricted space, it was unbearably hot and, as they were all still wearing their hats, it had been hard to see the lady standing before them. Consequently, not many of the Wrens could remember what Lady Mountbatten had said, except that she talked an awful lot about her husband, thanked them for what they were doing and hoped that the war would soon be over.

CHAPTER 26

Victory in Europe

The Galle Face [Hotel] *was decorated with flags & a huge illuminated V over the entrance. I think all Colombo was on the Galle Face Green, crowds of people. The State Council was floodlit in red, green & white & looked very attractive, but the clock tower was very well decorated with multi coloured fairy lights all round. Most of the Restaurants were closed & crowds of people were in the streets. We then went round to Town Hall which was just a blaze of light, floodlit in red, green & white, including the dome.*

– Diary entry, 9 May 1945

On Tuesday, 8 May 1945, the Wrens crowded into the recreation room at Kent House and waited in silence as an officer tuned in the radio. Winston Churchill began to speak:

'Yesterday morning at 2.41am at General Eisenhower's headquarters, General Jodl, the representative of the German High Command, and Grand Admiral Doenitz, the designated head of the German State, signed the act of unconditional surrender of all German land, sea and air forces in Europe to the Allied Expeditionary Force, and simultaneously to the Soviet High Command…

We may allow ourselves a brief period of rejoicing but let us not forget for a moment the toil and efforts that lie ahead. Japan with all her treachery and greed remains unsubdued… We must now devote all our strength and resources to the completion of our task both at home and abroad. Advance Britannia, Long live the cause of freedom. God Save the King.'

That night, Flora and many of the Wrens not on duty walked down Colpetty Road to Christ Church, now illuminated in floodlights with Allied flags festooning the tower. They were on their way to a thanksgiving service. Although they arrived well before ten o'clock, the church was already packed and they only just managed to crowd in at the back. Details of the service are preserved in the six-page Order of Service pasted into Flora's diary.

Did the prayers for all who had given their lives in the war, and for all those who were still engaged in battle, turn Flora's thoughts to: the merchant seaman from Rochdale; John, the RASC lieutenant who she hadn't seen since their day out at Kenya's White Sands; Tom and the other subbies aboard HMS *Carthage*? The war wasn't over for them, unless, of course, by now they were captured, injured... or dead.

Prayers were also said for a better world and for the guidance of those who would make peace in Europe. The last hymn was 'Now thank we all our God', followed by the National Anthem, then everyone knelt for the Blessing.

Although it was late when they got back to Kent House, the petty officer on duty just waved them past Regulating without comment. Back in the cabin, one of the girls produced a bottle of sherry. They had every intention of waiting up to hear the king's speech, but by one-thirty they were all sound asleep.

***

As they strolled through Fort the following evening, Flora and Johannes detoured around groups of staggering servicemen singing 'Land of Hope and Glory'. They walked along Prince Street, down Queen Street, and on to Galle Face Green. A band played and people were dancing; others stood on top of the cannons singing, and a Scotsman marched up and down the promenade playing the bagpipes.

Not everyone, however, was celebrating. Out at HMS *Anderson*, the wireless operators were still listening, the Holleriths were processing the punch-cards, the cryptanalysts were deep in concentration. The war with Japan was far from over.

From deciphered JN25 signals, the British had known for some time that Japan was withdrawing its troops from some of the outlying islands, to concentrate on defending its most lucrative conquests – those, like Malaya, that could provide oil and the other raw materials they badly needed. The operation to evacuate the Andaman and Nicobar Islands in the Indian Ocean was codenamed SHO (Akiraka)

On the night of 9 May 1945, while the rest of Colombo was celebrating, HMS *Anderson* picked up a signal. They knew it was about SHO (Akiraka). By the early hours of the morning, they knew that a heavy cruiser would leave Singapore on 10 May, and arrive in Port Blair on the Andaman Islands to pick up two army battalions two days later. The *Kurishoyo* would depart on 11 May carrying supplies for the Nicobar Islands, where it would load 450 army personnel for return to Singapore.

The heavy cruiser that sailed for the Andamans was the *Haguro*, and it left on the 9th, a day earlier than expected, but at HMS *Anderson* they were intercepting the signals and were able to keep the Royal Navy informed of its position. This gave a flotilla of destroyers enough time to plan their tactics and score several direct hits, with their torpedoes sinking the *Haguro* on the night of 16 May. The *Kurishoyo* escaped this time, only to be located again by deciphered JN25 signals and sunk by two destroyers a month later.

Apparently, a report of the sinking of a Japanese cruiser in the Indian Ocean, probably the *Haguro*, appeared in the local newspaper on 20 May. Flora, however, doesn't recall seeing it, and even if she had, she wouldn't have known how the Hollerith Wrens might have contributed. In fact, it would be many years before the part played by HMS *Anderson* would be acknowledged at all. At the time, all credit went to the commanders of the flotilla and the destroyer which fired the torpedoes. They both received distinguished service medals. Even an account of this incident in British official history published in 1969 makes no mention of how the destroyers knew the position of these two cruisers.

Unofficially, however, there was recognition, but it would not be until mid-July, when Flora was back home in England. Lord Mountbatten, Supreme Allied Commander South East Asia, visited HMS *Anderson* once more and told the Royal Naval codebreakers that they were 'worth ten divisions'.

***

Flora joined the queue in the waiting room. When her turn came, the medical officer looked up, nodded to a chair and asked what had brought her to see him. She rolled down her lisle stocking to reveal the tropical ulcer. He prescribed M&B tablets to treat the infection and told her to apply daily kaolin dressings.

When he asked if there was anything else, she said she was tired, yet she couldn't sleep. He reached over, placed a finger on her cheek to pull down the lower margin of her eye and muttered the word anaemia, then asked where she worked and how long she'd been overseas. She replied HMS *Anderson*, and that it would soon be two and a half years since she'd left Britain. He smiled, patted her hand and said he thought she'd done her bit for the war and he would be recommending lighter duties.

Lighter duties involved office work in WRNS administration – regular daytime hours, no more watches, not being on her feet for hours in the heat. By now, the badge sewn on Flora's left sleeve had not one but two anchors crossed over beneath a royal crown. She had been promoted to petty officer and was also entitled to wear a tricorn hat and brass buttons on her uniform jacket.

On 11 June 1945, the first Wrens who came out to operate the Hollerith, back in February 1943, were put on standby for the next draft back home to Britain. No one, however, was able to tell them how long they would have to wait. Their bags were all packed when, on the 12th, the navy invited a party of four Wrens to go out on exercise – no mention was made of the type of ship. It would be the first and probably the only time most of the Wrens had been at sea with the navy, so Flora and Pat were pleased to be off duty and able to go.

Flora's diary takes up the story:

Upon arrival at the jetty 8.30am we were met by a Lieut who said another party of 6 Wrens were also expected from one of the other quarters. Eventually they arrived & we were taken out in a small launch to the ship. We discovered they were three minesweepers going out on manoeuvres & two of the ships had sent invitations for the W.R.N.S. It was a perfect day but as we looked towards the breakwater were very dubious, the waves were just breaking continuously & dashing very high & when the first minesweeper was out of the harbour we could see her bobbing up & down just like a cork, it did not look too good at all. We were rather late leaving harbour as a wire was caught round the screw but we were all very interested to watch the diver go down to free the same.

Eventually we were going out of harbour & all very thrilled. The captain had put his cabin at our disposal & one of the stewards spent all his time making cups of tea & lime juice for any who wanted it – he did look after us well. We all thought we were good sailors but in the monsoon & on such a small ship we were soon disillusioned. One by one we had to give in & after a while the Captain's cabin looked just like a sickbay with corpses all over. They found cushions, pillows & even put up camp beds for us. We had to laugh & we must have looked funny when they came in to see how we were getting along.

Only two managed to make their way to lunch & even then they had to hurriedly retire, the rest of us just could not stand even the thought of food. The firing practice was just deafening & everything in the cabin shook, but the only damage was a bottle of ink which shattered. We were so annoyed we could not even stagger onto the deck & so did not see them sweeping.

On the return as we approached the harbour the wind dropped a little & the sea calmed & by the time we reached the entrance we all managed to get on deck & so feel we had achieved something. We arrived back about 7.30pm after being a whole day at sea & although it was a dreadful feeling to be so seasick once we were back in the Wrennery everyone was so jealous of the opportunity we had had it made us feel it had been well worth it. We were also somewhat consoled when we learned the party on the other minesweeper had been just as ill.

The following day, another party of Wrens was due to go on a similar outing – but at the last minute, with no explanation, the invitation was withdrawn.

***

The days dragged. When she'd first arrived, it had been all sunshine and sand, but now it was just heat and dust; the scenery had been breathtakingly beautiful, now it was foreign and alien; the work had been intriguing and challenging, now it was exhausting and monotonous. Flora just wanted to go home.

CHAPTER 27

Heading Home

> *Typical English weather when we got on deck, slight fog & drizzle & bitterly cold – everyone dressed in heavy coats & all looked rather blue. Docked at Southampton about 10.30am & were very surprised to see a Military Band waiting for us & after playing "God save the King"* [they] *carried on with a selection of light music until lunch time & it did cheer things up on such a dreary morning.*
>
> *– Diary entry, 11 July 1945*

On 18 June 1945, most of the SDX Wrens who had set out from Greenock on 21 February 1943 boarded a troopship bound for Britain. Of the original sixteen, six were missing: one had already returned home on a previous draft, another of their number had been sent to South Africa for health reasons and her sister, also an SDX Wren, was traveling home round the Cape to see her. Two of the three Wrens now married were being demobbed abroad, and one petty officer had signed up for another twelve months overseas. Flora records the first leg of the voyage in her diary:

> *We went on board the "Durban Castle" about 4pm & found we had very good accommodation, first class cabins for three or four persons & we were to travel as 2nd class. We had our own lounge – very small but quite handy. Meals were in the 1st Class the only difference being we did not get the choice of food & on some very hot days we did feel rather envious as we saw salads passing by & we had the usual stewed meat or roast. Suet puddings seemed to have haunted us all the time overseas & it was rather too much when these appeared in the Red Sea…*

The majority of passengers were service personnel including about 60 W.R.N.S. There were also a number of civilians including several children, the latter seemed very spoilt & the civilians took up a great deal of the deck space with deck chairs & deck space on a troopship is very limited. Several dances were arranged & a concert given towards the end of the voyage, also several film shows but everyone seemed quite contented to be on their way home & did not want entertainment.

The voyage until we reached Aden on the 25th June was very rough, the ship rolled & tossed & unless they were very good sailors they were ill – it was a dreadful feeling and for 5 days I could not look at food & when I did it was disastrous… & was I relieved when we reached calmer waters & the waves were no longer breaking over the upper decks.

We were very lucky passing through the Red Sea, there was a pleasant breeze & so we did not feel the heat too intense. Also once passed Aden there was no blackout & it was great to have the ports open at night & also lights on deck.

Thursday 28th June. We saw land most of the day, ranges of very barren hills and about 19.30 we reached Suez. It was rather thrilling to see lights ashore & see other ships all lit up. We were disappointed not to be allowed ashore & also very anxious to be on the way once more. We stayed there the night & left about 11.30 on June 29th & entered the canal. The canal is very narrow & on either side stretches of very barren scenery, sand, desert palms scattered here and there & an occasional encampment. A road runs along either side & it was quite an event to see a lorry or jeep go bouncing along. We saw a good number of Arabs & camels but it was very desolate. Passing of N.A.A.F.I. canteen which was built by the canal the few service personnel there came down to the edge of the jetty to wave to us, it must be very trying to watch the ships pass so closely on their way home when you are probably there for many months maybe years longer.

We arrived Port Said during the night of Friday the 29th June & once more we were not allowed ashore. Small boats were around the ship the whole of the day & a wonderful trade was being done in leather goods, handbags & zip bags chiefly, as they are made there. It was very amusing watching some of the transactions – they had to lower baskets on a string from the decks or ports, then they hoisted up the goods etc. from the small boat below & if suitable the money was lowered in the basket. It passed some of the time on watching as it seemed to go so slowly when we were not moving. We left Port Said at 18.30 after embarking further troops & were very thrilled to be once more on the way.

Even though it was now July, as they sailed through the Mediterranean everyone wrapped up in their winter woollies. On Tuesday a gale sprang up, and the Wrens feared they would have to take to their beds once more, but to their relief it didn't last long. During the night they passed Malta. On the following day the coast of Sicily was visible, but it was far too cold to sit on deck, so in the afternoon Flora climbed back into her bunk, getting up again in time for the evening's very amusing and most enjoyable concert party.

They passed through the Straits of Gibraltar in the early hours of 6 July, so none of the Wrens were awake to see the rock. By the time they sailed north up the Spanish coast, most of the girls had discarded their white, tropical uniforms and gone back into 'blues'.

To everyone's relief, the Bay of Biscay did not live up to its reputation and the Kwells and sick-bags weren't needed. They entered the channel at four o'clock on 9 July, the troops lining the deck rail to catch their first glimpse of England. It was after ten the next morning when they docked at Southampton with typical English fog and drizzle to greet them. On the dockside, a brass band played 'God Save the King'.

The return voyage had lasted twenty-three days, less than half the forty-seven days of their outward journey around the Cape to Mombasa, and then across the Indian Ocean to Ceylon.

It was the following day before they finally disembarked and caught the train to Waterloo. As they passed through the suburbs, Flora stared out at the devastation: a single chimney breast here, a staircase there, all rising up into nothing, the rest of the house reduced to rubble around it. How could she have forgotten the full horror in the years she'd been away?

With two hours to spare before the train to Rochester, the Wrens decided to take their trunks and suitcases to the station they'd be traveling home from and leave them in left luggage. It seemed pointless to lug them all the way down to the depot, only to bring them back again straight away when they went on leave. Flora hadn't, however, allowed for traffic jams on the taxi ride to and from King's Cross; when she arrived back at Charing Cross, their train had just left. During the three-quarters-of-an-hour wait for the next one she was befriended by the navy, and the luggage room attendant kept them all supplied with cups of tea and slices of apple tart.

At Rochester naval depot they collected their ration cards and travel warrants, before going home on twenty-three days' leave.

***

Halifax looked just the same – perhaps a bit grimier than she remembered, but all the buildings and streets were still intact, the mill chimneys still belched smoke. The family, however, had changed. The last two years had left more worry lines on her mother's face, more grey streaks in her hair. Flora hardly recognised the woman in the smart Red Cross uniform, her younger sister, Jessie.

Then there were the friends and acquaintances she'd grown up with that she would never see again. It was not long after Flora left Britain, but her mother said she couldn't bring herself to write in a letter about what had happened to the friend she'd known since infant school. Grieving for her husband lost at sea, his ship sunk by a U-boat in the Atlantic, she had taken her own life and their small son now lived with his grandparents. Flora watched the whirlpool in her cup as she continued to stir her tea much longer than necessary, and thought about how the war had ruined so many people's lives. To break the silence, her mother said that they should be thankful it was over now, and Flora snapped back that it wasn't… not out there.

Then it was all over. The world's first atomic bomb fell on Hiroshima on 6 August 1945, the second three days later on Nagasaki. At midnight on the 14th, Clement Attlee, the new Labour prime minister who had ousted Winston Churchill, announced: *'The last of our enemies is laid low.'* Emperor Hirohito of Japan had surrendered. As Britain held thanksgiving services and made plans for VJ Day, Flora though of the thanksgiving service they'd be holding in Christ Church and the revellers on Galle Face Green, thousands of miles away in Colombo.

At the end of their leave Flora and the other SDX Wrens reported for duty, but the war was over: the Bombe and the Hollerith lay idle. They were sent to Stanmore, where the officer in charge, not knowing what to do with them, sent them to a local hospital to mow the grass and weed the flower beds.

In October, the SDX Wrens were, one by one, summoned before the unit officer and asked about their plans for the future. Flora had thought she might continue to serve in the WRNS and look for another posting overseas. It was then that she was told that by the end of the year SDX would cease to exist, so she would need to change category and start again at the bottom, as a rating. Flora looked down at the brass buttons on her uniform and protested that she was a petty officer, only to be told that the war was over. It was different in peacetime.

Not that the Wrens' achievements during the war weren't appreciated. It was about this time that a letter was sent to all those serving abroad.

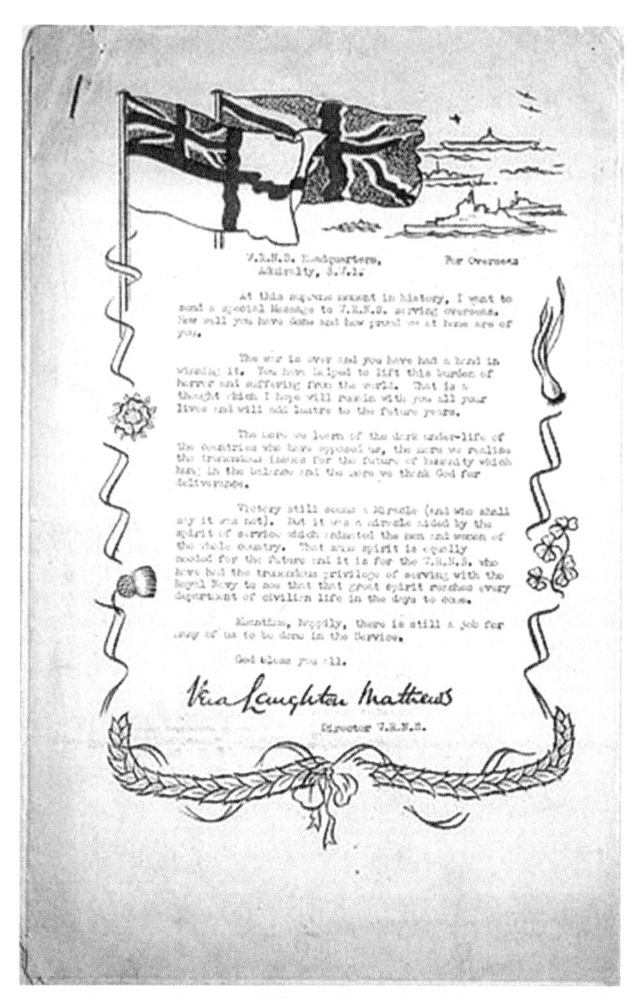

W.R.N.S. Headquarters, For Overseas
Admiralty, S.W.1.

At this supreme moment in history, I want to send a special Message to W.R.N.S. serving overseas. How well you have done and how proud we at home are of you.

The war is over and you have had a hand in winning it. You have helped to lift this burden of horror and suffering from the world. That is a thought which I hope will remain with you all your lives and will add lustre to the future years.

The more we learn of the dark under-life of the countries who have opposed us, the more we realise the tremendous issues for the future of humanity which hung in the balance and the more we thank God for deliverance.

Victory still seems a Miracle (and who shall say it was not). But it was a miracle aided by the spirit of service which animated the men and women of the whole country. That same spirit is equally needed for the future and it is for the W.R.N.S. who have had the tremendous privilege of serving with the Royal Navy to see that that great spirit reaches every department of civilian life in the days to come.

Meantime, happily, there is still a job for many of us to be done in the Service.

God bless you all.

Vera Laughton Mathews

Director W.R.N.S.

Letter to Overseas Wrens. Reproduced by courtesy of the National Museum of the Royal Navy, Portsmouth

Beneath the White Ensign and Union Jack, and within a border incorporating the rose of England, the thistle of Scotland, the leek of Wales and the shamrock of Ireland, were the following words:

W.R.N.S. Headquarters For Overseas
Admiralty S.W.1.

At this supreme moment in history, I want to send a special Message to W.R.N.S. serving overseas. How well you have done and how proud we at home are of you.

The war is over and you have had a hand in winning it. You have helped to lift this burden of horror and suffering from the world. That is a thought which I hope will remain with you all your lives and will add luster to the future years.

The more we learn of the dark under-life of the countries who have opposed us, the more we realize the tremendous issues for the future of humanity which hung in the balance and the more we thank God for deliverance.

Victory still seems a Miracle (and who shall say it was not). But it was a miracle aided by the spirit of service which animated the men and women of the whole country. That same spirit is equally needed for the future and it is for the W.R.N.S. who have had the tremendous privilege of serving with the Royal Navy to see that that great spirit reaches every department of civilian life in the days to come.

Meantime, happily, there is still a job for any of us to be done in the Service.

God bless you all.

Vera Laughton Mathews
Director W.R.N.S.

As Flora had already returned to Britain, she may never have seen a copy of this letter. She had already been allocated a release number but, like many of the other Wrens, Flora did not relish returning to civilian life, and was quite upset when her number appeared on the unit noticeboard indicating that her demob was imminent.

Each Wren was given two months' paid leave, to provide the money to tide them over while they found other employment, and a discharge certificate to serve as reference. At the demobilisation centre they collected their gratuity, clothing grant and coupons, civilian ration book, identity card and travel warrants and headed for home.

EPILOGUE

After the war, Flora found it hard to settle back into civilian life. In 1946, she volunteered for overseas service with the WRVS and was posted to Burma. In the '50s she emigrated to New Zealand, but she returned three years later to her home town of Halifax and spent the rest of her working life as a medical secretary in the NHS.

Although Flora had several proposals and was once engaged, she never married. Maybe no one could take the place of Johannes, the Dutch lieutenant. The last time he is mentioned in the diary is on VE Day, as they celebrated together on Galle Face Green in Colombo. I often wanted to ask her what happened to him, but whenever I broached the subject her eyes would mist over and she would turn away.

At her funeral in 2008, a family member told me that she believed Flora and Johannes had travelled back from Colombo on the same troopship, and during the voyage he had asked her to marry him. Flora accepted his proposal, but not his suggestion that they should ask the ship's captain to perform the ceremony onboard. They should wait until they were back home and have a proper wedding with their families present. But that never happened. Johannes arrived home to find his girlfriend still waiting, convinced that he'd be back to marry her once the war was over.

BIBLIOGRAPHY

Arunachalam, P., *Sketches of Ceylon History*, Colombo, Asian Educational Services, 2004.

Biggs, M.W., 'Coast Defences: Some Experiences in Peace and War', in *Royal Engineers Journal*, Vol. 108, No. 2, August 1994, p.201–8.

BR 1077: *Regulations and Instructions for the Women's Royal Naval Service to 31st December 1943* (copy held at Royal Naval Museum, Portsmouth).

Calvocoressi, Peter, *Top Secret Ultra*, Kidderminster: M&M Baldwin, 2001.

Chitty, Jean, *Kent House Colombo: Letters from a Wren May 1944 to November 1945*, Lymington: Belhaven, 1994.

Drummond, John, D., *Blue for a Girl: The story of WRNS*, London: W.H. Allen & Co Ltd., 1960.

Gibson, Perla, Siedle, *Durban's Lady in White: An Autobiography*, Herts: Aedificamus Press, 1991.

Hodgson, Margaret, *Scrapbook & Photograph album from WRNS Service overseas in Singapore, Colombo and Mombasa* (copies held at Royal Naval Museum, Portsmouth).

Jackson, Allan, *Facts about Durban*, 3rd ed., Durban: F.A.D. Publishing, 2007.

Jarvis, Sue, *Japanese Codes*, The Bletchley Park Trust Reports, Report No. 6 July 1997.

Hinsley, F.H., Thomas E.E., Ransom, C.F.G., & Knight, R.C., *British Intelligence in the Second World War*, Vol. I-III, London: HMSO, 1979–84.

Hinsley, F.H. & Stripp, Alan (eds.), *Codebreakers: the Inside Story of Bletchley Park,* Oxford: University Press, 1993.

Kahn, David, *The Codebreakers: The Story of Secret Writing,* London: Macmillan 1967, Weidenfeld & Nicholson 1966.

Kahn, David, *Seizing the Enigma*, London: Arrow, 1991.

Lamb, Christian, *I only joined for the hat,* London: Bene Factum Publishing Ltd., 2007.

Laughton-Mathews, Vera, *Blue Tapestry*, London: Hollis & Carter Ltd, 1949.

McKay, Sinclair, *The Secret Listeners: The Men and Women Posted Across the World to Intercept German Codes for Bletchley Park*, London: Arum Press, 2013.

McKay, Sinclair, *The Secret Life of Bletchley Park: the WWII Codebreaking Centre and the Men and Women who worked there,* London: Arum Press, 2013.

Mercer, Derrick, (ed.) *Chronicle of the 20th Century*, London: Dorling Kindersley, 1995.

Page, Gwendoline, *Growing Pains: A Teenager's War,* Sussex: The Book Guild Ltd, 1994.

Page, Gwendoline (ed.), *We kept the Secret*, Norfolk: Geo R Reeve Ltd, 2002.

Smith, Michael, *Station X: The Codebreakers of Bletchley Park*, London: Channel 4 Books, 1998.

Smith, Michael, *The Emperor's Codes,* London: Bantam Press, 2000.

Smith, Michael, *The Secrets of Station X: How the Bletchley Park Codebreakers Helped Win the War,* London: Biteback Publishing Ltd, 2011.

Stripp, Alan, *Codebreaker in the Far East*, Oxford: University Press, 1995.

Stuart-Mason, Ursula, *The Wrens 1917–77: A history of the Women's Royal Naval Service,* Reading: Educational Explorers, 1977.

Tomlinson, Michael, *The Most Dangerous Moment: The Japanese Assault on*

Ceylon 1942, London: Granada Publishing Ltd, 1979.

Winterbotham, F.W., *The Ultra Secret: The Inside Story of Operation Ultra, Bletchley Park and Enigma,* London: Weidenfield & Nicholson, 1999.

Winton, John, *Ultra in the Pacific,* London: Leo Cooper, 1993.

Young, Irene, *Enigma Variations: A Memoir of Love and War,* Mainstream Publishing, 1990.

GUIDEBOOKS, ETC.

Insight Guide: Kenya, 4th Edition, 1999.

Finley, Hugh and Crowther, Geoff, *East Africa*, 4th Edition, Lonely Planet Publications, Australia, 1997.

Ellis, Royston, *Sri Lanka by Rail*, Bradt Publications, England 1994.

ACKNOWLEDGEMENTS

My thanks go to the many individuals who helped in the research, writing and production of this book.

I am very grateful to marine archaeologist Hans-Martin Sommer, and to our guides, Omar Juma, and Ahmed Shee Ahmed, who helped us find the places where Flora worked and was billeted in Mombasa.

My thanks go to Priath Fernando for taking us on a tour of Colombo to visit the locations Flora mentions in her diary. He also introduced us to Lakshman and Pauline Wickremeratne, Jody De Saram and the late Prakrama Fernando, who kindly provided useful background information.

Sidath Thilakarathne was our guide organised by Genuine Srilankans Tours who drove us up country and arranged for us to visit the places where the Wrens spent their leave.

During visits to Bletchley Park, volunteer guides answered my questions, in particular Frank Falcon who also checked my description of the working of the Bombe. Guy Revell, Museum Archivist at the Bletchley Park Trust, provided advice and sourced photographs of the Bombe and the Hollerith. Michael Smith, author of several books on Bletchley Park, kindly gave permission for me to reproduce quotes from *The Emperor's Codes.*

At the National Museum of the Royal Navy in Portsmouth, senior curator Victoria Ingles located information about WRNS Rules and Regulations and the letter sent by Vera Laughton Mathews to the overseas Wrens in 1945.

Andrew McMurchy, a sergeant in the Army Intelligence Corps, provided useful background information on the Y service and deciphering German traffic.

I am also indebted to those who helped in the writing process: Helena Durham and Robbie Dewa read early drafts and made useful suggestions. Anne McDonnell provided invaluable advice on publication. Frances Thimann has read many versions and been a continual source of support and encouragement throughout. Dan Coxon copy-edited the manuscript, and Hannah Vaughan at TJ INK was responsible for overseeing the project. I am very grateful to Ian Wileman for his work in designing the cover.

My thanks also go to my family: to Katrina Merkelt, my granddaughter, for sketching a map of Mombasa as it was in 1943; and to Terry Brierley, my husband, for arranging for us to travel to the locations mentioned in the diaries, and for his patience over the many years it took to write this book.

Most of all, I am grateful to my aunt, Flora Crossley, for allowing me to read her diaries. Without her diligence in keeping a record of her time overseas and her memory for detail this story would never have been told.

As it has not been possible to contact all the people mentioned in this book and most have already passed away, some names have been changed.

The events described were recorded in my Aunt Flora's diary or related to me in our many chats about her wartime experiences. The background details have been extensively researched. As the events took place over seventy years ago, it was not possible to verify every detail, so I take full responsibility for any errors or assumptions.